01/05/15

D0297561

WAT

Please renew or return items by the date shown on your receipt

www.hertsdirect.org/libraries

Renewals and enquiries: 0300 123 4049

Textphone for hearing or speech impaired   0300 123 4041

Hertfordshire

H46 678 114 9

GIRLS
WITH
BALLS

TIM TATE

GIRLS
WITH
BALLS

THE SECRET HISTORY OF
WOMEN'S FOOTBALL

JOHN BLAKE

Published by John Blake Publishing Ltd,
3 Bramber Court, 2 Bramber Road,
London W14 9PB, England

www.johnblakepublishing.co.uk

www.facebook.com/Johnblakepub
twitter.com/johnblakepub

First published in hardback in 2013

ISBN: 978-1-78219-429-3

British Library Cataloguing-in-Publication Data:

A catalogue record for this book is available from the British Library.

Design by www.envydesign.co.uk

Printed in Great Britain by CPI Group (UK) Ltd

1 3 5 7 9 10 8 6 4 2

Papers used by John Blake Publishing are natural, recyclable products
made from wood grown in sustainable forests. The manufacturing processes
conform to the environmental regulations of the country of origin.

Every attempt has been made to contact the relevant copyright-holders, but
some were unobtainable. We would be grateful if the appropriate people
could contact us.

For Sam Tate
September 1982 – November 2012

CONTENTS

CONTENTS

INTRODUCTION

'The future is feminine'
– FEDERATION OF INTERNATIONAL FOOTBALL (FIFA),
JUNE 1995

Sepp Blatter was pleased. 'The future is feminine' had an impressive and authoritative ring to it. It was just the sort of soundbite certain to be picked up by the world's media, and would therefore ensure much-needed exposure for FIFA's Women's World Cup, then in its infancy. Blatter didn't, of course, believe it. But the career-minded sports administrator hadn't got to the position of being the favourite to win FIFA's forthcoming presidential election by allowing such minor matters as belief to over-trouble him. No, 'The future is feminine' was good and Sepp Blatter liked it.

He liked it so much that once elected he would go on to repeat it over the ensuing 15 years. The difference was that on these occasions – always timed to coincide with a major FIFA women's competition – he actually believed in the soundbite. And, in truth, he had good reason. Global men's football, FIFA's cash cow and the very reason for its existence, had to a large extent reached its maximum business potential. Television rights to the World Cup would, of course, continue to rise in price and fill FIFA's coffers but it had pretty much reached saturation level on every continent. If a new income stream was to be found, it wouldn't be in the men's game. Women's soccer – well, now, that could be a very different story, and a very profitable one, to boot. A new series of international football competitions meant new sponsorship and, most importantly, a whole raft of new television deals.

This isn't a book about FIFA. Fascinating though it is, other journalists and writers have devoted acres of newsprint and millions of words to the allegedly Machiavellian politics of the sport's supreme governing body. Nor is it a book about football – at least not in the sense of a traditional football book. Indeed, of all authors you could name I would probably be one of the least qualified to write about the technical skills and aspects of football, let alone the who-won-what-when statistics which are the staple ingredients of any conventional soccer book.

I am happy to admit that I haven't knowingly watched an entire football match since 1990 and would be hard put to name any of the leading players in national or international sides. In sport, my passion is, and always will be, rugby union – as a player (absurdly briefly), as a life-long spectator and for 10 joyous years as a coach. And so whilst there will be (for reasons that will become clear) at least passing references to, for example, the arcane mysteries of the offside rule, the development of the 4-4-2 formation, and the occasionally eye-watering finances involved in the game, this book is not written in the thrall of a life-long passion for all things football.

Instead it's a book about people: extraordinary figures from a dimly-remembered past, figures who were both of their time and who shaped it. But although it's a book about the past, and will dig deep into the loam of British social history, it's also about why the present is as it is.

As you might expect from the title, many of the characters in this story are women. Their struggle to play a sport they loved was fought out against a backdrop of huge social change in Britain. When women's football began – and it began surprisingly early in the overall history of the game – men alone had the vote and the only sporting activity considered suitable for girls was croquet, with the occasional dash of very demure cricket. When its golden era ended, surprisingly late, Britain had universal franchise and Barbara Cartland was driving racing cars round the Brooklands circuit.

The story of women's football reflects the story of the decades which transformed Britain from late Victorian claustrophobia into the open spaces of the 20th century. Other books have been published which examine small corners of this story: a list is included at the end and I heartily recommend each one. But each is somewhat hamstrung by the limits its author has placed on it, whether it be a privately-published account of the successes and failures of women footballers in the north-east of England during the First World War, or an academic assessment of the role of football femininity in the socio-political discourse.

This book attempts a more rounded picture by telling the truly extraordinary stories of early women footballers in the context both of their times and the development of football itself. We shall discover life imitating art and then art returning the compliment. Hit movies like *Gregory's Girl* or *Bend It Like Beckham* owe much (if possibly unknowingly) to the pioneering struggles of women from earlier generations.

But they also reflect the reality of those struggles being far from over. Because, as we shall see, the odd and, at times slightly disturbing, fact is that the struggle for a woman's right to wrest soccer away from the jealous grasp of men, if only for the love of playing it, continued long after this country woke up to the injustice of sexism, heard the pure, clear sense of feminism, and signed into law Acts of Parliament designed to stamp out inequality.

But above all this is the story of the longest-running secret in British football; a rattling yarn of determination and guts as well as jealousy, prejudice and betrayal. It is the story of devious men... and girls with balls.

Tim Tate
July 2013

CHAPTER ONE

Boxing Day, 1920, Goodison Park, Liverpool

Everton football ground is filled beyond capacity. Fifty-three thousand men, women and children pack its stands and draughty terraces. A further 14,000 would-be spectators are locked out of the ground and line the nearby streets. The 22 players need a police escort to get into the changing rooms. Pathé News cameras patrol the touchline. These extraordinary crowds – the biggest Liverpool has ever seen – have come to watch two local rival teams play a match for charity. But this is no normal derby match, much less a standard charity fixture. Eleven of the players are international celebrities: their team is the biggest draw in British, and world, football.

Yet they are all full-time factory workers, amateurs in an increasingly professional sport, and they are all women: the Dick, Kerr's Ladies of the Dick, Kerr & Co Ltd munitions works in Preston. (The company was founded by a Mr William

Dick and a Mr John Kerr, which explains the comma in the name). The male football establishment is terrified by them. And so it resolved to abolish women's football... forever.

On Monday, 9 May 1881, the *Glasgow Herald*, Scotland's second most popular daily newspaper, carried the following report:

LADIES INTERNATIONAL MATCH
SCOTLAND V ENGLAND

A rather novel football match took place at Easter Road, Edinburgh, on Saturday between teams of lady players representing England and Scotland – the former hailing from London, and the latter, it is said, from Glasgow.

A considerable amount of curiosity was evinced in the event, and upwards of a thousand persons witnessed it. The young ladies' ages appeared to range from eighteen to four-and-twenty, and they were very smartly dressed. The Scotch [sic] team wore blue jerseys, white knickerbockers, red stockings, a red belt, high-heeled boots and blue and white cowl; while their English sisters were dressed in blue and white jerseys, blue stockings and belt, high-heeled boots and red and white cowl.

The game, judged from a player's point of view, was a failure, but some of the individual members of the teams showed that they had a fair idea of the game. During the first half the Scotch [sic] team, playing against the wind, scored a goal and in the second half they added another two, making a total of three goals against their opponents' nothing. Misses St Clair and Cole scored the first two, and the third was due to Misses Stevenson and Wright.

There were many aspects to this 'rather novel' match that are revealing, as well some which presage the hostility to come. The first, and the most evident, was the instinctive newspaper response to view the game as little more than a curio – an entertainment somewhere between a fashion parade and a contemporary (if mild) Victorian freak show. But beneath that admittedly patronising view was a remarkable spirit of tolerance. The *Glasgow Herald* was by no means a liberal newspaper, its politics being somewhere in the middle of traditional Tory values. Yet there is no outrage expressed amid the typically arch prose; there are no condemnations, much less demands for a ban on the spectacle.

The second revealing aspect emerges from a reading of the team sheet. The *Herald* helpfully printed details of every player in the team, together with their positions. In addition to the necessity of a goalkeeper, both sides fielded two backs, two halfback and six forwards. This 6-2-2-1 formation tells us something about football itself in the late 19th century. Sides were heavily weighted in favour of a phalanx of attacking players – a formation which will become important as the story of women's football unfolds in the coming chapters. But that team sheet has something else to tell us. The few official histories of the women's game – as well as several unofficial ones – all record that the organiser of the fixture was a Scottish 'suffragist'[1] named Helen Matthews. All modern accounts suggest she not only set up the first Scottish women's team but was goalkeeper in all its early fixtures – including that first match at Hibernian FC's ground in Easter Road, Edinburgh. Yet nowhere is the name Helen Matthews on any team sheet. The reason for this is simple: despite the apparently benign response of the press, it wasn't safe for women to play football under their own names. Many of those listed on that team sheet appear to be pseudonyms – *noms de football*, adopted to protect the players' true identities.

It seems Helen Matthews took this subterfuge one step further. When she established the team she called it 'Mrs Graham's 11' and claimed to be the pseudonymous Mrs Graham. Yet if she did, as history suggests, play in its fixtures she must have assumed a double-alias. There are no Mrs Grahams anywhere in the side's records. It would appear to have been an act of extreme caution – paranoia almost. And yet the wisdom of hiding behind assumed names would very quickly become all too clear.

A week after its debut in Edinburgh, Mrs Graham's XI took to the field for a return match against England. This time the game was staged in Glasgow and team sheets show that many of the players had switched sides, somewhat undermining the claim for this to be a true international. But more worryingly, within the span of just seven days, public opinion appears to have turned against the women footballers.

On the morning of Friday, 20 May 1881, provincial newspapers across Britain carried reports of the match. (In those days provincial papers carried both national and international news, and unlike today's almost instant reporting, much of the news was several days old by the time it was published.) Under the headline 'Ladies' "International" Football Match', the *Nottinghamshire Guardian* informed its readers:

> What will probably be the first and last exhibition of a female football match in Glasgow took place on Monday evening at Shawfield Grounds. Upwards of 5,000 spectators were present, and the absence of the fair sex was

especially notable. The teams were supposed to be representatives of England and Scotland, and as the Scotch [sic] team had won the recent match in Edinburgh, some excitement was thereby caused as to the result of the encounter.

The meagre training of the teams did not augur much for proficiency of play, and if the display of football tactics was of a sorry description, it was only what might have been expected, and not much worse than some of the efforts of our noted football clubs. The costume was suitable and, at a distance the players could scarcely have been distinguished from those in ordinary football matches.

The game was continued without interruption till ends were changed, but the chaff of the spectators was anything but complimentary. Cries of 'Go it, Fanny!' and 'Well done, Nelly!' resounded from all parts of the field, but the players went on the even tenour [sic] of their way, regardless of interruptions.

Had the crowd's reaction been no more than this faintly bawdy banter, the story of women's football – and British football itself – might have been very different. But in an unsettling precursor of today's soccer hooliganism, in the 55th minute of the match ribaldry turned to violence.

At last a few roughs broke into the enclosure, and as these were followed by hundreds soon after, the players were roughly jostled, and had prematurely to take refuge in the omnibus which had conveyed them to the ground. Their troubles were not, however, yet ended, for the crowd tore up the stakes and threw them at the departing vehicle, and but for the presence of the police, some bodily injury to the females might have occurred. The team of four grey horses [pulling the omnibus] was driven rapidly from the ground amid the jeers of the crowd, and the players escaped with, let us hope, nothing worse than a serious fright.

Other provincial newspapers reported that the police action which saved the players involved a full baton charge by numerous constables. But they also reflected a feeling that by simply playing football, the women were somehow debasing the game. The popular publication *Bell's Life in London and Sporting Times* attacked 'the girls' utmost ignorance of the game'. It also directed its ire at the male officials – called umpires, rather than referees – whose whistles enforced rules. (It was common practice in nineteenth-century football for there to be more than one official in notional charge of a match.)

They, the paper stated baldly, were 'even more ignorant of the simple rudiments of the Association rules... there was never even such a thing as a corner-flag kick allowed, although the leather was repeatedly sent behind the goal line by the defending side'. As we shall shortly see, this sniffy verdict reflected not just contempt for the concept of women's soccer but an internecine war that, in 1881, was being fought for the very soul of football – a war being fought by powerful vested interests. Nonetheless, the views of the man in the street, at least insofar as they were reflected by their newspapers, were hardening, as this comment in the *Leeds Mercury* illustrates: 'Ladies' football has had an exceedingly short life, and not a very merry one. Public feeling has demonstrated against the unseemly exhibition in such a manner that the authorities are now frowning down the innovation.'

It was a blow to women's football and a setback for the nascent suffragist movement, although ironically, the day after the riot at the Glasgow match, Scottish women were given their first taste of political equality when the Queen signed into law the Woman's Franchise (Scotland) Bill, allowing rate-paying women to vote in local government elections. (English women had enjoyed this very limited right to vote for local councillors for almost two decades.)

A third match between the Scottish and English teams had been scheduled for 17 May at Kilmarnock Portland FC, but after the previous night's riots the club refused to allow the use of its pitch. If Scotland was now plainly off-limits, Helen Matthews decided to try her luck on the other side of the border. On Saturday, 21 May, five days after the Glasgow riot, Mrs Graham's XI and the self-proclaimed English team walked out on to the turf at Hole-i'th-wall, the home of Blackburn Olympic FC in Lancashire's Ribble Valley. The local *Blackburn Standard* newspaper was in attendance and reported:

FEMALES IN THE FOOTBALL FIELD
May 28, 1881

Woman's mission, according to some authorities, is to compete with man in every department of life, and some enterprising person has organised a team of 'lady' football players, who are understood to hail from Glasgow.

On Saturday afternoon these 'ladies' played a match on the ground of the Blackburn Olympic Club, at Hole-'the-wall, where some 4,000 people assembled to witness their exploits.

The ladies did not play well as a team, not, perhaps, having been trained to run in harness. There were no halfbacks or any halves whatever about the game, each

11

lady being in full possession of her position and playing her own game whenever she got a chance without much regard to the result.

Neither side scored up to the call of half-time but subsequently each side made a goal, though neither was allowed to count. Shortly before the time of closing there was an excited melee in front of the goal of the Scotch [sic] – it should be stated that the game was an international one – and a goal was neatly reckoned by the English team, who were declared the victors. Both sides soon afterwards scampered from the field.

Other than the distinctly sardonic references to 'ladies' – the speech-marks hinting at the question of whether suitably respectable women would put themselves on show in front of thousands of spectators – and the dismissive review of the tactical nous, the paper's verdict contained none of the bile and approbation which had followed the Glasgow match.

Encouraged, Helen Matthews scheduled a second game for the following Saturday, this time at Fairfield Athletic Grounds in Liverpool. But something appears to have happened during the intervening week. A few hundred spectators duly turned up: but there was no sign of the teams. Nor would there be for a full month afterwards. Then, on 20 June 1881, a notice appeared in the pages of the *Manchester Guardian*.

LADIES FOOTBALL MATCH

The Lady Players who were advertised to play during Whit-week will positively PLAY at Cheetham Football Ground, Totlow Fold, Great Cheetham Street, on MONDAY (today), TUESDAY, and WEDNESDAY, [June] 20, 21, 22. Admission 1s ad 2s^2. Kick-of [sic] 7.30pm.

The entrance fee was surprisingly expensive. Spectators at top-flight men's football matches paid a fraction of the 1 shilling (let alone 2 shillings) being charged at the Cheetham gate, reinforcing the impression that what was being staged was a spectacle rather than sport. No record exists of the first or third scheduled matches at Cheetham Football Ground, but on Monday, 20 June, the *Manchester Guardian* carried the following report. It was not good news.

DISORDERLY SCENE AT A WOMEN'S FOOTBALL MATCH

The score or so of young women who do not hesitate to gratify vulgar curiosity by taking part in what is termed a 'ladies' football match appeared last evening for the second time this week on the ground of the Cheetham Football Club, Tetlow Fold, Great Cheetham Street. The Club, however, had nothing to do with the affair.

The public had been invited by placard to witness a match between 'eleven of England and eleven of Scotland', the kick off to take place at half past seven pm. The players, attired in a costume which is neither graceful nor very becoming, were driven to the ground in a wagonette, and, as was to be expected, were followed by a crowd composed of youths eager to avail themselves of the opportunity for a little boisterous amusement.

Play – if kicking the ball about the field can be so described – was commenced pretty punctually. Very few persons paid for admission to the grounds, but a great multitude assembled in the road and struggled for sight of what was going on within the enclosure, whilst an equally large number gathered on the higher ground on the other side of the field for a similar purpose.

A number of police constables were present to maintain order and prevent anyone entering without paying, and for about an hour whilst this so-called match was being played they succeeded. There were frequent attempts, however, to elude the constables.

At length a great rush was made by those occupying the higher land, and the football ground was speedily taken possession of by the mob.

Apprehending a repetition of the rough treatment they have met with in other parts of the country the women no sooner heard the clamour which accompanied the rush than they also took to their heels and ran to where the wagonette was standing. This they reached before the crowd could overtake them, and amid the jeers of the multitude and much disorder they were immediately driven away.

This was a second riot, or at least near-riot, at a women's football match in a matter of just four weeks. Worse, it happened in a city which was already building a reputation for disorder, violence and crime. Manchester, the heart of 'King Cotton' (the backbone of the northern industrial revolution) was rapidly expanding. At the start of the 19th century its population was 322,000. Fifty years later it had topped one million and by 1881 was well on course to double that figure. The vast majority of this explosion of population comprised working class men, women and children. They were drawn into the sprawling slums of the city by work, generally ill-paid and frequently dangerous, in the cotton mills.

Crime and, to the Victorian mind most importantly, disorder were booming. The Lancashire Cotton Famine – a slump in the textile industry caused by disruption to cotton imports from

America during its civil war in the 1860s – had led to a lingering economic depression across the north-west. The fear of riots by the urban working class was never far from middle class minds, to the point where the dwellers in the slums they had created were termed 'dangerous classes', and was exacerbated by the spectre of unemployment and destitution. To some extent this fear was diffuse: a messy mix of concern with political disorder and the essentially Victorian obsession with maintaining what its leaders saw as the correct habits of restraint and obedience by the lower orders to their betters.

But it was a fear focused firmly on the relatively new concept of industrial cities which had been set out in 1844 by the Tory publication *Blackwoods Magazine* under the heading, 'Causes of the Increase of Crime': 'The restraints of character, relationship and vicinity are... lost in the crowd... Multitudes remove responsibility without weakening passion.' Beware, in other words, of the lack of restraint, and the unruly passions of the urban masses, concentrated in the filthy stews of the industrial revolution, which manifested themselves in criminality and widespread disorder.

It was against this background that Helen Matthews and her 'lady footballers' challenged the social order of the day. The open hostility of the *Manchester Guardian* is telling. The paper had been founded on liberal, non-conformist principles and (albeit under a different title) had 62 years earlier championed the cause of the city's unemployed when an army cavalry unit attacked a mass political rally at St Peter's Field, killing 15 people and injured up to 700 more.

By the time of the near-riot at Cheetham Football Club, the paper had been edited by one the legendary figures in the British press – C P Scott – who was transforming it into a radical voice on behalf of the urban working class. For the

Manchester Guardian to attack the very notion of women's football was to send a clear signal that the majority of public opinion was very firmly against it.

Even so, Helen Matthews was evidently not dissuaded. Two days after she and the other 21 lady footballers had taken refuge in their wagonette to flee from the baying crowd in Manchester, they set off on the 33-mile journey westwards to Liverpool, and in those pre-motor car, pre-tarmac road days it would have been a lengthy trek.

On Saturday, 25 June 1881, the *Liverpool Mercury* – like the *Manchester Guardian* a Liberal reformist paper with the self-declared mission of promoting 'continual and peaceful progress' – carried the following advert.

CATTLE MARKET INN ATHLETIC GROUNDS
STANLEY, LIVERPOOL
RETURN VISIT OF THE INTERNATIONAL
LADY FOOTBALL PLAYERS
ENGLAND V. SCOTLAND
TWO GRAND MATCHES
THIS DAY (SATURDAY) AND MONDAY NEXT
THE 25 AND 27TH INSTANT
Kick-off – Saturday at Five pm; Monday at 7.30pm
ADMISSION, ONE SHILLING

The claim to be a return fixture was, at best, misleading since the teams had failed to show up for their previous scheduled fixture in Liverpool. The *Manchester Guardian* acidly pointed this out in its report of the first 'grand match', noting that the low attendance to watch the women footballers was due 'to the disappointment caused a few weeks ago by their failure to keep

16

an engagement'. But the rest of the match report is revealing. After recounting how 'Scotland' had much the better of the game, spending almost the entire first half in 'English' territory, it notes that the Scottish players made 'several touchdowns and one goal' before the English, 'by a spirited dash, managed to get the ball through and make a goal'. The reference to 'touchdowns' indicates that these football matches were not being played under rules we would recognise in the game today, being more reminiscent of rugby. As we shall see shortly, this was both a crucial component of the hostility towards these women football pioneers and a reflection of the battle raging inside football itself in the 1880s.

For the record, Scotland won the match 2 goals to 1. Two days later the Scottish team won the second fixture 2 goals to nil. A third match was announced in the Liverpool press, scheduled for the following evening of Tuesday, 28 June. But unlike any of the previous matches, there were no reports of it in any of the local, regional or national press. Nor would there be any sight of the redoubtable Helen Matthews or Mrs Graham's X1 for another 14 years. From 1881 to almost the turn of the century, women's football seems to disappear. By the time it once again made headlines across the country, Britain would be a very different country: women's rights, loudly championed by the suffragette movement were attracting admiration and opprobrium in almost equal measure. But above all, football itself would have been re-invented.

CHAPTER TWO

'Football is all very well as a game for rough girls,
but is hardly suitable for delicate boys.'

— OSCAR WILDE

O n the morning of 26 October 1863, Mr Ebenezer Cobb
    Morley and 10 other solid and thoroughly respectable
professional men assembled in the Freemason's Tavern on Great
Queen Street, near London's Covent Garden. Their self-
proclaimed mission that autumnal morning was to set about
governing the ungovernable.

Morley, a solicitor from Hull, had moved to Barnes on the
south-west fringes of the capital five years earlier. A keen
footballer, he had promptly formed a club for like-minded
professional men from the leafy environs of Barnes and
Mortlake to enjoy the sport. There was, however, a problem:
they could find no other teams to play against. It wasn't that no
other clubs existed: London could at that time boast upwards
of a dozen clubs, and football was becoming well-established in
the provinces. Sheffield, in particular, was a northern bastion of
the game. The difficulty was that no one could agree on how to
play it. It was to settle that vexed question, ostensibly once and

for all, that Ebenezer Cobb Morley had summoned the great and the good to his meeting in the Freemason's Tavern.

Football has been played in Britain since the 12th century. The first documentary record of a football match in England was written in 1170 by William FitzStephen, a clerk to the then Archbishop of Canterbury, Thomas Beckett (indeed FitzStephen was present at his master's murder in the cathedral). FitzStephen was also something of an historian and penned one of the few contemporary accounts of life in London. In it he noted that during a visit to the capital he observed that 'after dinner all the youths of the city goes out into the fields for the very popular game of ball'. On further enquiry, FitzStephen discovered that every trade in the city boasted its own football team, writing:

> 'The elders, the fathers, and the men of wealth come on horseback to view the contests of their juniors, and in their fashion sport with the young men; and there seems to be aroused in these elders a stirring of natural heat by viewing so much activity and by participation in the joys of unrestrained youth.'

But it was not until a century later that another cleric recorded how the game was actually played. This (apparently anonymous) monk wrote that football was a game 'in which young men... propel a huge ball not by throwing it into the air, but by striking and rolling it along the ground, and that not with their hands but with their feet'. The game did not meet with the monk's approval: he described it as 'undignified and worthless' and noted that it often resulted in 'some loss, accident or disadvantage to the players themselves'. Such 'disadvantages' included the apparently frequent problem of players accidentally stabbing themselves to death by falling on their daggers.

The growing popularity of football – and the alarming toll of injuries or deaths – found its way to the court of King Edward II, who in 1314 was attempting to raise an army for that perennial favourite pastime of medieval monarchs, fighting the Scots. But since the young and able seemed more interested in football than the rather more militarily vital skill of practising the longbow, Edward took a dim view of such sport, complaining about 'certain tumults arising from great footballs in the fields of the public, from which many evils may arise'. His solution was simple and direct: he banned the game altogether.

Edward's son, Edward III, reintroduced the ban in 1331 in preparation for a new invasion of Scotland, and Henry IV did likewise in 1388. It apparently had little effect and so in 1410, his government imposed a fine of 20 shillings (£1, a vast sum at the time when a basic suit of armour cost £5) and six days' imprisonment for those caught playing football.

For the next 200 years the royal antipathy – based on the belief that it was far better for men to get themselves killed on regally-ordered battlefields than injured in the base sport of football – continued unabated. In 1414, Henry V pronounced a new decree requiring his subjects to practise archery rather than football. In 1477 his descendant, Edward IV, signed into law a new stipulation that 'no person shall practise any unlawful games such as dice, quoits, football and such games, but that every strong and able-bodied person shall practise with bow for the reason that the national defence depends upon such bowmen'.

To keep up the tradtion, Henry VII outlawed football in 1496 and his son, the corpulent and much-married Henry VIII, followed suit with a series of laws against playing the game in public places. At around the same time the church weighed in when, in 1531, puritan preacher Thomas Eliot pronounced that football caused 'beastly fury and extreme violence', and four years later the Bishop of Rochester demanded a new purge to suppress this 'evil game'.

Part of the problem for these good men of the cloth was that games were being played on the Sabbath day, but they were also concerned about the ever-present physical dangers of football. One such prelate, Philip Stubbs, included a detailed list of typical injuries in a 1553 book he cheerfully titled *Anatomy of Abuses*:

> Sometimes their necks are broken, sometimes their backs, sometimes their legs, sometimes their arms, sometimes one part is thrust out of joint, sometimes the noses gush out with blood... football encourages envy and hatred... sometimes fighting, murder and a great loss of blood.

Surviving records indicate that many young men ignored both the royal decrees and the imprecations of the church. In 1589, Hugh Case and William Shurlock were fined 2 shillings for playing football in St Werburgh's cemetery during the vicar's sermon. Ten years later a group of men in a village in Essex were fined for playing football on a Sunday, while similar prosecutions took place in Richmond, Bedford, Thirsk and Guisborough. In 1576 it was recorded in Ruislip that around a hundred people 'assembled themselves unlawfully and played a certain unlawful game, called football', while in Manchester in 1608 'a company of lewd and disordered persons... broke many men's windows' during an 'unlawful' game of football. The game was apparently such a significant problem that in 1618 the local council appointed special 'football officers' to police these laws.

Yet there were voices raised in public support of the game. Tellingly, in view of how football would develop in later centuries, Richard Mulcaster, the headmaster of one of the so-called 'Great Nine' public schools of England (Eton, Rugby, Winchester, Westminster, Harrow, Charterhouse, Shrewsbury, Merchant Taylors, and St Paul's-the-Fields) wrote in 1581 that football had 'great helps, both to health and strength'.

> '[it] strengtheneth and brawneth the whole body, and by provoking superfluities downward, it dischargeth the head, and upper parts, it is good for the bowels, and to drive the stone and gravel from both the bladder and kidneys.'

Nonetheless, England's rulers continued to ban the sport. Oliver Cromwell, fresh from defeating and then executing King Charles I in 1649, instructed the major-generals of his new Commonwealth to enforce the existing laws against football, lumping it in with bear-baiting, cock-fighting, horse-racing and wrestling in a list of sinful recreations. Only with the return of the kings to England in 1660 did the game begin gradually to re-assert itself across the country. Football once again became a staple part of life in pre-industrialised Britain.

But the game being played bore little or no resemblance to anything we would recognise as football today. It was, instead 'folk football', typically played on special days in the calendar – Shrove Tuesday being the biggest of all. These were wild and riotous affairs in which village competed against village or other seemingly-arbitrarily chosen groups of opposing teams, such as married men against bachelors. Those teams were elastic and vast, a heaving mass of hundreds of people, kicking, throwing, and carrying a wooden or leather ball stuffed with an inflated animal bladder across fields over streams and through narrow lanes. Such rules as existed were kept to a minimum and varied wildly from town to town, let alone county to county. Almost any degree of violence short of actual death was allowed.

The ostensible aim of this clash of mobs was somehow to force the 'ball' into a goal marked out at either end of the pitch. Sometimes the goals would be the balcony of the opponents' church. Given that the pitch itself could be several miles long and wide, and that the vast majority of those playing never actually saw the ball, scorelines tended to be at best very low and more frequently non-existent.

Folk football was played all over Britain in the 17th and 18th centuries – between rival villagers in the north of Scotland, and rival tradesmen in the streets of London, where the citizens of the capital were forced to protect their windows with hurdles and bushes. Derby, which was renowned for the game, has a particularly rich legacy of accounts of its annual Shrove Tuesday event. The match involved the inhabitants of St Peter's Parish in the south of the town against those from All Saints in the north – though each year large contingents of young men from surrounding villages came in to join either side.

The teams would assemble at lunchtime in separate inns in the town centre and, suitably refreshed, head off to the market place accompanied by peals of church bells. Despite the usually bitter February conditions players stripped off their outer garments to reveal bare arms and tightly strapped-up long trousers. In view of what was to come, these were sensible precautions. At 2pm sharp the bells stopped and silence briefly descended. The teams, generally hundreds, sometimes thousands strong, faced off against each other from either side of the square. And then, as one shell-shocked spectator later reported, the ball was thrown in the middle.

O ye Gods, what a riot! What pulling, hauling, tearing bawling! The ball is instantly surrounded by the 'dogs of war', who shortly form one solid and impenetrable mass of living clay: arms erect, eyes staring from their sockets, and mouths extended gasping for breath – just like so many madmen escaped from the asylum, and fighting for the recovery of their senses.

It was not an event for the faint-hearted. A French visitor to Derby wrote to a friend after experiencing, from a suitably safe distance, a typical match: 'If Englishmen called this playing it would be impossible to say what they would call fighting'. The goals were about a mile from the market square – All Saints' was a mill wheel in the western district of Markeaton Brook, St Peters' a garden gate slightly further south.

But it was a rare game that saw either side get anywhere close to them. The riotous brawl in the square itself would generally last at least an hour before the action moved in a whirlwind of destruction through the town's narrow streets. Frequently the ball ended up in the River Derwent, and both sides plunged into its presumably freezing waters and carried on the fight there. The *Derby Mercury*, a determinedly Tory newspaper dedicated to advocating the interests of agriculture, commerce, manufacturers and the Church of England, described what happened next.

Thus the combat would go on, hour after hour, fresh men taking the place of those who were exhausted, women rushing about in a state of frantic excitement, urging on their husbands and brothers, bringing them stimulants and refreshments, lending them petticoats to cover the naked limbs, and binding up their wounds.

But violence aside, folk football had one very particular quality: it was a game enjoyed by all classes, and social interaction between them was the order of the day. Whilst most of the local nobs and snobs preferred to stay on the edges of the action – often betting heavily on the outcome – many plunged into the fray. In 1762 one such 'gentleman' took out an advert in the *Derby Mercury*, offering a reward of one guinea (a gold coin worth 21 shillings – £1.05 in modern currency) for the return of a silver pocket watch he had lost in the heat of the battle.

However, from the end of the 18th century, both local councils and the national government in Westminster began to clamp down on folk football. In part, this was due to the growing problems of physical space. In the countryside the old open landscape was being carved up by the growing revolution in agriculture and by a succession of Enclosures Acts which created today's patchwork of walled and hedged fields. These effectively locked out the wide-roaming tradition of folk football.

Then, as the Industrial Revolution swept across Britain, cities grew and sprawled, sucking in men, women and children from the countryside to their narrow and fetid streets. Here there was simply no room for such a riotous free-for-all, and in 1835, Parliament passed a law specifically banning football on the highways.

But there were other factors at play. The newly-emerging Victorian middle class disapproved heartily of any blurring of social order, or orders. The working class was viewed with deep suspicion and fear – particularly as social unrest grew in parallel with industrial squalor. And these newly-powerful local burghers were imbued, too, with a sense of a moral crusade against what they viewed as the bestial antics of the lower orders: they were serious men, in serious times and firmly opposed to frivolity. Which may explain why, in Manchester in 1844, a proposal to set aside a few acres for the playing of traditional games was dismissed by the local council on the grounds that it might be 'an encouragement to too much levity'.

And when a year later, again in Derby, the lower orders refused to be put in their properly determined place and dared to defy the ban on the Shrove Tuesday football match, the town mayor, William Mousley, was forced first publicly to read the Riot Act[3] and then to call in two troops of Dragoons to disperse the players. When the game's ringleaders were finally arrested and then charged, they came perilously close to being transported out of England to the penal colonies of Australia. Within a decade, football as a sport for the working man had been almost entirely snuffed out across the length and breadth of the land.

Football, however, was still being played, but as the 19th century unfolded it was shifting from the ordinary masses and was being adopted by the upper classes. If, as the Duke of Wellington allegedly asserted, the Battle of Waterloo had been won on the playing fields of Eton, those self-same playing fields, and others at rival establishments, were now growing the seeds of football.

Public school life in the early part of the century could be summed up with the three B's: Bullying, Brutality and Buggery. Violence and abuse, both physical and sexual, was endemic at the Great Nine institutions. And there was, of course, the infamous 'fagging': the enslavement of the youngest pupils (often no older than 8) by the more senior boys. Fags were required to do their masters' bidding – be that cooking meals, polishing their boots or assuaging their adolescent lusts. School staff exercised absolutely no control over these activities. One young and tormented fag described in a letter home in 1824 his master's habit of donning a pair of spurs, mounting his victim and forcing him to carry him around the dormitory before attempting to jump over a marked-out 'gap' without dislodging his rider. Should he fail, the youngster told his parents, the older boy 'spurs us violently. My thigh is now quite sore with the inroads made by that dreadful spur.'

But this blatant violence was not confined to the dorms. Between 1768 and 1832, there were 21 separate mass riots at Eton, many involving firearms, as the pupils (all scions of the aristocracy) fought pitched battles for supremacy over the staff, who were invariably drawn from the middle classes, one rung beneath them on the social ladder. In 1815, the local, and armed, militias were called in to quell disorder at both Rugby and Winchester.

In part this was due to the remarkable lack of teaching which took place. By 1830, for example, Eton schoolboys were in the classroom for just 11 hours a week. Nor, as yet, did the schools provide a sporting outlet for their pupils' energies. Most actively prohibited the playing of games, preferring to leave their charges to the traditional aristocratic pastime of roaming the countryside with shotguns (known in those days as fowling-pieces) or a good afternoon's entertainment of tormenting the populace of surrounding villages.

But eventually, probably led by the reforming influence of Thomas Arnold, headmaster of Rugby, the public schools began to institute both a proper timetable and to encourage school sports: cricket in the summer and football in the winter months. Unfortunately, fuelled by a prejudice even more virulent than the disdain they felt for the lower orders, each school determinedly developed its own unique set of rules. And so football at Harrow was played with a 'ball' in the shape of a church cassock which could not be handled except by catching to earn a free-kick; while Eton footballers were required to pass their more conventionally spherical ball with their hands. At Winchester, fags were required to form a human wall around the field and flap the ball back to the feet of players who were forbidden to dribble it with their feet, whilst Rugby schoolboys could dribble, kick or even run with the ball – without the assistance of a shield of shivering children.

While all school football involved propelling the ball into, or over, a marked-out goal-line, there was no common size, shape or position of the goals. And Eton – which would later proclaim itself to have been the incubator of modern football – also instituted an additional method of scoring (probably because their strenuously stringent off-side rule resulted in a distinct dearth of goals). This involved getting the ball behind any part of the opponent's goal line and touching it with a hand. They called it a 'rouge'.

Whatever their inter-organisational shortcomings, the Great Nine public schools unquestionably rescued and resurrected the game of folk football and, in theory, at least, civilised it. (The fact that public school football was just as, and probably even more, violent than the game it replaced was conveniently ignored). And from the late 1820s onwards it became a fixed part of the lives of the schools' privileged pupils. Fixed being the operative word: each school carefully wrote down, refined and then re-defined its peculiar set of rules.

Not surprisingly, these young men wanted to pursue their favourite sport when they moved from school to university, and as a result, Cambridge – which with Oxford was the favoured choice for young gentlemen – formed a football club in the late 1830s. The problem was that each new member brought with him the rules he had been taught (often painfully) at his respective school and chaos ensued. H C Malden, one of the very earliest Cambridge players, would subsequently note: 'The result was dire confusion. Every man played by the rules he had been accustomed to at his public school. I remember how the Eton men howled at the Rugby men for handling the ball.'

A common code was clearly needed. But it took until 1848 for the Cambridge players, led by Malden, to begin work on one: 'We met in my rooms at 4pm, anticipating a long meeting. I cleared the tables and provided pens, ink and paper. Every man brought a copy of his school rules, or knew them by heart, and our progress in framing new rules was slow. We broke up five minutes before midnight.'

It would take several further meetings for the Cambridge Code to be agreed. When, finally, the ink was dry the new rules were an amalgam of the varying school traditions. Catching was allowed, though a player had immediately to kick the ball and was not permitted to run with it, as happened at Rugby. The curious Eton Rouge was dispensed with. Goalposts were – for the first time – to be connected with a piece of string across the top, and for a goal to be scored it had to pass under it. And a strict off-side rule – reflecting the Victorian horror at any 'sneaky' play – was instituted. 'No player,' the new Code stressed, 'is allowed to loiter between the ball and the adversary's goal.' Traditional football histories rightly point to the establishment of the Cambridge Code as the first step along the road to a uniform set of football rules. But they also tend to imply that this road was a smooth and untroubled one. The reality was the exact opposite.

The Cambridge men sent out their hard-worked effort to all the public schools. None showed the remotest interest in it. The reason was that staple of the English upper-classes:

snobbery. Each school not only viewed the others as rivals but in many cases as social inferiors. If there was any discernible underpinning to this rigid hierarchy it was age. Eton, as the oldest public school, was at the top of the pecking order, with Shrewsbury and Rugby viewed as Johnny-come-lately interlopers. It was a structure so rigid that it evoked extraordinary passion. When, in 1858, a correspondent to *Bell's Life* had the temerity to suggest that the Great Nine should agree to 'fixed laws' for the game of football, the readers' responses were so ill-tempered that the paper's editor pronounced that 'we consider them better unpublished'. He then declared the entire subject out of bounds.

As late as 1866 – three full years after Ebenezer Morley and 10 other London worthies met in the Freemason's Tavern to form a Football Association which should rule the game with a common code – Westminster School disdainfully declined an invitation from Shrewsbury for a football match, with the chilling response that it did not recognise the upstart as a public school. All in all, the task facing the founders of the FA that morning on 26 October was much more than a simple feat of organisation. Whether they knew it or not they were trundling on to a field so mystical, so exclusive and so wilfully obscure that it would not just defy their efforts but labour mightily to de-rail them.

CHAPTER THREE

*'If you do away with hacking you will do away with all
the courage and pluck from the game, and... bring over a lot of
Frenchmen who would beat you with a week's practice.'*
— Francis Maule Campbell, Blackheath FC,
26 October 1863

The choice of the Freemasons' Tavern was, accidentally or not, remarkably apposite for the meeting that founded the FA. The inn reputedly stood at 61-65 Great Queen Street, at the centre of London's Masonic world. Almost half of the south side of the road was occupied by Freemasons' Hall, headquarters of the United Grand Lodge of England. The north side was dominated by the premises of a Masonic regalia manufacturer, shops selling Masonic regalia, and a number of Masonic charities. The Tavern was frequently used by Freemasons for receptions and dinners. (There is some dispute about the actual location of the Freemasons' Tavern, with some sources suggesting it was on the site of the Freemasons Arms pub which stands today in nearby Long Acre. Given the internecine squabbles that would characterise just about every step of the FA's early existence it seems entirely appropriate that there is no agreement on exactly where it was born.)

Freemasonry in the mid-Victorian era retained much of the

pomp, circumstance and quasi-religious trappings of its origins, but was also becoming a reliable path to business networking. And business, or 'trade' as the Victorian aristocracy would have termed it, was very much what characterised Ebenezer Morley and his ilk.

In many ways Morley was the very model of a modern Victorian. Resolutely middle class (he had not attended public school) he was a Justice of the Peace and was a pillar of his little community, serving as clerk to the Conservators of Barnes Common (though he would subsequently be hauled before local magistrates to explain why one pond on the Common was 'in such a state as to be a nuisance and injurious to health'.).

Ranged alongside him that October morning were the representatives of 10 London football clubs: Blackheath, Perceval House, Kensington School, the War Office, Crystal Palace, Forest of Leytonstone (later known as the Wanderers and who will go on to play an important part in the story of football), Surbiton, The Crusaders, Blackheath Proprietary School and the archly-named No Names Club of Kilburn. Morley himself was the official delegate of Barnes FC.

Many of these representatives were cut from the same social cloth as Ebenezer Morley: educated in a variety of 'ordinary' schools, often having quit education by the age of 15 without troubling a university, and now carving a niche for themselves in trade or in the distinctly non-upper class professions. But, in tune with their times, they saw themselves as having a moral duty – a middle class white man's burden – of taming all that was unruly in society and of converting the lawless to the true path of rectitude. They were, as Percy Young, one of football's most prolific authors, put it: 'Men of prejudice, seeing themselves as patricians, heirs to the doctrine of leadership and so law-givers by at least semi-divine right.'[4]

Morley had written to *Bell's Life* inviting all interested parties to attend his meeting, which would aim not just to form an association of football clubs but to create a common set of rules by which the game might be played. Conscious of their vital role in keeping the sport alive and literally kicking, he had also invited the public schools. In that, as in much else, the energetic Mr Morley was to be disappointed. Eight of the Great Nine loftily ignored his letter altogether; only Charterhouse sent a representative, but with strict instructions that he was only there to observe and must not take part in the discussions, much less join any association which might assume the right to tell public schools how to play *their* sport.

And there, in a nutshell was the problem. John Cartwright, a then influential journalist for *The Field*, summed it up for his readers that autumn: 'It is impossible to report progress: the matter stands in precisely the same position as it stood years ago... [Public school rivalry] hangs clog-like at the heels of football.' Undaunted, the coming men of football pressed on.

The Football Association was formed with Ebenezer Morley as its secretary. Membership was fixed at one guinea (£1.05p) – a fee which granted the right for member clubs to send two representatives to the next meeting. And the newly-instituted Association got down to the business of formulating rules based on a blend of being played at public schools, universities and the clubs themselves. It proved to be an Herculean task and quite beyond agreement. There was one particular sticking point. It concerned a staple element of public school football: hacking.

With admirable efficiency of language this rule, carefully codified by the public schools, did exactly what the word suggested. Players were allowed – in fact, encouraged – to hack brutally at the shins and legs of their opponents. The eminent nineteenth-century journalist and writer James Brinsley Richards, who spent seven less than happy years at Eton, later recalled[5]: 'I have had my shins hacked till they were all blue and bleeding, and caused me the most maddening pain... I think there was a broken leg or collar bone in the school at least once a year. Sprained ankles and partial concussions of the brain, causing sick, nervous headaches, were of daily occurrence.'

At the meeting in the Freemasons' Tavern, Morley proposed the unthinkable: outlawing these acts of unremitting violence. 'If we have "hacking", no one who has arrived at the years of discretion will play at football and it will be entirely relinquished to schoolboys.' Against him, Morley faced a vociferous, if minority, faction led by Francis Campbell from Blackheath FC. Campbell argued that 'hacking is the true football' and that it encouraged 'masculine toughness'. He thundered that the proposal to ban hacking emanated from 'those who like their pipes or grog or schnapps more than the manly game of football'; and, for good measure, issued a dire warning that to abolish it would only ensure an entirely unwelcome influx of (obviously less masculine) players from France.

In what would become a time-honoured tradition, the new Football Association decided that it could not decide. A further meeting would need to be held the following month before it could issue its much-vaunted code of rules. But in truth, very little attention was being devoted to this new self-crowned 'authority'. The British Newspaper Library keeps copies of almost every published paper in the country. Search its records for 'Football Association' in October 1863 and just two results emerge.

The *Chelmsford Chronicle* reported that the meeting had taken place (though it devoted less than a column inch to the story, and its position at the bottom of a page under a story revealing that a German man had married a German girl before emigrating to America, rather suggested the FA might not be commanding too many headlines in the near future). While the *Exeter Flying Post* commented:

> Football is just now receiving considerable attention: the clubs of the metropolis being anxious that a certain set of rules should be adopted by all football players, and a Football Association has been formed for the purpose of setting the desired code. The great public schools have their respective rules which it is thought desirable to assimilate; but this proposal has, in some instances, been received with reticence.

But the reticence of Ebenezer Morley and his supporters to adopt the brutality which characterised the playing fields of Eton was nothing in comparison to the contempt with which the public schools themselves dismissed his efforts. Less than a month after the inaugural meeting of the Football Association, a letter dripping with disdain appeared in columns of *Sporting Life*:

> 'I do not think the meetings in London are attended by people or clubs of sufficient influence to cause their suggestions to be generally acted upon... [who] are they to dictate rules to Eton, Harrow, Winchester, etc ?'

Even so, these upstart men of trade were determined to do so. On 24 November, the abandoned first attempt at a rules meeting was resumed, and this time Morley's faction won the day. A list of 13 'Football Association Laws' was duly issued. Hacking and running with the ball in hand were banned, which so incensed Francis Campbell that he withdrew Blackheath FC from the FA and it would go on to become London's first Rugby Football Club. But catching the ball and making a simultaneous mark in the ground with the heel (a manoeuvre which allowed the catcher a free kick) was permitted.

Morley's triumph has led to him being dubbed (by the FA, amongst others) 'the father of modern football'. But at the time he – and his Football Association – were voices crying in the sporting wilderness. Six days after the new rules were promulgated, the annual Oxford vs Cambridge football match took place at Eton. It paid not the slightest heed to the new 'laws' of the game. Instead it continued the public school traditions. On the opening whistle, half a dozen players from each side squared up to each other the in the centre of the field. They then locked arms, crouched down and formed a scrum (known in Eton parlance as a 'bully'). When the ball was thrown in between the opposing packs there was a mass kicking – not at the ball (the heaving, sweating mass of players was forbidden to hook the ball out of the bully) but at each other's shins. Nor was passing allowed, thanks to an eye-wateringly complex off-side rule. The sole aim was to form a V-shaped phalanx of players behind the lead forward and then drive this wedge through the opposing team. Occasionally the ball would get kicked free of this mass brawl, and the bully would set off in hot pursuit to start all over again.

Hardly surprisingly, the game ended as a 0-0 draw, with only a 'rouge' by Oxford winning the fixture. A beautiful game it was not. But unlike the formation of the FA, it was reported enthusiastically in the press. The correspondent for *Bell's Life* pronounced: 'The peculiarities of the game now played at Eton... were never seen to greater effect than during this contest... Both the victors and the vanquished retired from the field covered with honour, much dirt, and many kicks and bruises, but there were no broken legs.'

For the next four years the new Football Association was almost completely ignored and its attempt to create a universal set of rules was barely acknowledged. Whilst matches were held under the FA code (Ebenezer Morley played in the first recorded game, against Richmond in 1863) by the end of 1866 the Association had just 10 member clubs, many of whom were agitating to revert to their own original laws. The situation was so bad that at the 1867 AGM, Morley suggested the FA might as well be dissolved altogether.

But salvation was at hand. And it came from a hitherto disregarded source. The city of Sheffield was, in this mid-Victorian era, a powerhouse of the industrial revolution. Leeds, centre of the wool and textiles business, or Manchester, home to the cotton trade, might be the more powerfully beating hearts of the age, but Sheffield had carved itself a reputation, and many small fortunes, from steel.

In 1857, Nathaniel Creswick then chairman of the local Silver Plate Company, had helped form Sheffield Football Club. In a remarkably short order it would boast 57 members, all sons of well-to-do industrialists; and by the early 1860s several long-established Sheffield cricket clubs had branched out to form their own football teams. While Ebenezer Morley laboured mightily to get London to notice non-public school football, in Sheffield the game was thriving.

Not that it was played under FA rules. Creswick would later record that he had written to all the Great Nine public schools, asking for a copy of their rule books; and then he had sat down to write his own code, drawing on what he saw as the best bits of each. Contemporary local press reports indicate that what was being played in Sheffield was a crude version of public school football: it was certainly just as violent.

In December 1862, a local derby match between Sheffield FC and their bitterest rivals, Hallam, descended into a riot. A Hallam player deliberately fouled Nathaniel Creswick (not, history records, a stranger to punch-ups on the turf) and after a brief exchange of views, Creswick punched his opposite number in the face so hard that blood flowed freely. Cue an invasion of the pitch and an all-round fist-fight involving players and spectators.

By 1866, Morley's beleaguered group of London clubs had evidently heard of Sheffield and on 31 March that year a representative team from the capital played Sheffield FC in Battersea Park. It was, apparently, just as violent as the Sheffield-Hallam fixture, and *Bell's Life* reported that 'some of the London team got rather severely kicked and knocked about'. But it was played under FA rules, thus providing a much-needed boost to the Association's reputation.

The following autumn, just as Ebenezer Morley was losing hope, Sheffield gave the FA another shot in the arm. Just six people turned up at the Association's AGM that year, but one of them was a delegate from Sheffield FC. He brought with him a letter which detailed the vibrant football scene in the city but most importantly, he pledged the clubs' allegiance to and support for the Football Association. It would be a turning point for the FA's fortunes, and one which Morley recognised by announcing that Sheffield was 'the greatest stronghold of football in England'. But, like a footballing Trojan Horse, Sheffield's life-line would also contain the seeds to a new and almost-fatal conflict. It was a battle for the very soul of the game which would scar the FA for decades to come and play a fundamental part in the hostility towards women's football. Its root cause was money.

From 1867 – when it introduced new rule changes that definitively marked the Association game as different from Rugby Football – the FA began to prosper. More and more clubs were formed in the capital, and Sheffield's example had encouraged contact between London and Scotland, where a rash of new clubs had emerged. But the key characteristic of all these clubs, and their players, was their class. Some, like the Wanderers, were exclusively the preserve of the aristocracy. Its notice in the London newspapers seeking out new players stated: 'Varsity men [by which it meant Oxford and Cambridge] living in the capital. Anyone else need not apply.'

The rest of the London teams were resolutely middle class, formed by and for the sons of prosperous industrial families and who, like the ex-Varsity men, could afford the luxury of time devoted to football. Of the vast mass of British people for whom time not working equated with poverty, hunger or destitution, there was little or no sign. Football was, at this stage in its life, emphatically not the game of 'the people'.

But in Sheffield, there were early indications of democratisation. By 1867 there were already suggestions being put forward that if a player was injured during a game (not unlikely since, rule changes notwithstanding, football was still largely centred around a flying phalanx of players charging at the opposition) he should be compensated for time lost at work. This could only mean that the sport was being slowly infiltrated by working class players.

As football spread across the Pennines and into the cotton towns of Lancashire, this change in the social make-up of teams grew more marked. The new strongholds of Blackburn, Bolton and Preston were predominantly working class teams and by the mid-1870s an under-the-counter system of illicit payments was growing.

In part this was because crowds were now paying in significant numbers to watch football matches – which made it difficult for clubs to justify profiting from the work of amateur players – and partly because it was recognised that football was becoming more and more competitive. What traditionalists viewed with horror as professionalism began with 'shamateurism': clubs first began paying players extravagant expenses and then moved on to paying them for time lost at work. It was a short hop from there to a club director hiring a promising footballer to occupy a non-existent job at his factory while really occupying himself with football.

If this had been kept to a local level it would probably have flown under the not-terribly perceptive radar of the Football Association. But it was only a matter of time before clubs began importing players from outside their home towns and counties, or more accurately, countries. Scotland was seen as a major source of footballing talent. This was probably because north of the border players concentrated on a skill viewed with deep suspicion in England: passing the ball. The first player to be lured south was probably a Glasgow shipyard worker called James Lang. In 1876, he was tempted to Sheffield by a notional job at a local knife factory, but was in reality a full-time footballer for the Wednesday club. According to the club's first official historian, Lang's working life was 'chiefly devoted to football and reading the news of the day in the papers'. The Scotsman was subsequently remarkably candid, admitting that, 'I'm not going to say that I crossed the border to play for nothing, because you would not believe me if I did.' Notionally, all teams were still resolutely amateur. Rule 15 of the Football Association code was explicit:

> Any member of a club receiving remuneration or consideration of any sort above his actual expenses, and any wages actually lost by any such player taking part in any match, shall be de-barred from taking part in either Cup, Inter-Association or International contests and any club employing such a player shall be excluded from this Association.

But by 1882, professional football players – most frequently poached by clubs in the Lancashire cotton belt – were an open secret. The wording of an advert in *The Scotsman* in October that year was typical: 'Football player (a good full-back) wanted for a club in Northeast Lancashire. To a really good man who can teach well, liberal wages will be given.'

The club was probably Preston North End, then both prosperous and ambitious. Its chairman, William Sudell, had set out to create the first unashamedly professional side, and before long had turned North End into both a profitable business and the pre-eminent team in Britain. The fact that this took place in Preston – then a dirty and distinctly unsanitary mill town with a population which had multiplied five-fold in the previous 50 years and which had a concurrent history of bloody-minded non-conformism – would, as we shall see, be important in the story of women's football. But for the moment it found itself at the centre of the row over professional men's football. And it was a row which threatened to tear the FA apart.

Goaded by what was happening in plain sight, in October

1882, the FA set up its first enquiry into the practice of unlawful professionalism. In what would become its trademark style, it instituted a sub-committee to investigate the Lancashire clubs: they responded by submitting sets of bogus accounts. The sub-committee's efforts were abandoned. But a year later, Preston North End was sweeping all before it in the FA Cup: report after report of one-sided matches played against notably untrained teams of ex-public school amateurs began to pile up. By the start of 1884, North End had made it through to the fourth round of the Cup.

The fixture – to be played at Preston's Deepdale ground on 19 January – pitted Sudell's side against Upton Park, a team of London-based graduates of the Great Nine public schools. It drew a crowd of more than 10,000 paying spectators and ended, after extra time, in a 1-1 draw. A re-match would have to be arranged. But the next day Preston North End received a letter from the Football Association signed by FA secretary Charles Alcock, stating: 'I beg to inform you that I have this morning received a protest from the Upton Park Club against your club on the grounds of professionalism. It will be placed before the committee at their next meeting.'

The simmering tension between football's *soi-disant* old custodians – the patrician and privileged alumni of the rich public schools in the south – and the nouveau rich *arrivistes* of the clubs in the north had been simmering for years. Alcock was a member of the former. An ex-Harrovian and founder member of the Forest Club, which would subsequently become the Wanderers, the leading truly-amateur side, Charles Alcock was in no doubt about the gentlemanly qualities required to be 'one of us'. Writing later about the recruitment process for Wanderers' sister cricket club, The Butterflies, he explained: 'Someone would come into our study and say, "I say you fellows, can I be a Butterfly?" Whereupon, if he was a good fellow, we used to say, "My dear fellow, you are one".'

Alcock was also the driving force behind the Football Association in the years after its near demise. He had helped create the FA Cup and presided over the introduction of international matches. But the England sides selected by Alcock and his privileged chums were resolutely stuffed with 'gentlemen'. So much so that when a working class player, Billy Mosforth from Sheffield, was selected to appear for his country, the rest of the team refused to pass the ball to him. When, in an 1879 fixture against Scotland, Mosforth finally complained to his team captain – an ex- Harrow and Cambridge man called Alfred Lyttleton – he received the languid response: 'I am playing for my own pleasure, sir.'

Now Alcock was at the heart of an argument over professionalism which was being played out in the pages of newspapers across the land. When, after a 90-minute interrogation of William Sudell by the FA sub-committee, Preston North End was expelled from the FA Cup, the Lancashire press was outraged. *Football Field,* a paper published in the nearby town of Bolton, remarked sarcastically: 'Our notion of what constitutes fair play may differ from those held in the south of England', while the *Preston Herald* reported Sudell's view that 'whoever prompted the action against North End [was] a contemptible fellow'.

On the other side of the argument, *The Graphic*, a London-based national newspaper with a strong social reform agenda, argued: 'Football is a sufficiently dangerous game already, without the employment of hired professionals, who, to maintain their credit and earn their wages, must necessarily feel bound to exhibit unnecessary energy.'

And the magnificently named regional paper, *The Hull Packet and East Riding Times*, put it even more bluntly: 'Rough and unfair play, a disregard of the rules, disgraceful rows, and abuse of the umpires[6] and referees, can all be traced, directly or indirectly, to the presence in certain teams of paid professional players, to whom a love of the game and fair play are of very small importance as compared to the absolute necessity of winning a match and dividing the gate [money].'

At first, faced with what appeared to be an argument which would split the Football Association in two – just as a decade earlier the row over handling had led to the breakaway Rugby Football Union – Alcock backed the old guard. But by 1885 the writing was on the wall: the FA had to modernise or beat itself to death. At a succession of special general meetings, Alcock nailed his colours to the mast, declaring: 'I cannot be called a supporter of professionalism... but until professionalism is legalized the deadlock which now exists will continue.... I object to the argument that it is immoral to work for a living and I cannot see why men should not, with that object, labour at football...'

Eventually, the modernising faction triumphed. Professionalism was legalised over the vehement objections of gentlemen players that it was not only immoral but would promote illegality and corruption. The FA breathed a sigh of relief. But within a decade the spectre would return to haunt the now-thriving professional game. It would re-affirm the worst fears of the die-hard traditionalists – and it would come from the troublesome town of Preston.

At 5.30pm on the afternoon of 20 March 1895, William Sudell – the driving force behind North End's rampant success – was arrested. He was charged with embezzlement and falsifying accounts at the mill where he was manager. According to the evidence at his trial, he had stolen the then astronomical sum of £5,326 – all of which he spent on keeping Preston North End at the top of the game. On Wednesday, 10 April, having admitted the charges, Sudell 'threw himself upon the mercy of the court and pleaded for leniency' (to quote the *Burnley Express*). Mercy was not forthcoming: he was sent to prison for three years.

It was against this deeply unpromising backdrop – a darkly coloured cloth of financial corruption and the demands of traditionalists to reverse the damage to 'their' game – that women footballers would once again step into the spotlight. And once again, they would face the anger of the sporting establishment.

CHAPTER FOUR

'Their costumes were modest and becoming,
but that is the only praise we can afford them.'

– The London *Evening Standard*,
Monday, 25 March 1895

On Thursday, 1 January 1895, the influential liberal London daily newspaper *The Westminster Gazette* published news of a new footballing project. The report was syndicated across the country and abroad. This version was published the following day in the leading Irish daily of the age, *Freeman's Journal*:

A LADIES' FOOOTBALL CLUB
A number of sturdy young ladies have recently banded themselves together for the purposes of carrying on a football club exclusively for representatives of the fair sex. One of the leading spirits of this new and hitherto unprecedented venture is Lady Florence Dixie, who is the president of the club, but as her ladyship does not contemplate... active participation in the game, a representative of the *Westminster Gazette* called upon Miss Honeyball, the originator and secretary of the club to learn some particulars.

49

'The game will be played in the ordinary way,' Miss Honeyball replied. 'In fact, if we improve as we seem to be doing, we hope to be able to oppose some weak male teams before long. The only difference will be that we shall confine each match to sixty minutes. Of course we only play under Association rules.

'As for the danger, the girls don't feel that at all, and as regards the weather, I can assure you we don't allow that to interfere with our practice. Why, we turned out last Monday, when the ground was covered with several inches of snow and it was freezing hard. The ground man laughed at us, and said we were mad. So far we haven't had a single accident.

'We are all most enthusiastic and we play for the sake of pure sport only, and that reminds me that I must tell you that the club is constituted solely for the enjoyment of amateurs. I hope eventually to be able to pay the members travelling expenses, but many of the girls declare that they will not accept a penny for fear of being dubbed professionals. At present every girl pays her own expenses. We have a match coming on shortly, and in view of it are practising regularly twice a week.'

At this point, the unnamed reporter felt it necessary to interrupt and challenge his interviewee on the issue of safety.

'I mean no disparagement, Miss Honeyball, but it would be interesting to know if the ladies take any extra precautions in the way of protecting themselves from the hard knocks and tumbles which are absolutely essential to a game which requires strength besides science?'

'No, we do not attempt to fortify ourselves against

accidents any more than men. We wear proper football boots, with the corrugated toe and heel. At first some of the girls wore high-heeled and pointed boots, but these have been abandoned. We also wear ankle pads and shin guards, shirts and blue knickerbockers after the style of the divided skirt. Red brewers' caps are worn on the head, and the hair is securely fastened up with hairpins, so you see we are fully prepared for the fray.'

Next, the intrepid newspaperman probed the all-important question of social standing.

'Do you find that the club is increasing in popularity? And, by the way, from what class is your club principally recruited?

'The game is undoubtedly growing in favour with girls. At present the Ladies Football Club numbers twenty-two members, the oldest of whom is twenty-eight years of age and the youngest is fourteen, but I am anxious to get up a reserve team. Perhaps you would like to know the weight of the heaviest lady footballer. Well, she is eleven stone. The players belong chiefly to the middle class. There are also four or five married ladies who are regular players.'

This, alas, proved one step too far for the reporter. Evidently shocked, he interrupted the determined Miss Honeyball's list of facts, exclaiming: 'The husbands – what about them!' But the secretary of the newly-founded British Ladies' Football Club was dismissive.

'What have they got to do with it? Why shouldn't ladies play football as well as men? I may tell you we are all homely girls. We don't want any la-di-da members. We play the game in the proper spirit. We allow charging, but no bad temper is ever displayed, and I have never heard a cross word spoken.'

There was, as we shall see, both much more and much less to Miss Honeyball than met the eyes of the evidently aghast representative of the *Westminster Gazette*. But two things were certain. Much more would be heard of the British Ladies' Football Club over the next two years. And its members were about to hear some very cross words indeed.

In the 14 years since Helen Matthews' attempts to storm the male bastion of football with Mrs Graham's XI, the sport had changed dramatically. Professionalism was here to stay (despite grumblings of unease) and much of the old public school game had either been consigned to history or had been taken up as Rugby Football with its own quite separate structures. True, 'charging', the tactic by which a player (or, more frequently, several players) were allowed deliberately to run at the opposition and knock them down like skittles in a bowling alley, was still practised. But for the most part, football in the mid-1890s was recognisably the game played today.

In the non-sporting world, everyday life was still resolutely male-dominated. Britain remained very much a man's world. If a modern woman of the 21st century were to be parachuted 150 years back into the past, she would struggle to recognise the condition of late nineteenth-century women as anything other than a miserable existence. From cradle to grave, women were forced to obey men, financially, legally and sexually.

Although by the mid-1850s, women outnumbered men by 360,000 (the population breakdown being 9.14m and 8.78m respectively) girls received less education than boys, were barred from universities, and most could obtain only low-paid jobs. They could not enter professions, since these were all closed to women. In short, the sole purpose of most women was to marry and reproduce. As a result, the vast majority of even middle or upper class women had no independent means of subsistence. A wealthy widow or spinster was a lucky exception. A woman who remained single – and 30 per cent of women over 20 were unmarried – attracted social disapproval and pity in just about equal measure. Frequently they were pressured to emigrate to England's vast colonial Empire where men outnumbered women and a 'suitable match' might be found. Certainly, out of wedlock she could not live with a man, nor have children.

Most women had little choice but to marry, and in so doing the woman's body 'belonged' to the husband. Not only was this enshrined in law, but the woman herself agreed to it verbally: written into the marriage ceremony was a vow to obey her husband, which every woman was required to swear before God as well as earthly witnesses, and it would take until the late 20th century for women to obtain the right to omit that promise from their wedding vows.

Every man had the right to force his wife into sex and childbirth. He could take her children without reason and send them to be raised elsewhere. He could spend the family's money freely on a mistress or on prostitutes. Mere adultery was not grounds for a woman to divorce a man (although by law it was sufficient grounds for a man to divorce his wife). Except in extremely rare cases, women could not obtain a divorce and, until 1891, if she ran away from an intolerable marriage the police could capture and return her, and her husband could imprison her. All this was sanctioned by church, law, custom, history, and approved of by society in general. Nor was it the result of ancient, outdated laws: in 1857 a new Divorce Act specifically restated this inequality. Attempts at rebellion from the social mores were swiftly – and legally – crushed by fathers, husbands, even brothers. Judge William Blackstone had announced that husbands could administer 'moderate correction' to disobedient wives, and there were other means. As late as 1895, the father of Edith Lanchester – a proto-feminist who was politically opposed to marriage – paid for her to have her kidnapped and committed to a lunatic asylum for cohabiting with a man. In short, if a woman was unhappy with her situation, and very many were, there was almost nothing she could do about it.

But if life was oppressive for middle and upper-class women, for those several rungs below them in the ranks of the Victorian social order it was infinitely worse. Girls started work between the ages of about 8 to 12 and continued until marriage. After that, a woman's fate depended on her husband. If he earned enough to support her she would usually cease work, otherwise she worked all her life, with only short, often repeated, breaks to give birth.

Because they were barred from all well-paid work, the majority of women were forced into a very small range of occupations. Around 50 per cent went into domestic service as parlour-maids, scullery-maids or kitchen skivvies. Most of the rest were consumed by the voracious factories which powered the nation and the Empire, or endured the back-breaking toil of agricultural labour. Almost the only skilled work for women was in the bespoke clothing trade, but even that was ill-paid and considered to be of low social status.

In 1890, Florence Fenwick Miller, a midwife turned journalist, gave a speech to the National Liberal Club in which she summed up woman's lot succinctly:

Under exclusively man-made laws women have been reduced to the most abject condition of legal slavery in which it is possible for human beings to be held... under the arbitrary domination of another's will, and dependent for decent treatment exclusively on the goodness of heart of the individual master.

Aside from innate male prejudice, there was another stereotypical (and, given the popularity of visiting prostitutes, distinctly hypocritical) Victorian sensibility at play. Women – at least in the abstract – were effectively worshipped. They were presumed, and expected, to be as radiant as an angel, as dainty as a fairy. And this almost mystical concept was given physical form in their clothes. Victorian women wore layers upon on layers, fold upon fold of cloth – literally hidden under the multiple, impenetrable mysteries of corsets and petticoats.

Women's clothing symbolised their constricted lives. Between 1856 and 1878, aristocratic women's lower bodies were imprisoned in a cage of crinoline – a cumbersome and humiliating creation which, when the woman sat down, rode up embarrassingly at the front. The skirts, which were fastened elaborately on top of this structure, were so wide that many women burned to death after the material caught fire from an open grate or candle.

There were attempts at reform. In 1851, Elizabeth Miller, an American, designed what would become known as 'rational dress' – a knee-length skirt worn over baggy, Turkish-style 'harem' trousers. Briefly publicised and worn by a fellow-American, Amelia Bloomer (whose name would thereafter be used to describe these pantaloons) it provoked howls of outrage on both sides of the Atlantic. Male society was simply not ready for even the merest hint that a woman might possess legs.

Thirty years after Amelia Bloomer caused consternation, two English society ladies took up the fight once again. Florence, Viscountess Harberton, then in her early forties, had been a long-standing campaigner for women's rights, and her friend, Mrs E M King, had publicly pronounced traditional Victorian women's garments as fit only for 'savages'. In 1881, they formed a new organisation, the Rational Dress Society (though it was also sometimes called the Rational Dress Association). Its forming charter announced:

> The Rational Dress Society protests… against crinolines or crinolettes of any kind as ugly and deforming… [It] requires all to be dressed healthily, comfortably, and beautifully, to seek what conduces to birth, comfort and beauty in our dress as a duty to ourselves and each other.

In fact its initial aims were, to the modern eye, remarkably modest: to reduce by half the weight of underwear a woman was required to put on. This would still leave them carrying a full seven pounds (3.17 kilograms) of netherwear, but it is a sign of the times that the proposal was viewed as far too radical for any 'decent' woman to contemplate. And there the cause of sartorial emancipation might have ended but for the arrival of an unlikely saviour: the bicycle.

Two-wheeled personal transport had been in existence since Baron Karl von Drais, a civil servant to the Grand Duke of Baden in Germany, unveiled his *laufmaschine* (literally: running machine) in 1817. But since it, and subsequent updates on the design, required the rider to propel it by means of pushing his feet against the ground, it remained the preserve of a relatively small class of wealthy aristocratic dandies across Europe.

The first real pedal-powered bicycle emerged in France in 1863, and it would, 30 years on, begin to set women free. These early bicycles, however, were deliberately aimed at – and intended to be the sole preserve of – men. The machines were uncomfortable and frankly dangerous. The high-wheeler, of which the penny-farthing would be the apogee and which became popular during the 1870s, required the rider to sit several feet above the ground, and was universally considered completely inappropriate to both the dress and physical anatomy of ladies.

Then, in 1880, the 'Safety Bike' was born. Unlike penny farthings, which had no gears and a huge front wheel, and were thus the frequent cause of serious injury, Safeties had a chain drive, normal shaped wheels and a diamond frame, so could be ridden with ease and didn't require a course in gymnastics to mount them. Its arrival coincided with the emergence of the middle class and cycling very quickly became a Victorian craze – at least among those able to afford the purchase price of between £10 and £20, roughly the same amount as a carthorse. Cycling magazines and periodicals began to appear on news-stands and the pastime of cycling became a central motif of (often comic) novels.

But there were two immediate difficulties – problems which swiftly became publicly-debated moral panics. And both related to the possibility that women might mount these new and liberating machines. The first concerned the obvious (at least to male Victorian minds) dangers of actually allowing a woman to straddle something. At this stage in the late 19th century, nicely brought up young ladies were discouraged even as children from sitting on see-saws or riding on hobby horses for fear that it would either damage their reproductive organs or promote undesirable sexual pleasure.

The guardians of British morality paled: the results of sitting astride a machine and then leaning forward were too horrible to contemplate. Why, surely, the constant friction of the saddle would ineluctably unleash whole troops of nymphomaniacs riding round Britain in a state of frenzied arousal? And then there was the effect on their solemn and binding duty to bear children. One French expert pronounced firmly that cycling would ruin the 'feminine organs of matrimonial necessity' – and after all, those Frenchies knew a thing or two about that sort of thing.

Still, perhaps there was a way forward. Women had ridden horses side-saddle for centuries: maybe they could do likewise with these new bicycles? To respond to this societal pressure, bicycle manufacturers began to develop and market machines which could be ridden side-saddle – although this undoubtedly made them both ugly and unstable. And for those women who still brazenly insisted on outraging public decency by sitting astride, a new range of products appeared which were designed to eliminate 'harmful pressure', including saddles with so many holes in them they were almost unrideable.

Finally, in 1889, the Coventry-based Starley Bros introduced the unfortunately named Psycho Ladies' Bicycle, which offered a proper step-through frame and which tackled at least part of the modesty problem by forcing the cyclist to sit bolt upright in a pose which definitively ensured no unseemly physical pleasure could be obtained. But the Psycho Bicycle only exaggerated the remaining problem: legs. Women had these, hidden somewhere underneath all those skirts and petticoats, but riding a bicycle plainly revealed at least the ankle end of these inflammatory limbs; and that just wouldn't do at all. Again, the new breed of bicycle entrepreneur stepped in with a temporary, if utterly impractical, solution called The Cherry's Screen. This was a device, shaped like a pair of wings, and designed to block the sight of a lady's ankles from view, thus safeguarding the nation's moral health. But it was simply too cumbersome to be of any real value; and besides, it didn't address what was really at the heart of the problem.

Since the start of the 19th century, women had been required to conform to a brutal clothing regimen. The upper body was tight-laced into whalebone corsets so as both to ensure its safety from a casually prying hand and simultaneously to present to admiring males an appealing 'wasp' waist. The fact that this required a feat of engineering which caused immense pain and physical damage[7] was apparently beside the point. Below the waist was the complex structure of undergarments, covered by a full-length skirt.

Since cycling was now a fully-fledged national obsession – and since otherwise respectable ladies were intent on indulging in it – they plainly needed guidance on how to dress. And so emerged a small army of writers, men and women, eager and willing to advise. One, Frances 'Fanny' Erskine Inglis, who married Spanish nobility and became the Marquise of Calderón de la Barca, pronounced on the question of corsets: 'Some wise people say that corsets should be discarded for cycling. This is not correct. There should be no approach to tight-lacing, but a pair of woollen-cased corsets afford great support; they keep the figure from going all abroad, and protect the vital parts from chills.'

But voluminous skirts posed an even more quotidian danger. Even on a step-through frame, wearing a typical Victorian skirt while bicycling had rather the same outcome as attaching a sail to the handlebars: it blew or toppled the machine over. And even if the rider managed to stay upright the fabric would invariably become tangled in the back wheel – with the same result.

In an attempt to unchain women, literally and metaphorically, the Rational Dress Society tried to deal with both the cycling problem and the corsetry issue at once. 'What,' asked the redoubtable Lady Harberton, 'can be the true state of intelligence of a creature which deliberately loads itself with quantities of useless material round its legs... and then, in order to correct the ugliness of such a dress, squeezes in its body until the vital functions can only be carried on imperfectly?'

The society's solution was the re-introduction of Amelia Bloomer's failed experiment with pantaloons, this time safely tied at the ankle and covered with a slightly shortened skirt. This was not a particularly successful resolution of women's cycling problems, but it was the first wedge in the crack of public attitudes that would – eventually – lead to women wearing trousers. More immediately, its real importance was that it paved the way for Miss Honeyball and her team of knickerbocker-clad lady footballers. Without the effort and determination of Lady Harberton and the Rational Dress Society, no woman would have dared step on to a football pitch clad in anything other than corsets and skirts.

There was a further connection between the British Ladies' Football Club and the Rational Dress Movement. The club's president was Lady Florence Caroline Dixie, daughter of the 8th Marquess of Queensbury and one of the most remarkable women of the era. Born in 1855, Lady Florence Douglas (as she was then) seems to have been pre-destined for an unusually eventful life. Her father, then the solidly upright MP for Great Marlow, committed suicide when Florence was five years old. Two years later her mother took the then unthinkable step of converting herself and her youngest children, Florence included, to Roman Catholicism – and whisked them out of the country to live in Paris.

This led the children's guardians to threaten Lady Queensberry with the loss of her children, a very real possibility given the state of women's rights at the time. This, and a subsequent unhappily claustrophobic education at the hands of severe nuns, sharpened the young Florence's political views. Suffragism, rational dress and a passionate love of sport dominated her life from then on.

Marriage, in 1875, to the suitably aristocratic Sir Alexander Dixie, Baronet, did nothing to quell this ardour. In 1878, she and her husband turned their backs on the stultifying London 'season' and set off for a year's big game hunting in Patagonia. Lady Florence proved to be an uncomfortably good shot. Two years after her return (complete with a pet jaguar she somewhat unfairly called Alfums) she was hired as the field correspondent of the London *Morning Post* and sent to South Africa to report on the Boer War. Oddly, given all that she was exposed to and in the light of her otherwise radical views, she remained an old-fashioned imperialist. But there was nothing traditional in her views on women. In the preface to a novel published in 1890 she wrote:

Nature has unmistakeably given to woman a greater brain power. This is at once perceivable in childhood... Yet man deliberately sets himself to stunt that early evidence of mental capacity, by laying down the law that woman's education shall be on a lower level than that of man's... I maintain to honourable gentlemen that this procedure is arbitrary and cruel, and false to Nature. I characterise it by the strong word of Infamous. It has been the means of sending to their graves unknown, unknelled, and unnamed, thousands of women whose high intellects have been wasted, and whose powers for good have been paralysed and undeveloped.

GIRLS WITH BALLS

It was perhaps inevitable that football and Florence Dixie would collide. There was a strong sporting tradition in her family: her eldest brother, the 9th Marquess of Queensbury, was a keen amateur boxer and his endorsement of the sport's first set of rules has gone under his name ever since. (He was also the man who would destroy Oscar Wilde by accusing him of being a sodomite.) According to the remarkably confident Miss Honeyball, when Lady Florence was asked to be the president of the new British Ladies' Football Club, she agreed on the sole premise that 'the girls should enter into the spirit of the game with heart and soul'.

Early in February 1895, Dixie penned a heartfelt and lengthy article which was published in the campaigning London evening paper the *Pall Mall Gazette*:

> There is no reason why football should not be played by women, and played well too, provided they dress rationally and relegate to limbo the strait-jacket attire in which fashion delights to attire them. For, for women to attempt any kind of free movement in fashion's dress means the making of themselves ridiculous, even as men would so make themselves did they play cricket or football arrayed in skirts and their attendant flummeries.
>
> I cannot conceive a game more calculated to improve the physique of women than that of football. In Association Football a player must be light and swift of foot, agile, wiry and in good condition; and are not these physical requisites the very characteristics of good health most to be desired for women? To lack them is a misfortune, to attain them an ambition, which all lacking them should have; and certainly, football is the surest way of securing them.

In that school of the future, which, looking ahead, I see arising on the golden hilltops of progress above the mists of prejudice, football will be considered as natural a game for girls as for boys.

Lady Florence was nothing if not an optimist. Nor was she the only one. The secretary of the British Ladies' Football Club – now given her full name of Miss Nettie J Honeyball and apparently residing at 27 Weston Park in the London suburb of Crouch End – gave interview after interview setting out an even more ambitious agenda, including this in the *Daily Sketch* on 6 February 1895:

There is nothing of the farcical nature about the British Ladies' Football Club. I founded the association late last year, with the fixed resolve of proving to the world that women are not the 'ornamental' and 'useless' creatures men have pictured. I must confess, my convictions on all matters, where the exes are so widely divided, are all on the side of emancipation and I look forward to the time when ladies may sit in Parliament and have a voice in the direction of affairs, especially those which concern them most.

In this, Nettie Honeyball was well in advance of her time. Although the women's suffrage movement had been founded more than 20 years earlier it had very little in the way of a public profile and even less support. It would take another decade before suffragettes, led by Emmeline and Sylvia Pankhurst, would force the issue on to the front pages.

That February in 1895, the dreams of 'the golden hilltops of progress' so boldly put forward by Miss Honeyball and Lady

Florence Dixie were about to receive a sharp lesson in the political realities of the day. They had set about the task of creating a real football team with resolution. They had persuaded Tottenham Hotspur's centre-half, J W Julian, then a player of national renown, to coach them and they trained every weekday in a park next to the Alexandra Park racecourse at Hornsey. They had divided their players into two teams, loosely based on where the women originally hailed from, and billed their first match as North vs South (of London). They had also applied to Charles Alcock, the secretary and driving force behind the Football Association, for permission to play this inaugural game at the Oval – home of Surrey County Cricket Club (of which the energetic Mr Alcock was also a mainstay) and Forest Football Club.

But while the FA was, for the moment, content to keep silent on the propriety of women playing football, Charles Alcock was adamant that no such spectacle could take place on his hallowed turf. His refusal brought a typically tart response from Florence Dixie: 'Mr Alcock declares that his committee cannot allow ladies to play on the Oval. I suppose their presence would desecrate this happy hunting-ground of the male foot! Be that as it may, women must not foot it in there; so says Mr Alcock's committee.'

Instead, with the assistance of a Bloomsbury solicitor, Charles de Lyons Pyke, the British Ladies' Football Club was finally given permission to play at the Nightingale Lane ground in Crouch End. The match date was fixed for 23 March, but in the intervening weeks a steady stream of protests appeared in the pages of newspapers all across England. It began in the regional press, and on Saturday, 9 February, the *York Herald* weighed in:

The British Ladies' Football Club evidently means business. Lady Florence Dixie, in consenting to act as president, expressly stipulated that the girls should enter into the spirit of the game with heart and soul; and Miss Nettie Honeyball, the secretary and captain, very emphatically denies that there is anything of the farcical nature about the club. Miss Honeyball says that she has had no trouble in obtaining members and that the number is now close upon thirty, the ages varying from fifteen to six and twenty.

The costume is a sort of blue serge knickerbocker, with a jersey of cardinal red, or pale blue. Mr Julian, a well-known halfback, is acting as coach, and the fair captain is confident that the association will not collapse. But she also seems to anticipate the period when big League football clubs will be composed of both male and female players. We sincerely trust that she may prove a false prophet.

Twelve days later the *Evening Telegraph and Star*, based in that powerhouse of men's football, Sheffield, reported suggestions that the team's president was being leant on to withdraw her support:

It is not thought that footballing by ladies will be a great success, and some grave attempts are being made to induce Lady Florence Dixie to abandon her scheme. There is not much chance of her doing anything so reasonable. She will persist until failure meets her all round. But the test will not come until ladies' teams are willing to play in public, and to be stared at. Perhaps the Dixie Association will never emerge from its privacy to brave this terrible test.

The next day the paper renewed its attack. Under the headlines 'Can women play football ?' and 'A reply to Lady Florence Dixie', the writer denounced the idea that football could in any way be good for the health of women:

> For boys and young men I hold that Association football is the finest out-door game yet invented. Will it be 'calculated to improve the physique of women' that they should charge each other? Yet charging is an essential of the game, for otherwise a little practice would enable any player to dribble from one end of the field to the other.
>
> A man charges with his chest and shoulders, and checks with his hip. Will the doctors tell us that these portions of a woman's body are fit for such rough purpose? Even gentlemen are not particularly refined when playing football... Accidents more or less serious will happen however fairly the game is played. 'Nothing adventure, nothing win.' This is what football means to men. Is the same thing to be true of women – one cannot say ladies in such connection?

Within 24 hours the controversy had moved to the pages of the fashionable and influential London press. On Saturday, 23 February, the *Pall Mall Gazette* gave a prominent position to a lengthy letter from a correspondent signing himself 'No Goal'.

> I do not wish to be rude to Lady Florence Dixie, for whose views I have the sincerest commiseration – but I feel that it is high time so poor 'man, proud man' pointed out to her the absolute absurdity of her arguments in favour of 'footer for the fair'...
>
> A woman sometimes waddles like a duck and

sometimes like a chicken – it all depends on her weight. She is physically incapable of stretching her legs sufficiently to take the stride masculine... the smaller a woman's foot is the prouder she is of it, and very naturally. I dearly love to see her feet come peeping in and out of her skirts, as the poet says 'like little mice' (delicious simile!).

I don't think lady-footballers will ever be able to 'shoot' goals. In order to score a 'point' they will find it necessary, I fear, to charge the enemy's goal en masse and simply hustle the ball through... Sir, I have seen two women fight and never wish to witness a like scene again, and I think that the aspect of two lovely girls, flushed and mud-bespattered, causing their rounded shoulders to collide ever and anon with brutal force, would be a most deplorable one. The whole thing is so foreign to the poetry of life – if poetry can be said to exist when an educated and refined lady urges her sisters to don men's attire and play men's games.

Women may boat, women may ride – they can do both gracefully – but women may not, with an advantage to themselves, ride a bicycle or kick a football. These pastimes are beyond them... Let women 'keep' books, write books, paint pictures, ride horses and row boats, but for the love of heaven stay them from making sights of themselves on the football field, or objects of ridicule on the bicycle saddle.

Faced with what appeared to be a tide of public opinion turning against women's football, Nettie Honeyball began to woo the press by inviting journalists to observe her preparations for the first match.

GIRLS WITH BALLS

The *Pall Mall Budget* – a weekly illustrated arts magazine with the then expensive cover price of sixpence (2.5p) – took up the offer. By the end of February its report had been syndicated across the country. The following version of the original article was published in the *Sheffield Evening Telegraph and Star* on 27 February 1895.

'I have this room entirely for my own use,' explained Miss Nettie J. Honeyball, the secretary of the British Ladies' Football Club to a representative of the *Pall Mall Budget*, who looked around for the cigarette ash pans, the box of cigars or other indications of the New Woman, but they were entirely absent.

I found Miss Honeyball... hard at work making the costumes for her teams. She was good enough to show the garments to me. The blouse (I think she called it a shirt) was made for one team of dark and light blue, while the opposing team will be arrayed in glorious red and white. Thus on the field the red, white and blue will be represented. The knickerbockers are made of blue serge, very full, drawn up at the knees by elastic bands, and thus when worn have much the appearance of the divided skirt. The cap is of the 'brewers' type, the stockings are black and thick-ribbed, and the boots are much the same kind as are usually worn by football players, only that being made specially for the fair wearers they are lighter and smaller.

'The members of the club,' Miss Honeyball said, 'have come from all parts of London and the suburbs, and even from the country. They are chiefly young ladies of independent means, whose parents can afford to keep them without work, though a few are married women.

'Our first match will be on March 16, on the Crouch End ground. I have had letters from all parts of the country – some very nice and flattering, and some very disagreeable, and one so very offensive that I have been obliged to hand it over to the police'.

The appointed day came and went with no sign of the promised match. Shortly afterwards, though, posters began appearing across London advertising what would today be recognised as the organisers covering their bet: the ladies' match, they announced, would be preceded by a more regular fixture between the very male teams of Crouch End and the 3rd Grenadier Guards. The date was now set for Saturday, 23 March. The following Monday, readers of both national and regional newspapers were treated to the correspondents' verdict. The opening paragraphs of London morning paper, the *Daily Sketch,* set the tone:

> There was an astonishing sight in the neighbourhood of the Nightingale Lane Ground, Crouch End, on Saturday afternoon. Crouch End itself rubbed its eyes and pinched its arms. The intelligent foreigner might have been excused for imagining some State function was taking place – a Drawing-Room, for example. All through the afternoon train-loads of excited people journeyed over from all parts, and the respectable array of carriages, cabs, and other vehicles marked a record in the history of Football. Yet all that this huge throng of ten thousand had gathered to see was the opening match of the British Ladies' Football Club.
>
> It would be idle to attempt any description of the play. The first few minutes were sufficient to show that football by women, if the British Ladies be taken as a criterion, is

totally out of the question. A footballer requires speed, judgement, skill, and pluck. Not one of these four qualities was apparent on Saturday.

For the most part, the ladies wandered aimlessly over the field at an ungraceful jog-trot. A smaller ball than usual was utilised, but the strongest among them could propel it no further than a few yards. The most elementary rules of the game were unknown, and the referee, Mr. C. Squires, spent a most agonising time.

Hours later the London *Evening Standard* weighed in:

To say football was played would be stating more than the real truth. Several of the ladies showed a great lack of knowledge of the rules, and the match was little more than a burlesque, although the ladies were terribly in earnest. Their costumes were modest and becoming, but that is the only praise we can afford them.

Play in the first half was beyond criticism and, indeed, description... Goals were occasionally taken, in a kind of inconsequential way but there was never any development of exciting play, which might have distracted the attention of the spectators from the fair players to the game.

After remarking on a fight that broke out in the crowd, the *Standard* drily reported the final score as seven to one in favour of the North team. The patrician derision of the London press was almost universally matched in the regions. The *Manchester Guardian* announced that, 'When the novelty has worn off, I do not think women's football will attract the crowds.' The *Jarrow Express*, channelling the *Evening Standard*, was even less charitable:

The members of the British Ladies' Football Club have played their first match in public. We hope it will be their last. There will always be curiosity to see women do unwomanly things, and it is not surprising that the match was attended by a crowd numbering several thousands, very few of whom would like to have their own sisters or daughters exhibiting themselves on the football field.

Some of these young persons appeared to possess only an elementary knowledge of the game and its laws, and, for the present at all events, the club is quite unlikely to attract spectators for the sake of the play. How long it will continue to attract them for reasons unconnected with sport is another matter, but it is significant that a considerable proportion of those present left the field at half-time. The laughter was easy, and the amusement was rather coarse; but these are waning delights, and we shall be surprised if a second display wins even so equivocal a success as the first.

The only exception to the negative reporting was in the *Sporting Man* magazine. In a much more tolerant spirit, it commented:

True, young men would run harder and kick more strongly, but, beyond this, I cannot believe that they would show any greater knowledge of the game or skill in its execution. I don't think the lady footballer is to be snuffed out by a number of leading articles written by old men out of sympathy both with football as a game and the aspirations of the young new women. If the lady footballer dies, she will die hard.

That was, perhaps, an unfortunate turn of phrase, since simultaneously the *British Medical Journal* published an editorial condemning women's football on the grounds that it could cause severe – possibly life-threatening – injury, adding: 'We can in no way sanction the reckless exposure to violence, of organs which the common experience of women had led them in every way to protect.'

Other than demonstrating that women's football could attract headlines and crowds in almost equal measure, there were two small nuggets of important fact in the reams of derogatory reporting. The first was one which would dog the British Ladies' Football Club for the rest of its life: the identity, or rather the sex, of what all the papers agreed was the team's star player.

According to the London *Evening Standard*: 'The North... included a small boy, who was the cleverest player on the field', while *Lloyd's Weekly News* maintained that this player was, 'Miss Daisy Allen, a little girl of 14, whom the spectators, judging from the boyish manner in which she played, nicknamed Tommy.' In the weeks to follow, 'Tommy', whether boy or girl, would be much sought after by crowds of spectators and the gentlemen of the press. But his, or her, identity would not be the last time that the British Ladies' Football Club was found to be hiding its players behind false names.

The second notable point to emerge concerned one of the youngster's fellow players. This time all the newspapers agreed on the identity of the lady and her undoubted skill at football. It turned out to be 'Mrs Graham' – or, more exactly, Helen Matthews – the Scottish suffragist who had led the first, doomed attempts at women's football more than a decade earlier. She had, it transpired made the journey from Glasgow to London to be part of Nettie Honeyball's team. That, like the

Tommy controversy, would have long-lasting and distinctly unfavourable results.

For the moment, though, the British Ladies' Football Club was in a positive mood. So much so that it was decided to go on the road and take the women's game to counties throughout the land. In the 26 weeks between the inaugural March fixture and the end of September it played an astonishing 34 games throughout England as well as in Scotland and Northern Ireland. No male footballer of the time took part in so many games in a season – let alone ones which were as far apart as Montrose on the Scottish east coast and Bristol in the south-west of England[8]. It re-affirmed Nettie Honeyball's assertion that the players were all of sufficient financial means to devote such time and effort to playing amateur football; it was also a solid affirmation of their stamina – and the remarkable efficiency of the Victorian railway network.

Press reporters followed the team wherever it turned up to play. Whilst all devoted substantial column inches to the women's outfits, their real obsession was with the identity, and sex, of Tommy. Ever since the Crouch End game, there had been speculation as to whether the Ladies' star player was a boy or a girl. Accurate reporting wasn't helped by the apparently cavalier approach of Nettie Honeyball: her team sheets variously billed their prolific goal scorer as 'Miss N. Gilbert' or 'Miss Daisy Allen'. Her given age ranged anywhere from 10 to 15. The confusion increased during the match in Doncaster on 24 April. Contemporary reports say that one particularly interested spectator got himself close to the front of the crowd and asked one of the other players 'Is the little 'un a girl?' He received the confusing response: 'Yes, he is'.

Within days of this report, *Lloyd's Weekly News* claimed to settle the matter once and for all. Persistent investigative journalism by its correspondent had revealed that Tommy (aka: Miss Gilbert and/or Miss Allen) was in fact the 13-year-old son of one of the lady footballers. For good measure, the paper stated that his surname was Richardson. Whether or not these rigorous enquiries had unearthed a very male flaw in the self-proclaimed all-female team is open to doubt. Photographs of the British Ladies' Football Club members, taken at various matches on their tour, very clearly show that all were women. And the Club continued to trek, untroubled, from town to town; and it also continued to field 'Miss Gilbert/Miss Allen' without ever bothering to denounce the report in *Lloyd's Weekly News*.

But if the raging press controversy over Tommy's sex was brushed away, other problems began to emerge. The first was an ill-omen for ladies' football and its relationship with the male custodians of the game – and one which presaged by 20 years the FA's ruthless suppression of the women's game. It began innocuously enough when a fixture was announced at Maze Hill, Greenwich – home to London's Royal Ordnance (male) Football Club. Press notices and posters advertised the game and on 18 April a crowd of between 3,000 and 4,000 drifted into the ground. Kick-off was set for 5pm: but there was no sign of any of the British Ladies' Football Club.

The team had played the previous evening in Walsall, some 140 miles away from Greenwich. But as the London crowd shifted restlessly, a telegram was delivered to the Royal Ordnance clubhouse. It read: 'Crouch End 5.13pm. Storm raging here. Must scratch – Honeyball'. This is puzzling. Although the winter of 1895 had been exceptionally cold – heavy snows had fallen all over the country and thousands of people skated on the frozen Serpentine in central London – by mid-April the weather had returned to normal. Whilst detailed meteorological records for the capital on 18 April are not available, two days later the FA Cup final was played at Crystal Palace on what was described as a 'beautiful spring day'.

When Nettie Honeyball's telegram was received, the Royal Ordnance Club convened an immediate and somewhat panicky emergency committee meeting. With 3,000 spectators, each of whom had paid to watch the game, milling around outside, a return telegram was dispatched to the British Ladies' Football Club secretary seeking both an explanation and a new date for the fixture[9]. But Nettie Honeyball failed to respond. The crowd was informed that the match would not be played, and the Club closed up for the evening. By noon the next day there was still no word from the women's football team. Royal Ordnance sent a second telegram marked urgent. This too seems to have been ignored. It was time for more direct action.

The British Ladies' Football Club was due to play its next match at the ground of New Brompton FC in Gillingham, Kent. The Royal Ordnance committee sent another telegram to the club and discovered, by return telegram, that Miss Honeyball and her team were due to arrive shortly at a London train station. Royal Ordnance dispatched its secretary, Mr G R Wagstaffe, to meet and confront them. But when he did, Nettie Honeyball was uncooperative. She rebuffed his complaints and insisted he speak directly to the team's manager – a hitherto unknown individual called Alfred Hewitt Smith. When he was finally run to earth, G R Wagstaffe was in no mood for argument. After threatening legal action, he forced the unfortunate Mr Smith to sign an undertaking – in front of witnesses – agreeing to re-schedule the fixture, and to covering all the costs of Royal Ordnance. It read:

On behalf of the British Ladies' Football Association [there is no explanation for this slight change of name, from 'Club' to 'Association'] I Alfred Hewitt Smith, ratify the following agreement. That the British Ladies' Football Association will play a match on the ground of the Royal Ordnance Football Club, on Thursday May 2nd, 1895, and that after the expenses of the Royal Ordnance Football Club for printing and postage have been deducted from the gross gates, the remainder shall be divided in equal moieties between the Royal Ordnance Football Club and local charities.

There was one problem with this agreement, and it once again brought women's football into conflict with Charles Alcock and the Football Association. The proposed date of 2 May was just into the official closed season for football. The FA refused permission for the game to take place, and since Royal Ordnance was a member of the Association, Alcock's word was law.

In what would shortly become a disturbingly familiar scenario for the British Ladies' Football Club, Royal Ordnance referred the matter to its lawyers. A new telegram was sent to Nettie Honeyball warning that unless her team played the long-promised match by the end of April (and therefore before the closed season) she and the ladies' club would be summoned to court. Evidently chastened, Honeyball this time replied by immediate return telegram and the date of Monday, 29 April was inserted into the team's already frenetic schedule of games.

The strains of so many fixtures in such a short period were already beginning to show. On several occasions the British Ladies had turned up at least two players short of a full 22. They had begun to draft in goalkeepers from whichever club was hosting their game. What wasn't in doubt was the women's box-office appeal. Report after report, in town after town up and down the country, recorded gates of between 2,000 and 10,000 paying spectators. What they got for their ticket price was, by near universal opinion, undoubtedly entertaining if very poor sport. A report in the *Reading Mercury* on Saturday, 20 April of their game on Easter Monday at Reading's Caversham ground, was typical:

> Nineteen young women, one boy, and two men trifled with a football for 40 minutes as an Easter holiday diversion at Caversham on Monday last. It would be straining a point to describe their performances as football, but seeing that they represented the British Ladies' Football Association (President, Lady Florence Dixie) it may be presumed that they intended to give a display of the national winter pastime.
>
> They played to an audience of 3,000 women and 2,000 men. Those present were in attendance from curiosity to see the New Woman make an exhibition of herself, not of her football. Consequently the numbers dwindled from 5,000 at the beginning to 2,500 at half-time and 500 at the close of proceedings. This was perhaps not unnatural, for in order to emphasise the femininity of the performance the teams were 45 minutes late.
>
> They also wore, pinned to the back of their hair, conical shaped caps which had a knack of falling off whenever a performer – generally by accident – 'headed' the ball. This necessitated a delay in the proceedings while two or three of the opposing forwards assisted in re-pinning the cap.
>
> To enter into the details of the game would be tedious

and even impossible... The principle part of the football executed on the occasion was that of the boy who is cited on the cards as 'Miss P. Smith' but is habitually addressed both by players and lookers-on as 'Tommy'. As burlesque, feminine football is on the whole tiresome.

Still the team soldiered on. It appears to have ignored the FA's ban on games taking place in the closed season (though a match at Sheffield's Bramall Lane was cancelled after Charles Alcock and his committee sent a telegram to the club warning that 'it was contrary to the rules that the Lady Footballers should play on their ground in May') and played to sizeable crowds across the north-east, Yorkshire, the south-west, and over the border in Scotland.

But there appears to have been a power struggle raging inside the British Ladies. Nettie Honeyball disappears from all team sheets after 13 May 1895. Given that she, backed by Florence Dixie, was the originator and driving force behind women's football, it's time to delve a little more deeply into her background. At first glance this should be simple. She was, after all, the very high-profile front woman for the team. There are literally dozens of interviews with her and at least one carefully staged portrait photograph. This shows her to be a young woman of average height for her times, probably in her mid to late twenties and, according to an interview in the *Daily Graphic*, tipping the scales at 11 stone (a fraction under 70kg). A report in the *Leeds Mercury* tells us that she had a brother who accompanied the team on its travels and acted as both organiser and occasional spokesman.

And thanks to the interview with Florence Dixie (and surviving contemporary posters advertising the matches) we also know exactly where Nettie J Honeyball was living when she announced the formation of her team of women footballers: 27 Weston Park, Crouch End, North London. Which is where the mystery begins.

The 1895 census reveals no trace of a Nettie Honeyball (or indeed any other woman) at 27 Weston Park. Instead it lists the occupant as one Arthur Tilbury Smith, a carpenter. The only other person listed in the house was his son, Alfred Hewitt Smith, the same name as the manager of the British Ladies' Football Club in the confrontation between Royal Ordnance on the platform of a London railway station.

Diligent genealogical research by Patrick Brennan[10] posed three immediate questions. Was Alfred Hewitt Smith the 'brother' of Nettie Honeyball referred to in the press? Could she have married into the family, thereby making him her brother-in-law? Or could the two be man and wife? Even if Nettie Honeyball was a pseudonym, the first option seems unlikely: Arthur Tilbury Smith did have a daughter, whom he named Phoebe, but in 1895 she was just 13 years old.

There were two brothers in the family besides Alfred, but both Frederick and William are shown to have been married to women with the first names of Jessie and Alice respectively. Nor could Alfred Hewitt Smith be Nettie Honeyball's husband: in 1896 he married another member of the British Ladies' Football Club, Hannah Oliphant. So who *was* Nettie J Honeyball?

The name itself was unusual: Patrick Brennan's research indicates that between 1865 and 1875 (between which dates she would have to have been born, to fit the details given in any of the press reports) just 11 girls with the surname Honeyball were registered in London. None were given Christian names which bore any resemblance to Nettie (nor, in case this was a nickname, to Annette, Janet, Jeanette). Brennan did find two possible candidates: the 1891 census listed a Janetta Honeyball. She was then 21 – therefore in the right age range – and she was recorded as boarding at a grocery shop in Lambeth Walk, where she was employed as a cashier.

But this hardly fits with Nettie Honeyball's claims that all the women players were middle or upper class, with sufficient resources (or parental finance) to support themselves on their UK-wide tour. Additionally, there is no sign of her in censuses after this date; nor did Brennan find any record of her marrying or dying between 1896 and 1901. This Miss Honeyball seems simply to have disappeared without trace.

The second possibility was a Nellie Honeyball, listed in the 1881 census as having been born in London in 1874. By the time of the formation of the British Ladies' Football Club she would have been just 20. But the confidence and maturity evident in the Nettie Honeyball interviews, coupled with the undoubted fact that in Victorian times a 20-year-old middle class woman was still to all intents and purposes the equivalent of a modern-day adolescent, render her an unlikely candidate. Added to which, all census records for the period show her living in solidly working class areas. Then there is the curious coincidence of Alfred Hewitt Smith, alleged team manager of the British Ladies, living at the address given for the otherwise invisible Miss Honeyball. Added together, these separate strands point to a reasonable conclusion: Nettie Honeyball never really existed.

Recent research carried out in conjunction with the Scottish Women's Football Association suggests that Nettie Honeyball was a fiction invented by Alfred Hewitt Smith and his younger sister Phoebe. In this distinctly plausible theory, the Smiths came up with the idea of a women's football team, but since

Alfred was plainly a man, and Phoebe far too young, they needed a suitable figurehead to launch the project and attract players. The advantage of this person being entirely fictional was that if – as had happened a decade earlier in Scotland to Mrs Graham's XI – trouble got out of hand 'Nettie Honeyball' could simply vanish. Certainly, as troubles began to mount halfway through the British Ladies' Football Club's inaugural tour her name disappeared from the team sheet.

What makes the position more complicated was the emergence in the press of 'Mrs Graham' (in reality the Scottish suffragist, Helen Matthews) as one of the leading lights of the club. Correspondent after correspondent filed reports highlighting her genuine footballing prowess: along with the diminutive Tommy she was singled out as the team's best player. And by the time the touring side reached Scotland, fixtures appear to be booked under her name, either as well as or in place of the British Ladies' Football Club. Nor was the tour going smoothly. Money was beginning to become an issue. On Friday, 31 May 1895, the *Glasgow Evening Telegraph* reported the outcome of a legal action involving the women footballers:

> Yesterday in the Glasgow Small Debts Court, Mr A. B. Lennox, of Newcastle, manager of the British Ladies' Football Cub, sued the office-bearers of the Cowlairs F.C. for £15, restricted to £12, as repayment of money withheld on the occasion of the match, played by the lady players on the Cowlairs field, Springfield Park, on Saturday afternoon, 4th inst. After a conference, the defenders agreed to pay half the sum sued for, and an amicable arrangement was come to.

Throughout the remainder of 1895, the touring side continued its trek up and down the country led by Mrs Graham. But while the crowds still flocked to watch the matches, the tone of press reports took a sharper, less amused view of the exhibitions. A report in the *Luton Times and Advertiser* on 22 November was all-too-typical:

> It was chiefly the daring novelty and unconventionality of the thing which attracted a large crowd to the British Ladies' football match on Wednesday. I doubt if one-tenth of those present on that occasion would go to see a repetition of the performance.
>
> Personally, I expected little or nothing, and therefore was not disappointed. Some portions of the play were laughable... All the applause was lavished on little 'Tommy', the Reds' centre forward who tricked and dodged and passed like a veteran... If Mrs Graham could only get together an eleven composed of maidens of 'Tommy's' calibre, well, then we should see some life and fun in the game. The 'gate' on Wednesday, I hear, amounted to £46, and of this Mrs Graham takes half, not a bad haul.

By the time of this match, there appears to have been a split between the team founded by Nettie Honeyball, with the backing of Lady Florence Dixie, and Mrs Graham's new model side. And, in a manner which pointed forward to tours by fractious ex-members of modern rock bands, each claiming the right to use the group's name, there were now two rival touring women's teams. A few days before the Luton game the *Hull Daily Mail* had printed a lengthy interview with what it described as the *Capitanessa* of the Lady Footballers.

[She] is named Mrs Helen Graham. She played in goal on Saturday and her nut-brown locks were hanging down her back. She was out and away the best man [sic] of the twenty-two, and her achievements would have done credit to a capable Preston North Ender. I asked Mrs Graham to interpret for me the 'idea' of her teams.

'We were organised,' she explained, 'to show that the game of Association football can be played by women as scientifically as by men. We have had some bad luck. We are now in our second season, though a counter-organisation has been formed, and is yet in the field. Lady Florence Dixie originally allowed her name to be identified with us, but when the difference arose with the other team, she withdrew her support, as both teams were using her name.'

'That is unfortunate,' said I. 'I was under the impression that Miss Nettie Honeyball was your captain?'

'No, she is no longer connected with us in any way, and I am both captain and secretary. I have lived in a football atmosphere all my life – I am only 23 now – and brothers of mine have played with the Millwall Athletic and Preston North End.'

'Are any of your members, besides yourself, married?' I asked. 'Yes, several, though all except myself play as "Miss". We have had a great many difficulties and prejudices to contend against, notably in Scotland (I belong to Scotland, you know), where at one place we were stoned by the women. It is so difficult for them to understand that a girl may be respectable and yet play football.'

By the spring of 1896, Mrs Graham's side was in the middle of a strenuous country-wide tour, under the title of The Original

Ladies' Footballers. Then on 13 May an advertisement appeared in the *Freemans Journal* and the *Daily Commercial Advertiser* in Dublin advising readers that the British Ladies' Football Club (President Lady Florence Dixie), would appear for the first time in Dublin at the City and Suburban Grounds Jones's Road, on Saturday, 16 May. Admission was set at either sixpence or one shilling (with a remarkably steep two shillings for the 'Special Grand Stand'). Unfortunately, the Dixie team emulated its earlier reputation of failing to turn up, the players having managed to miss the boat at Holyhead.

When they eventually did appear on the following Monday and Tuesday the two games played seemed to have been a resounding triumph. A further advertisement appeared announcing that 'Owing to the great success of the Lady Footballers' a farewell match (presumably meaning a farewell to Ireland) had been arranged for Saturday, 23 May, the opponents to be a team of 'Dublin gentlemen'. Local press reports show that in that fixture the ladies defeated the gentlemen by 7 goals to 2.

Meanwhile, Mrs Graham's XI was busying itself in Scotland – and seemed once again to be attracting the sort of violence which had dogged Helen Matthews's attempts at establishing women's football. On 31 May, *Reynolds Weekly Newspaper* reported the unfortunate events at a match in Ayrshire 12 days earlier.

We have got the lady footballers in the North, but though they seem to be well content with us, we are not impressed by them. When they appeared at Irvine there was quite a little riot. One of the ladies got a black eye from some ruffian, the crowd of savages broke in, and the players would not go on. They were badly hustled, and had a regular struggle in order to get back to the clubhouse. Such is civilization in Scotland up to date under the auspices of Presbyterianism.

South of the border, the (self-styled) 'official' British Ladies' Football Club was yet again displaying their organisational difficulties. On 23 June, Channel Islands newspaper *The Star* reported that the team would play a side from the Guernsey Rangers FC on 30 July. But on the day of the match *The Star* had to report that they had missed their train at Swansea and the match would be postponed. If that wasn't bad enough, they soon once again ran into buffers of the sporting establishment. The Club had attempted to stage matches at Bideford and Exmouth rugby clubs in Devon, but on 3 July a committee of the Devon Rugby Union announced that 'Under the English Laws such matches cannot be allowed; and further, the Committee strongly disapprove of any such matches being entertained.'

Whatever its merits on the field, women's football was now turning into a sorry farce. On 16 July 1896, the *Belfast News Letter* carried an update on the progress of Mrs Graham's XI in Scotland: 'The lady football team is at Gourock in a destitute condition, where Mrs Graham, their captain, is down with scarlet fever.' And things were shortly to get worse. Two months later a diminished squad set off on a tour of the English West Country. A match at Wellington, Somerset, on 19 September set the tone, with the press describing the game as 'a complete fiasco'. The team travelled on to Exeter, but constant rain meant the fixture had to be cancelled. The team decided to stay put in the town, hoping the weather would lift: it would prove a remarkably bad decision. The *Belfast News Letter* returned to the sorry story with an update:

The ladies' football club known to Belfast has fallen upon evil days. A meeting at Exeter was spoiled by the rain, at least so the ladies tell the story, and the expenses of the club, while remaining in the city hoping against hope for a match with liberal gate money, outran the joint resource. When the funds were utterly exhausted, and it was equally impossible to remain or to go away, the club appealed to the Mayor for assistance.

His Worship said that if there had been but two distressed damsels he might have done something, but that really when it came to six of them, he did not see his way to being generous. Eventually some friends came to the rescue, and the players were restored to the bosoms of their respective families.

It was hardly a positive advert for women's football. Not only were there just six players in the side, but to be begging for a handout to pay a £16 hotel bill was hardly likely to endear them to a public increasingly hostile to the very idea of women players. Further ignominy was heaped on them when the railway company, to which they owed money, was reported to have taken away some of their clothes in lieu of payment. There would be no more matches in 1896, and just three attempts at games the following year. These were billed as Ladies vs Gentlemen and were clearly no more than a light-hearted novelty exhibition. They drew crowds of a few hundred – a far cry from the glory days of 1895 and the mass appeal of women's football.

With the benefit of hindsight, they *were* glory days. Women's determination to throw off their corsets and step out from the claustrophobic embrace of Victorian men had not just been demonstrated but been honoured. In spite of the subterfuge of

false names, women had bravely made a very public demand
for something closer to equality.

That equality wasn't only sexual: although there are only the
scantest of mentions, it appears that in some matches either
Mrs Graham or Nettie Honeyball included a black woman
footballer called Carrie Boustead. Since only two black players
were then plying their trade in the men's game – and with no
little difficulty – it was an act of real bravery for the already
distrusted ladies' teams to feature this double-affront to
contemporary mores (and indeed a very real statement of
courage by Miss Boustead herself). But at the end of the 19th
century this hindsight was utterly invisible. Instead, from 1897
onwards the only mention of the once proud British Ladies'
Football Club and the very determined Miss Graham was in
the police courts.

On 5 April 1900, newspapers carried reports of a case at
Liverpool Sessions: a local businessman, Alfred John Bailey, was
summoned for having forged court documents in relation to a
dispute over an unpaid bill owed to a friend by Mrs Graham's
team. The *Angus Evening Telegraph* told its readers:

> The documents complained of were sent by the defendant
> to persons who were owing accounts to Mr Sugg [the
> proprietor of a sporting goods shop]... and although... no
> judgement had been obtained, the party was informed in
> the official-looking paper that 'having failed to comply
> with the order of the court' she had rendered herself liable
> to being imprisoned or have her goods seized.
>
> One of the parties to whom the document was sent was
> Miss Helen Graham Matthews, who, on being called,
> stated that formerly she was a professional lady footballer

and the Secretary of a ladies football club. She explained that Mr Sugg lent a number of jerseys to the team of lady footballers for a match which they were to play at Manchester, and as several of the garments went missing the officials of the Club resolved to keep the lot and pay for them. The Treasurer, however, afterwards went off with the Club's money, and the jerseys remained unpaid.

Two weeks later the unfortunate Mr Bailey was bound over: no record of his sentence exists. It was a sad and miserable end to what had started with a view, as Lady Florence Dixie put it, of 'the golden hilltops of progress above the mists of prejudice'. Women's football had died with not a bang, but a whimper. It would take the blood and filth of a world war for it to be re-born.

CHAPTER FIVE

'The Guns! Thank Gawd, the Guns!'
– RUDYARD KIPLING, 'UBIQUE'

On the morning of Friday, 14 May 1915, the most influential newspaper in Britain – and, at the time, quite possibly the world – published a major scoop. It revealed the previously top secret truth about the single greatest threat to winning the war against Germany: 'Want of an unlimited supply of high explosives... [is] a fatal bar to our success. We need more high explosives, more howitzers and more men.'

The report in *The Times* that morning, filed by telegraph by its military correspondent, Lieutenant Colonel Charles à Court Repington, was based on an interview he had conducted with British Commander-in-Chief, Sir John French. The two men were personal friends, and French had given the journalist unprecedented access to the British Expeditionary Force (as it was then known) on the Western Front. While representatives from all other newspapers were banned from the Front, French ensured that Repington was able to witness, first hand, the Battle of Aubers Ridge.

The attack was an unmitigated disaster for the British troops. In the course of just one day 11,000 men died in a hail of machine gun fire from the heavily-fortified German trenches opposite. 'We found the enemy much more strongly posted than we expected,' Repington reported. 'We had not sufficient high explosives to level his parapet to the ground... and when our infantry gallantly stormed the trenches... they found a garrison undismayed, any entanglements still intact. And Maxims [German machine guns] on all sides ready to pour in a hail of bullets.'

The Times' report caused an immediate storm. Questions were asked in the House of Commons, and newspapers across Britain picked up the story giving it increasing currency. 'The Shell Scandal', as it quickly became known, would soon bring down the ruling Liberal government, re-kindle the fires of feminine suffrage, and lead to a wholesale re-organisation of British industry. But it would also have another, unforeseeable effect: it would herald a golden age of women's football.

When Britain declared war on Germany on Tuesday, 4 August 1914, public reaction, while apprehensive, was largely jubilant. The crisis, which had begun at the end of July when Austria invaded Serbia, picked up an unstoppable momentum over the ensuing British Bank Holiday weekend. The holiday Monday was warm and sunny and London was thronged with people eager to hear the latest news. Michael MacDonagh, who found himself in the middle of huge crowds in Parliament Street and Whitehall, would later write in an account of the capital during World War 1[11]: '[They were] highly excited and rather boisterous... young men in straw hats and girls in calico dresses… all were already touched with war fever.'

The Times reported that the 'demonstration of patriotism

and loyalty became almost ecstatic'. Even the Prime Minister, H H Asquith, observed how, while he travelled between Parliament and Downing Street, he was 'always escorted and surrounded by crowds of loafers and holidaymakers'. Reports in regional papers, filed by news agencies, described a rush of young men to join up: 'The HQ of the London recruiting district in Great Scotland Yard were besieged from an early hour yesterday by hundreds of applicants anxious to enlist. Towards the forenoon, the numbers increased, and the sight of the ever-increasing stream pouring into the building attracted considerable interest.'

Conventional history suggests that this unseemly glee at the declaration of a war which would ultimately kill more than eight and half million men (and maim 21m) was in part due to the belief that it would be a short, sharp conflict. The phrase 'it'll all be over by Christmas' has assumed a too-tragic ring of naive hubris[12]. And there are records which indicate that, at a popular level, at least, the comforting cliché was widely used. Aubrey Smith, who would survive the war and write an account of his experiences in *Four Years on the Western Front by 'A Rifleman'* (1922), remembered:

> We were a very jolly party in those days [September to October 1914] and we felt that we were having a glorified holiday. For one thing, we thought the War would soon be over and that there was only a remote possibility of our being required.
>
> As the messenger said to me when I called at the office one day in October: 'There are twenty millions fighting together, and, if everyone only fired ten rounds a day, it makes two hundred million cartridges fired daily. Now, sir, how can they keep that up till Christmas?'

But in the War Office and in the corridors of government, Britain's leaders knew better. Field-Marshall Earl Haig had told the assembled top brass and politicians at the Council of War on 5 August that since Great Britain and Germany were fighting for their very existences, the war would inevitably be a prolonged and drawn-out struggle, and one which would need all the country's – and its then-mighty Empire – strength to win.

Six weeks later, the Chancellor ofthe Exchequer, David Lloyd George, made a speech warning that: 'It will not be easy. It will be a long job. It will be a terrible war. But in the end we shall march through terror to triumph. We shall need all our qualities, every quality that Britain and its people possess. Prudence in council, daring in action, tenacity in purpose, courage in defeat, moderation in victory, in all things faith, and we shall win.'

The problem was that – however jubilant the populace or gloomy their leaders – Britain simply wasn't ready for war, or at least not the sort of industrialised mass-slaughter it was about to embark on. For a start, the British army was an entirely volunteer force and no amount of painfully enthusiastic volunteering was going to provide enough fodder for the cannons. And those cannons – or rather their modern equivalent, heavy artillery – were also distinctly inadequate.

In 1899 this branch of the army had been modernised (to bring it into line with rival continental forces) with a Royal Warrant ordering the creation of three separate units: the Royal Garrison Artillery, the Royal Field Artillery and the Royal Horse Artillery. But by the outbreak of war, prevailing military thinking was still guided by the Victorian belief that mounted cavalry charges were the key to winning battles.

It didn't take long before these out-dated tactics became redundant. After the first few months, troops from all armies fighting along the Western Front, began to dig themselves into deep and fortified trenches, protected by barbed wire and machine guns. Charging these emplacements was suicidal (not that this stopped the commanders from ordering their troops to do it). The only way to improve the chances of success was to bombard enemy positions with artillery shells. In battle after battle both sides rained down shells on the other, each gun firing several rounds per minute, at speeds of up to 1,700 miles an hour. The result was carnage.

First World War shells were designed to burst in huge chunks of red-hot metal. These caused appalling and morale-sapping dismemberments and injury. Shrapnel shells that exploded in the air above the trenches, sprayed balls in all directions with the specific purpose of wounding rather than destroying emplacements. High explosive shells were fired to obliterate dugouts and other earthworks: they also created massive concussion waves that could kill a man up to 30 yards away. Often, the men killed by concussion had no visible sign of injury and their colleagues were reported to be particularly demoralised by finding a mass of bodies killed seemingly without cause. In the early battles on the Western Front, these artillery bombardments accounted for 60 per cent of all deaths and casualties.

The writer Henri Barbusse, who fought in the French army on the Western Front, described in his book *Le Feu* (1916) the effects of being under artillery fire: 'The noise was so monstrously resounding that one felt annihilated by the mere sound of the downpour of thunder.' The appetite of these guns was voracious. To maintain a sufficiently destructive bombardment – one that gave the infantry at least a fighting chance of storming the enemy's trenches – required a vast number of shells. British arms manufacturers, still on a largely peacetime footing even in the second year of the war, simply couldn't keep up with demand.

By March 1915, as Sir John French plotted tactics for a forthcoming battle to recapture Neuve-Chapelle in the Artois region, it was evident that the British Expeditionary Force didn't have enough shells to cut the necessary swathe through German lines. At 7.30am on 10 March, the British guns launched a 35-minute artillery bombardment followed by an infantry assault.

The German defences in the centre were quickly overrun and Neuve-Chapelle was secured. A cavalry brigade was made ready to exploit the expected rout. But two German companies of 200 men and a machine gun had survived the shelling, and as a result of their firepower, the attack ground to a halt before being abandoned three days later. Just over a mile of previously lost territory had been regained. But the human cost was high: of the 40,000 British and Indian troops who fought in the battle 11,200 were killed or wounded.

Sir John French laid the blame squarely on the lack of artillery firepower. Although more rounds were fired by the British in this one relatively short battle than during the entire five years of the Boer Wars, it was simply not enough. And it was the abject failure at Neuve-Chapelle which led him to invite *The Times* to witness the next (equally fruitless) assault at Aubers Ridge – and to leak the explosive (no pun intended) story of the shortage of shells.

The effect of *The Times'* shocking revelation in Britain was both immediate and long-term. Within 10 days the Shell Scandal caused the downfall of the Liberal government, and a new coalition administration set up an entirely new department in Whitehall – the Ministry of Munitions, headed by David Lloyd George.

An enquiry into the state of shell production swiftly revealed that although artillery shells were designed to be recycled and spent shells were returned to the munitions factory for re-filling, the industry was undermined by a major systemic problem: competition. Government arms factories tended to concentrate on small arms, whilst private munitions firms were producing poor-quality munitions in wholly insufficient numbers, largely due to a completely uncoordinated approach. As a result, in the first eight months of the war just 2m artillery rounds had been sent to France, and many of these were duds which failed to fire.

Lloyd George realised that the industrialised nature of fighting on the Western Front dictated a centrally-controlled system to deliver faster production of far more – and far more reliable – shells. The question was how? The organisational issue was (relatively) easy. In July 1915, Parliament passed the Munitions of War Act which brought all private arms companies under the close direction of the Ministry and the power to compel other civilian-based industries to switch to production of shells. The new law initially met fierce resistance from industrialists, who were less than happy at having their production lines altered by government fiat. Workers and trades unions – especially on Scotland's Clydeside – were also hostile. The Act not only gave the Ministry power to set low pay rates for munitions work, but also imposed criminal sanctions for anyone deemed to be taking time off or generally shirking their duties. But Lloyd George bought off the unions by bringing their officials on to the Ministry's pay roll and by conceding some power to them over the sex of munitions workers.

However, the simple fact was, there weren't enough men to fill the benches at the new or expanded munitions factories. The position was made even more acute when on 2 March

1916, the Military Service Act introducing compulsory conscription of all men between 18 and 41 years of age came into force (with exemptions for married men, widowers with children, ministers of religion or anyone working in a reserved occupation). Britain needed its women.

Over ten years had passed since Lady Florence Dixie had attempted to usher in the age of the New Woman via football ground turnstiles. In that time the country had seen the passing of its queen, and the birth of a new era – Edwardian Britain – which was, on the surface at least, a much brighter and more cheerful place. Out had gone the widow's weeds of an elderly monarch still mourning the husband she had lost 40 years earlier. In came a fashion-conscious, frequently hedonistic king who imbued the realm with a spirit of optimism.

But beneath the veneer of this British Belle Époque, how much had really changed? For women, not much. For the most part, Edwardian women of all social classes were still expected to defer to men and, generally, be little more than ornaments on their spouses' arms, or in their beds. True, the wealthier ones were gaining access to higher education, but for the vast mass of the female population, life was essentially just as it had been for their mothers and grandmothers before them: marriage, childbearing, and their treatment dependent on what kind of man they married.

The abuse of women – verbal (expressed in patronising put-downs at home, in the street and in the increasingly popular music halls) physical or sexual (prostitution in London reached its apogee in the Edwardian era) – was rife in all levels of society. A woman could still be incarcerated in an asylum on little more than the word of her husband and a doctor (usually male). It wasn't that women (at least working class women) didn't work: the census showed that during the Edwardian era 55 per cent of single women and 14 per cent of wives were in paid employment. But while there were a few financially-privileged women who became doctors, for the most part the professions remained closed to them.

Nor had the suffragism movement, championed by women such as Helen Matthews (alias Mrs Graham), brought the vote any closer. As a result a new, much more direct and vociferous movement had emerged: the suffragettes. Led by Emmeline Pankhurst and quite prepared to engage in acts of civil disobedience, vandalism, and hunger strikes when jailed, suffragettes finally pushed women's rights into the headlines.

But the government's 'Cat and Mouse Act', by which women were force-fed, released and then re-arrested, ensured that the status quo remained largely untroubled. On Thursday, 15 July 1915, Mrs Pankhurst, having been released from prison only a few days earlier, addressed an outdoor meeting at the London Pavilion. Putting aside her differences with a government which had repeatedly incarcerated her, she told the crowd that women were 'not being utilised for war purposes in this country to the extent they might be... If the services they freely offer are accepted, many men would be released for the proper business of men, to fight for their country'.

But despite their evident patriotism, the suffragettes were still fighting the overwhelming tide of public opinion, in the ruling classes and within trade unions. Women's role in society was still seen as completely apart from – beneath, even – that of men. In sum, and viewed with hindsight, the Edwardian era was the last bastion of near-universal male dominance. And yet it was on women that the British war effort would now substantially rely.

CHAPTER SIX

So we are at the benches, and our pals are in the trenches
And all our work serves the end,
And mere women too, are here to help us throughout
In our efforts our world to defend

– 'THE MUNITIONS WORKERS SONG'
(POPULAR FIRST WORLD WAR BALLAD)

In the weeks leading up to Christmas Day 1917, British troops dug in along the Western Front began to receive packages of food and clothing sent from home. These comfort parcels – delivered at the astonishing rate of 50,000 per day – were a vital lifeline, and a much-needed boost to morale.

One private spoke for all his fellow soldiers when he sent a letter home explaining how much the lovingly chosen and wrapped packages meant: 'I think my idea of hell would be the Front without parcels.' Even when packages were addressed to a man who had been killed, the brutality and desperation of the trenches ensured that they were usually consumed by the survivors.

GIRLS WITH BALLS

That Christmas, troops from all armies – British, American, Canadian, Australian and their enemies from the Axis countries – were in dire need of cheer. 1917 had been a brutal and bloody year with major battles at Vimy Ridge, Ypres and Passchendaele, as well as vicious fighting at numerous, if less resonant, other points on the Front. All had claimed nearly a million casualties. All along the line, men hunkered down and found what little comfort was available. Unlike previous years, there would be no game of football between British and German troops: no fleeting fraternisation in the hell of No Man's Land. British High Command had deemed it bad for morale.

On the home front, the comfort and morale of British soldiers was uppermost in the public's mind. And in the run up to Christmas, a notice was posted at Deepdale, the ground of Preston North End Football Club, announcing 'A Great Holiday Attraction'. A women's football match was to be played between the ladies of Coulthard's Foundry and those of Dick, Kerr's munitions works on Christmas Day, with the proceeds going to the Moor Park Voluntary Aid Detachment Hospital for Wounded Soldiers. It was not the first game of ladies' football to be played during the First World War and it would by no means be the last.

On 27 January 1916, the British government introduced the Military Service Act. All voluntary enlistment into the armed forces was stopped. Instead, the Act stated that all unmarried British men aged between 18 and 41 were now deemed to have enlisted. They were – although the Act didn't use the term – effectively conscripted. These new enforced recruits were not given a choice of which service, regiment or unit they joined (as had been the case with volunteers), although if a man stated a preference for the navy it was given priority over the army to take him. The Act was further extended to include married men three months later.

A system of appeals tribunals was established to hear cases of men who claimed to be disqualified on the grounds of ill-health, occupation or conscientious objection. Some trades were deemed to be vital to the war economy and anyone working in these so-called Starred Occupations was exempted from the call up. But the Act failed to deliver the necessary manpower to feed in to the human mincing machine of the Western Front. Only 43,000 of the men initially called up actually qualified for service in the army when they arrived at the barracks. Worse still, another 93,000 failed to respond to the call-up and courts up and down the land began to fill with cases against these proto-deserters. A further 748,587 men claimed some form of exemption, miring the tribunals in perpetual hearings.

Eventually, 1,433,827 men were listed as being in Starred Occupations, or were seriously ill. Many had even already been discharged from the army on these grounds. The manpower needs of the British war effort were simply never met. But the government's need wasn't just for bodies to throw into the trenches. Ever since the Shell Crisis and its resulting aftershocks, huge efforts to increase the production of artillery rounds – and to reduce their purchase price by the War Office – had been a national priority. But how, given the simultaneous conscription, could this need be met? Munitions manufacturing was a traditionally male occupation, and more than that, a skilled male occupation.

The answer to both problems was set out in another law, The Munitions of War Act, which had been passed in July 1915. In addition to giving the government control over the industry, it had enabled it to dictate the price of munitions. At the start of 1915, the price for one 18lb (just over 8 kilograms) high explosive shell – the standard projectile for British artillery – was 32 shillings. By the end of the year the War Ministry had reduced that per item cost to 12 shillings and sixpence.

This plainly had an effect on the munitions companies' profits. Thirty-two shillings was the average weekly wage earned by a skilled (male) worker. Each shell sold to the government therefore paid handsomely for the cost of production – and since, as we have seen, every battle involved hurling tens or even hundreds of thousands of artillery rounds at the enemy, war was, for some, a very profitable business indeed.

Reducing the price of shells by almost two-thirds made a sizeable hole in the companies' accounts. The only solution was to reduce costs, and that meant drafting in unskilled, non-traditional forms of labour. In the boardrooms of armaments manufacturers there was much unhappiness about this development. But on the shop floor, the reaction was stubbornly hostile: trades unions were vehemently opposed to undercutting the position of skilled workers.

Minister of Munitions Lloyd George, the canniest of politicians, pressed the unions hard, until they finally consented to a scheme of 'dilutions': this would allow munitions companies to draft in strictly limited unskilled workers to 'dilute' the otherwise full-strength labour force. But he also saw that he could satisfy the demands of the suffragettes for women's rights. It was he who had encouraged Mrs Pankhurst to hold a meeting at the London Pavilion which she had used to call for women to be allowed to serve their country by working in war industries.

Women wanted to work – indeed working class women had always worked. Women were also available in very large numbers. From the very start of the war, trades which had traditionally employed them, such as in the manufacture of clothing and luxury goods, suffered a sharp downturn. Within a few months more than 50,000 women were laid off. Lloyd George would have his replacements for the men being sent to die in France.

Although many middle class women now moved into the still-warm seats of male clerical workers, working class women were frequently drafted into more hands-on occupations as munitions companies opened their gates. And the policy proved successful. According to government figures, by the end of 1916 more than 897,000 women had filled the jobs vacated by men. By 1918 that figure would reach a little over 1m, and of these more than 700,000 worked in the munitions industry. By the end of the war 80 per cent of all weapons and shells were being produced by women. The press dubbed them 'munitionettes'.

Munitions work by its very nature was hazardous and the factories were noisy and chaotic. The stories of women munitions workers have been assembled in a remarkable archive at London's Imperial War Museum, of which Elsa Thomas's first impressions of the vast Woolwich Arsenal in London are typical:

> I never was so frightened in my life as when I went to the Arsenal. And they took us into a workshop and all I could see was a little cap and a huge pressing machine. And this little boy was pulling and pulling – making copper caps. These copper caps fell there just like glittering things falling… Well that's what my first experience was. I thought, 'Oh, I could never do this.' The lathes up above,

you know, frightened [me]. I thought, 'I shall never do this, no I shall never do this.'

And when they got over the shock of the environment, the women discovered that the work was enormously physical. Elsie McIntyre, who filled shells at the Barnbow Factory in Leeds, recalled:

> When it first opened in the early part of the war, we had to stem the powder into shells with broom handles and mallets. You see, you'd have your shell and the broom handle, your tin of powder. And you'd put a bit in, stem it down, put a bit more in, stem it down. It took you all your time to get it all in. It was very hard work.

What Elsie McIntyre and her fellow-workers were stuffing into the shells was extraordinarily dangerous – Tri Nitro Toluene, or TNT, was in theory a fairly stable explosive, but when all was said and done it was still an explosive. Kathleen Gilbert, who went to work at the Park Royal shell filling station in West London, described how she was taught to handle the material:

> They used to give us domes of glass on the table with holes for your hands to go through, and you filled up the gains. Gains were something like cartridges but bigger. You filled them up with this black rock stuff. You all had to change when you went in. You had to strip and change into other clothes because you weren't allowed a little tiny bit of metal on you at all, not one hook or eye or anything. And of course they had corsets in those days with wires in them, you see. And you had to finish up with an overall and put your head covering on.

Despite these precautions, accidents, including fatal explosions, were far from uncommon. Twelve women were killed when one East London munitions factory blew up, and by the end of 1918 the death toll among munitionettes topped 200. Even more deadly than the constant risk of explosion, the TNT shell-filling brought with it exposure to highly toxic chemicals. Beatrice Lee, who worked at the Yorkshire Copper Works, recalled the effects on her:

> It wasn't what you'd call a healthy job. Because, well, at that time my hair was jet black and I used to have to bend over the boshes with the acid. You've seen the style today where people have their hair bleached at the front, well my hair went like that, just at the front with bending over the boshes where the acid was, because we used to have to put the tubes in this hot acid. Well, the hot tubes used to make the acid hot and then the fumes used to come up. It was a very unhealthy job.

In 1917, Lilian Miles and her sister Grace worked on the production line at a munitions company. Before long, Grace became sick. Lilian describes how she tried to get the illness investigated:

> She went to the doctor and the doctor said that she was under the influence of alcohol because she was falling about and she couldn't hold herself up, she was falling about. So the doctor told her to come back again when she was sober. Well I went down to the doctor and I said to him, I said, 'She doesn't drink.' 'Well,' he said, 'I think she was under the influence of drink.' And I said she wasn't.
> 'There's something wrong with her,' I said, 'because

she's falling about all the while.' And of course she was only 19, she wasn't 20.... [eventually] he had a specialist to her and they took her in the hospital. She died in terrible agony. She died in terrible pain and they said that they reckoned that black powder it burnt the back of her throat away. And the continual breathing of this black powder it sort of burnt the back of her throat away.

Munitionettes like these were instantly recognisable wherever they went. The chemical base of TNT contained an ingredient which turned their skins vivid yellow. Caroline Rennles, who was employed at the Slade Green TNT Factory in Kent, encountered a mixed reaction to her appearance:

Well of course we all had bright yellow faces, you see, 'cos we had no gas masks in those times and all our hair here... The manager used to say, 'Tuck that hair under!' you know, and you used to almost look like nuns. And you know what when you're young... So it was all bright ginger, all our front hair, you know. And all our faces were bright yellow – they used to call us canaries. Well, when we come off our little old train, like, the big main train would be coming through and it would be packed, you know, with different people. So of course the porters, like, they knew that we were all munitions kids, you know. So they'd say, 'Go on, girl, hop in there,' like, and they used to open the first class carriages, you know.

And there'd be all, oh, there'd be all the officers sitting there and, you know, some of them used to look at us as though we was insects, know what I mean? And others used to mutter, 'Oh well they're doing their bit.' As I say, some was quite nice and others, you know, used to treat us as though we was scum of the earth. 'Course we, all our clothes like, we couldn't wear like good clothes because the powder used to seep into your clothes, know what I mean? But you couldn't wear nothing posh there really.

Women also found that they were discriminated against in the very factories that were ruining their health. They were doing the same hard and dirty jobs as men, but they were treated very differently. Sibbald Stewart, who worked alongside munitionettes at Elswick Ordnance Factory in Glasgow, vividly described the conditions they all faced together:

We started off at six in the morning and we worked 'til about six at night. Twelve hours on the machine and the night shift came on and took over from us and gone on over midnight. So, two twelve-hour days for each machine in the twenty-four hours. Oh, a break for half an hour at midnight in the night shift, but you'd a full hour's break at lunchtime on the day shift. The only breaks, yes, no cups of tea in the morning or afternoon... Heavy going! It was tiring work, it was tiring of course they were heavy – they were 72 pounds weight per shell, the shell case alone. It was heavy going.

Male munitions workers like Sibbald Stewart received an average weekly wage of £4 6s 6d, but for women doing the same job, the pay was just £2 2s 4d. Unsurprisingly, women munitions workers began to organise into their own versions of the male trade unions, and to lobby for more equal treatment. But they also began moving on to other, traditionally male, turf: they began to play football.

GIRLS WITH BALLS

In the years since Helen Graham Matthews and Nettie Honeyball had last kicked a ball in public, football had changed considerably. Professionalism was now universally accepted, if sometimes grudgingly. Upper-class players – notably from the Wanderers – horrified by the spectacle of rough artisans being paid to play what they considered to be their rightful sport, had formed a breakaway Amateur Football Association in 1907, and in what would shortly become a signature act, the FA had promptly outlawed it. Meanwhile, teams in towns and cities across Britain had developed substantial followings.

Those loyal supporters, too, had changed in character. The crowd at the first FA Cup Final in March 1872 had been overwhelmingly rich and privileged: adorning the heads of the 2,000 spectators was a veritable forest of top hats, and the few ladies present were attired in all the bustled and corseted finery of the Victorian aristocracy. By the outbreak of the First World War, Saturday afternoon football crowds were several times larger and in overwhelming proportions working class. Football – at least the Association variety – had become the people's game once more.

The Football Association itself was, somewhat inevitably, immune to this democratisation. It was still dominated by the rich and well-to-do, but to some extent it was beginning to appear that it had rather lost justification for its existence. The Association rules – born of a bitter feud between public school alumni and the more proletarian northern clubs – had long since been tightened and engraved in universally accepted code, leaving little need for policing by the good men and true of the FA. (The last major change being a new rule in 1892 which prohibited charging at, and knocking over, goalkeepers.) What's more, the weekly routine of fixtures had been wrested away from FA control by the formation of the Football League in 1888: it governed the season's matches and leagues quite independently. All that remained of the FA's once-mighty purview was its annual Challenge Cup.

Having little or no real purpose has never stopped the administrators of any sport. The FA was led by Charles Clegg, a wealthy Sheffield solicitor and simultaneously President of the British Temperance League. It now involved itself in something truly close to the hearts of its august management: money. (Clegg managed to be both privileged and carry a chip on his shoulder. A forthright and self-important man, he is remembered for barking out such truisms as 'no one ever gets lost on a straight road'.)

Luring players from one club to another with ever-larger pay packets had become the norm. In 1901, to combat this self-evident evil, the FA had issued a new ordinance: a maximum wage. The cap was set at £4 per week, and for good measure the FA also outlawed the paying of bonuses to players. If Clegg and his compatriots – all from an unimpeachably mercantile background – had thought this would end the issue they were remarkably naive about the essential nature of capitalism. Football was now a business, and businesses have always been happy to bend the rules on the road to success.

Unquestionably the leading club at the time was Manchester City, led by the equally confirmed best footballer in Britain, Billy Meredith. The FA had suspected for several years that City was flouting the maximum wage and hiding its crimes with clever – or downright misleading – accountancy. In 1904, matters came to a head. Financial 'discrepancies' were found in the transfer of two players from Glossop FC to City. An FA enquiry fined the club £250 and ordered the suspension of five of its directors. But that was just the beginning. Charles Clegg announced that far from being over, the FA's investigations into Manchester City were ongoing, but refused to give any further detail. 'The nature of the allegations,' he pronounced loftily, 'could not be indicated at this stage.'

In August, the FA dropped its bombshell: the report of its enquiries revealed that Billy Meredith had offered a £10 bribe to the captain of Aston Villa to 'throw' a vital match against City. It imposed a 12-month ban on Meredith and instructed City's management that he was not, under any circumstances, to receive any pay. To add injury to this insult, it also forced City to take on the Association's own auditor as its accountant. Its aim in doing so was to prise open the club's distinctly murky books.

By 1906, Meredith was both broke and resentful. On 19 March he dropped his own bombshell, when, in an interview with *Athletic News* he revealed 'with a frankness that amounts to fearlessness' that Manchester City had deliberately ignored the FA's maximum wage rule. 'The club put aside the rule that no player should receive more than £4 a week,' he told the paper. 'From 1902, I had been paid £6 a week. The season we carried off the [FA] Cup I also received £53 in bonuses for games won and drawn. Altogether the club paid in bonuses £654 12s 6d. The team delivered the goods and the club paid for the goods delivered and both sides were satisfied.'

On 4 June, *Athletic News* carried the inevitable outcome. Under the headline 'Enormous Offences; Overwhelming Sentences', it reported that the entire Manchester City board had been removed from football (including one life ban), 17 of its players were also suspended for the remainder of the season, and fines were imposed on them totalling £900. The club was disgraced and would be essentially ruined for the next 30 years.

But Billy Meredith hadn't finished with the Football Association. At the conclusion of his ban he had joined an up-and-coming outfit on the other side of Manchester: it would become Manchester United. And together with Charlie Roberts, another United star striker, Meredith decided it was time a little player-power penetrated the respectable halls of the FA. In the summer of 1907 he sent a circular to all professional footballers: it proposed the formation of a player's union.

> Personally, I really don't think that the gentlemen who sit on the FA Council have ever at all realised how absurdly autocratic, unfair and unjust has been their attitude towards the players. Ask any man who has to attend an FA Commission to tell you what he thinks about it. They have always treated the player as though he were a mere boy, or a sensible machine, or a trained animal.
>
> When they were displeased they just cracked the whip or gave him a slap. They never dreamed that the man might be able to explain things if he were given a fair chance and that if he did give a good explanation he might be man enough to resent his treatment if that explanation were merely pushed aside with a contemptuous laugh.

Billy Meredith's very public declaration of war received support from the sporting press. *Athletic News* declared: 'We cannot conceive of any player with a grain of sense refusing to support the establishment of a body for the protection of his own interests'. That phrase 'his own interests' would shortly be the key to a bitter battle with the FA, for Charles Clegg believed that the divine right to determine everyone's interests in the game of football had been bestowed on the FA and the FA alone.

On 2 December 1907, the Association Football Players' Union was formally established. Almost immediately 700 professional footballers joined it – a figure which would rise to 1,300 within a year.

The FA might harbour a very distinct ill-will to the new organisation but it could not lawfully ban it. Instead it waited for Meredith and his friends to march on to its territory; and by the start of 1909 the Players' Union had set up camp squarely on FA turf. Injured players had, for some time, been entitled to receive their wages while recovering from incapacitation. But clubs frequently failed to do so, and the mechanism by which a player could appeal to the FA to enforce his right to injury pay was slow and cumbersome. The Players' Union decided to by-pass this route and assist players in suing their employers in the courts via the relatively new Workman's Compensation Act.

Unfortunately, Rule 48 of the Football Association Constitution prohibited players from going to court without the prior approval of the FA. To Meredith and Roberts this was manifestly unjust: the Workman's Compensation Act was the law of the land, and no citizen should be denied its protection. But to Charles Clegg – already caricatured by the press as 'the Napoleon of the Football Association' – the issue was much more important than mere legislation. It was about who governed football. And to Clegg there was only one answer.

In February 1909, the FA ordered the Union not to take any cases to court. The Union refused to comply with this edict and in March the FA retaliated by withdrawing official recognition of the Union. Rumours of a nationwide football strike began to circulate in the press. In May, Clegg and the FA Council ordered all the Union's officials – all professional players – to resign or face suspension from football. Led by Meredith and the equally troublesome (at least from the Clegg's point of view) Roberts, the players voted to defy the FA. Roberts had already been in trouble with the self-proclaimed masters of football over his choice of shorts. In a hint of what would shortly follow, the FA had attempted to ban him from wearing tight-fitting brief shorts because they were deemed unseemly for the game. Roberts had defied the pronouncement.

The FA duly punished the Union's players by suspending them and stopping their pay. The players responded by affiliating their Union to the General Federation of Trades Unions. The GFTU had been set up by the TUC nearly a decade before precisely to help smaller unions fight battles with their employers. Meredith had a contract to write a column for the popular *Weekly News* which he used to castigate the Football Association: 'The FA have been ruling us just as the bad barons of old ruled their people, and it's only just being brought home to them that it won't do any longer. The player refuses any longer to be treated as if he were both child and slave.'

Throughout the summer of 1907, the Union and the FA fought a series of skirmishes in round table negotiations. But Charles Clegg was a first class, and highly devious, political operator. Using tried and tested dirty tricks, he began to drive a wedge between the radical faction of the Union, led by Meredith and Roberts from Manchester United, and the more moderate (or at least less well-known) members. On 31 August he summoned all professional players to a mass meeting at the Grand Hotel in Birmingham: all, that is, but the troublesome Manchester United players. Those who, like Charlie Roberts, tried to attend were simply turned away at the door.

The divide-and-rule tactic worked well. Clegg brokered a deal which greatly damaged the Players Union and the livelihoods of its members. It was to be the beginning of the end of player power. Three years later, when the Union again challenged the FA in the courts – this time over the transfer system which essentially bound players to clubs for the latter's benefit – it was soundly defeated and came close to bankruptcy.

By the start of the First World War there was no doubting who were the masters of football. The wealthy, conservative and privileged men of the FA were once again the rulers of the people's sport and the sole arbiters of who could play it. And it was on to this turf that women footballers – working class to the tip of their boots – were about to step.

CHAPTER SEVEN

'The pace... has the same effect as a slow
moving Kinema-picture.'
– *LANCASHIRE DAILY POST*, 27 DECEMBER 1917

I n October 1917, Grace Sibbert was presented with a challenge. She was 26 years old and had been married for almost four years. Her husband, John, had volunteered early in the war, joining the Loyal North Lancashire Regiment. He had fought in the Somme Offensive – the brutal, bloody and largely unproductive battle which claimed the lives of hundreds of thousands on either side. (The first day of the offensive, 1 July 1916, was the worst day in British army history, with almost 60,000 men killed or wounded.)

John Sibbert was, in some ways, lucky. He was captured during the battle and marched off to a German prisoner of war camp. What happened to him thereafter is unrecorded, but whilst he may have escaped a squalid death in the Picardy mud, British soldiers interned as prisoners of war typically endured starvation, torture and, all too frequently, death. What is known is that at some point, Grace was advised of her husband's capture.

She was, by then, a munitionette, one of thousands who had responded to a government poster campaign bearing the message 'On Her Their Lives Depend' and depicting an attractive young woman donning overalls and cap, superimposed on a photo of an artillery soldier loading shells into a field gun. Grace joined Dick, Kerr's Munitions Works in Preston, Lancashire. By the time her husband was captured, the town's newspaper was filled with reports of wounded 'Tommies' being brought to the town's Moor Park Hospital.

These were, of course, pre-National Health days. Moor Park was a Voluntary Aid Detachment (VAD) establishment, staffed largely by non-professional medical personnel and housed in a pavilion provided by the Royal Lancashire Agricultural Society. It was initially intended to care for just 35 patients, but as the war continued and the shipments of walking wounded grew daily, new wards were built. Some of the work was funded by public subscription, some by donations from local manufacturing companies – which goes some way to explain why the hospital's matron suggested to Grace Sibbert that the women of Dick, Kerr's might care to help by holding a fundraising concert.

Dick, Kerr & Co Ltd was itself a significant contributor to the war effort. The company had been set up in Scotland in 1885 by its founders William Bruce Dick and John Kerr, specialising in construction of steam engines, trams and railway appliances. Throughout the years until the outbreak of war, as a public company its shares had been quoted daily in the financial press. Under the Munitions of War Act, Dick, Kerr rapidly turned from railway engines to munitions, employing hundreds of workers at its factories in Glasgow and Preston.

Many of those were men in Starred Occupations – designated vital to the war effort. And many of them, in

Preston at least, were in the habit of kicking a football around in the company yard during tea breaks. According to the semi-official historian of Dick, Kerr's, Gail Newsham[13], Grace Sibbert and her fellow munitionettes dared one day to tease the men about their footballing prowess and venture that the 'girls' could do better. Which is when she was issued with her challenge: prove it.

Since this apparently coincided with the request for assistance from Moor Park's matron, Grace Sibbert decided to combine the two. A Dick, Kerr's Ladies team would be formed and, if suitable female opposition from another local works could be procured, a match would be played, under Football Association rules, in aid of the hospital's funds.

On that score, at least, Grace Sibbert would have had no worries. As we shall see, from the start of 1917 as more and more women were drafted into manufacturing, ladies football teams sprang up all over the country. They were, by and large, tolerated – if not actively supported – by the FA. True, it had in 1902 issued an edict that no football involving mixed teams was permitted (a ruling that, for players from the age of 11 upwards, is still in force today) but in the prevailing drive towards everyone doing their bit for the war, the FA turned a tactful blind eye to the numerous and frequent breaches of its ordinance.

Sibbert would, had she reflected on it, have also been reassured that the fixture would fulfil its purpose of raising money. Women's football had novelty value, and the relatively recent history of the British Football Ladies' Club proved that, for all the scorn heaped upon it, the spectacle of female footballers drew paying crowds in their thousands.

Added to all of which was the dolorous position of male football during the First World War. When Britain declared war on Germany on 4 August 1914, the Football Association and the Football Leagues[14] were preparing themselves for the start of the season. Both the Leagues and the FA decided to carry on as normal with their respective competitions.

Recruitment to the armed forces was, as we have seen, on a purely voluntary basis, and professional clubs were reluctant to release players, with whom they had just signed new year-long contracts. Faced with this opposition, the Ministry of War declared that professional footballers could only join up if the clubs agreed to cancel their contracts.

Almost immediately the clubs, the Football League and the Football Association came under sustained pressure from the press as well as the great and good of British society. In a sermon at St Swithun's Church, East Grinstead, on 30 August 1914, the Reverend W Youard urged footballers to follow the lead of the Rugby Unions who had already instructed their (admittedly amateur) players to join up.

> I would say to every able-bodied young man in East Grinstead to offer yourself without delay in the service of your country. The Welsh Rugby Union Committee has passed a resolution declaring it the duty of all football players to join immediately. Blackheath Rugby Football Club has cancelled all its matches for the same reason. That is the right spirit. I hope it will be imitated by our own clubs. Go straight to the recruiting officer and offer yourself. That is the plain duty of every able-bodied young man today.

On 6 September, the author Arthur Conan Doyle followed up with a national appeal for all sportsmen to heed the need of their country.

There was a time for all things in the world. There was a time for games, there was a time for business, and there was a time for domestic life. There was a time for everything, but there is only time for one thing now, and that thing is war. If the cricketer had a straight eye let him look along the barrel of a rifle. If a footballer had strength of limb let them serve and march in the field of battle.

Newspapers, already inflamed with jingo-istic patriotism leapt aboard the bandwagon, some suggesting that those who did not join up were 'contributing to a German victory'. Others – notably the regional press – contented themselves with reporting the increasingly frequent emotional pleas of the people's betters. The *Stratford Express* of 2 December carried the following notice:

The Bishop of Chelmsford paid a visit in Bethnal Green on Sunday afternoon, when he addressed the men's service at St James Church, where he was accorded a hearty welcome. The Bishop, in an address on Duty, spoke of the magnificent response that had been made to the call to duty from the King. All must play their part. They must not let their brothers go to the front and themselves remain indifferent. He felt that the cry against professional football at the present time was right. He could not understand men who had any feeling, any respect for their country, men in the prime of life, taking large salaries at a time like this for kicking a ball about. It seemed to him something incongruous and unworthy. He wanted them to be true to their duty, their duty to their home and family.

But not all of the press was convinced. Five days after the Bishop of Chelmsford invoked God to inveigh against wartime football, *Athletic News* warned its readers:

> The whole agitation is nothing less than an attempt by the ruling classes to stop the recreation on one day in the week of the masses... What do they care for the poor man's sport? The poor are giving their lives for this country in thousands. In many cases they have nothing else... There are those who could bear arms, but who have to stay at home and work for the army's requirements, and the country's needs. These should, according to a small clique of virulent snobs, be deprived of the one distraction that they have had for over thirty years.

Football, it seemed, was more important than religion or country or warfare. The game itself once more split along the familiar fault line of gentlemen and players. While professional footballers were locked into their clubs and prevented from joining up, the patrician amateurs – public school men, one and all – had no such problems.

One such leading gentleman, the former England soccer international and all-round sportsman Charles Burgess Fry, called for the abolition of football, demanding that all professional contracts be annulled and that no one below 40 be allowed to attend matches. (Although since Fry would go on to become an ardent fan of the Nazis and invited the Hitler Youth to visit the Royal Navy training ship of which he was director, his pronouncements might, perhaps, be taken with a pinch of historical salt.)

Then on 12 December 1914, William Joynson-Hicks, Tory MP and chairman of the Automobile Association, founded the

17th Service (Football) Battalion of the Middlesex Regiment, or as it became known 'The Football Battalion'. Its motto was unequivocal: 'The charge at football is good, that with a bayonet finer.'

Writing in his invaluable *Soccer History* magazine, Ian Nannestad says: 'The organisers hoped to enlist a full battalion of 1,350 men, apparently from the ranks of both amateur and professional players and staunch supporters of senior clubs. Recruitment at the time was principally aimed at unmarried men, of whom there were estimated to be around 600 amongst the ranks of professional footballers. A significant proportion of these were based in the north of England, although the battalion announced it would only recruit men from clubs south of the River Trent. Initial interest was high, with 400 to 500 present at the meeting, but of these only 35 enlisted on the day, and by the end of the year *The Sportsman* recorded just 34 additional names.'

The Football Battalion would fight through many of the bloodiest battles of the war. When the shooting was over it was estimated that 500 of its 600 volunteers had been killed.

Whether due to stinging criticism in the press or simply the ever-growing weariness of war, attendances at football matches fell dramatically during the second-half of the 1914-15 season. The professional clubs, conscious of the need to be seen to do something to support the war effort, began holding regular collections for war relief funds, and supporters were often subjected to speeches by local dignitaries encouraging them to enlist. Football grounds were made available to the army for drill practice and, in many stadia, miniature rifle ranges were set up on the pitch.

But support was clearly draining away. As a result, the

Football Leagues and the FA decided to suspend professional soccer until peace was won. Thousands of professional footballers were now out of work: many heeded the call of their country and volunteered. Although figures aren't strictly reliable, an estimated 2,000 of Britain's 5,000 professional football players 'took the King's Shilling' following the abandonment of the 1915-16 season. Amateur leagues continued largely unaffected but the major clubs essentially shut their gates and closed down for the duration. All of which left a significant gap in the market – a gap which munitionettes had begun to fill.

The first recorded match is believed to have taken place on Christmas Day 1916 in the Cumbrian town of Ulverston when women from a local munitions factory took on (and beat) a team picked from the rest of the female population. That game appears to have fired the starting gun for women's teams to form all over Britain. Throughout 1917 local newspapers, if not the national dailies, reported scores of ladies football fixtures, each drawing large crowds and raising substantial funds for war charities. Press reporting was largely favourable. An entry in Scotland's popular Sunday paper, *The Post,* on 10 June 1917 was typical.

A sports gala held at Fir Park, Motherwell, yesterday afternoon lacked nothing in the way of variety. The meeting was promoted by the National Projectile Factory, Mossend, and was attended by a crowd of 10,000 spectators... Sergeant Angus, V.C.[15], kicked off the ball in the ladies football match, which proved quite an attraction. The sports were in aid of war charities and should be the means of providing a large return for this laudable purpose.

Nor was this good nature confined to journalists: the letters columns began to fill up with expressions of gratitude.

> To The Editor of *The Midland Daily Telegraph*: Monday, September 24, 1917
>
> Sir, After the splendid exhibition displayed by the ladies on the Butts ground on Saturday last, I feel confident that (with your assistance in giving it publicity) another tournament could be arranged on practically the same lines, the proceeds to be donated to some charitable object. Judging from the number of spectators who witnessed the tournament and who, in their applause, encouraged the players, a good 'gate' would be the result... These ladies, who are doing so much for the country, should be encouraged in their sport.

But what emerges from these newspaper columns is a clear picture of ladies' football as little more than a novelty – one which was undoubtedly doing its bit for the war effort, but a novelty nonetheless. Matches were often played in deliberately absurd costumes, or with comic handicaps such as strapping players' arms behind their backs. In this, the women footballers were seen as following an established tradition. Bizarrely, given the era and its chauvinistic attitudes to women, there had been for some years a flourishing trade in female boxing or wrestling exhibitions. Women's football seems initially to have been accepted under this general umbrella rather than as serious sport. A report in the *Essex Newsman* on Saturday, 10 March 1917 captures the flavour:

> Lady footballers have great attractive qualities. Not, of course, for the 'classy' character of their play, but in the

main for reasons which wild horses would not drag from yours truly.

I may say at once that a Ladies' Football match seems to appeal to a very wide circle, at least it did on Saturday at the Coval Lane Ground, Chelmsford... 'Say,' shouted one youth, 'she in the white shorts looks tasty.' Immediately 'she' was the observed of all observers and by general consent it was admitted that the youth knew a good thing when he saw it.

I will go further and say that all the players 'looked tasty'. Good looks predominated and generally the thought of most of the men present was 'How happy could I be with either, were t'other dear charmer away'. And judged by the results of the match the ladies, whatever their football was like, scored heavily. The 'gate' for the Red Cross Hospital amounted to between £18 and £20, and I hope they will have a few more shots at the price.

There were though, apparent rumblings of discontent amidst the general approval. Women's teams tended to wear baggy chemises over long and equally baggy 'knickers'[16] (sometimes with the addition of an overskirt) and topped with a mob cap. However modest this uniform might be – particularly when compared to short shorts favoured by Charlie Roberts – there was still evidently enough female flesh on show to cause concern over public morals. A letter published in the *Blyth News* on 30 August 1917 gives both a snapshot of these mutterings and a stout defence of munitionette footballers in the north-east. That it was written by a man, signed 'Munitioneer', who claimed to work alongside the women, made it all the more powerful.

I have heard, more than once, some very uncharitable and uncalled-for criticism of the respectability of the young women playing these matches, certain of the 'unco guid'[17] asserting that it is not decent for them to appear in public in 'knickers'! – pardon my mentioning the article of clothing that has raised their ire.

May I say that these girls are doing an excellent work of charity in playing. We cannot all subscribe hard cash to the hundred and one deserving funds now calling for our support. They are doing their bit by work: all honour to them.

I should like to suggest that they are more decently dressed in the 'unmentionable' garments than their prurient minded critics who are parading the streets in blouses open nearly to the waist and skirts too short for a girl of 12. I am working with these girls [the munitionettes] and I am proud of it. Some of them are a bit boisterous, but they all have hearts as big as a lion. If some of the weak-minded and weak-kneed could only have seen them stick in manfully during the recent inclement weather they would feel reassured that there is no possible doubt of our winning the war while we have such women (heroines I call them) as mothers of the race.
– MUNITIONEER

Notwithstanding this gallant defence, it is clear that the very existence of women, often young and unmarried, in the previously all-male sanctuaries of manufacturing did cause concern. Munitionettes – already subject to strict controls due to the nature of the materials they handled – were also carefully monitored by both in-house moral supervisors and by the Women's Police Service.

Departure from the standards expected of women (not, of course, imposed on men) resulted in being reported or, potentially, taken to court. Not for nothing were all women's football teams constantly accompanied by an official chaperone.

The self-anointed great and good men who sat on the Football Association's various committees do not appear to have taken any offence at the mushrooming of women's teams. Nor did the FA or the Football Leagues prevent ladies matches being played at the major clubs' grounds. Indeed, at local level at least some FA officials were actively supportive. On 26 May 1917, Durham County Football Association – the regional body affiliated to the London headquarters – held its annual general meeting. Its secretary, one W Spedding, criticised those within the county who were still demanding that all football should be stopped for the duration of the war.

The local press reported that Mr Spedding pointed to lady footballers as a shining example of how the sport was doing its bit for Britain. He noted that even though these women's football clubs were not affiliated to their local Football Associations, 'their enthusiasm was stimulating, and was assisting the others to bear with fortitude their own burdens'. And to underline his point, Mr Spedding extended his best wishes to the munitionettes and expressed fervent hope that 'their charitable efforts would be crowned with success'.

It seems that as long as women's football was no more than light-hearted public entertainment, aimed solely at supporting Britain's fighting men, the attitude of the sport's authorities was variously one of benign indifference or (somewhat patronising) congratulation. But within a few years this tolerance would evaporate: and the catalyst would be Grace Sibbert's new team, Dick, Kerr's Ladies.

Grace Sibbert's acceptance of the challenge laid down by the munitions company's male workers wasn't entirely hubris. The women had already been playing kick-about soccer in Dick, Kerr's factory yard. Alice Norris, who joined the team aged 14 and became one of its fixtures, later recalled: 'We used to play at shooting at the cloakroom windows. They were little square windows and if the boys beat us at putting a window through we had to buy them a packet of Woodbines[18], but if we beat them they had to buy us a bar of Five Boys chocolate[19].'

Sibbert arranged for the Christmas Day match to be played against the neighbouring Arundel Coulthard factory girls. Early in November 1917, she secured the agreement of Preston North End for the use of its Deepdale ground, and the club also took responsibility for putting up official North End posters to advertise it, provided the Dick, Kerr's Ladies paid £5 towards the cost – a charge it then almost immediately rescinded.

Whether Grace Sibbert realised how popular the proposed fixture would be we can only guess. What is recorded is that on that Christmas Day afternoon 10,000 men, women and children paid to pass through the turnstiles. Two days later the *Lancashire Daily Post* carried the longest report of any women's game since the days of Nettie Honeyball and the British Ladies' Football Club.

> After the Christmas dinner the crowd were in the right humour for enjoying this distinctly war-time novelty. There was a tendency amongst the players at the start to giggle, but they soon settled down to the game in earnest. Dick, Kerr's were not long in showing that they suffered less than their opponents from stage fright, and they had a better all-round idea of the game. Woman for woman they were also speedier, and had a larger share of that

quality, which in football slang is known as 'heftiness'. Quite a number of their shots at goal would not have disgraced the regular professional except in direction, and even professionals have been known on occasion to be a trifle wide of the target.

Their forward work, indeed, was often surprisingly good, one or two of the ladies displaying quite admirable ball control, whilst combination was by no means a negligible quality. Coulthards were strongest in defence, the backs battling against long odds, never giving in, and the goalkeeper doing remarkably well, but the forwards, who were understood to have sadly disappointed their friends, were clearly affected with nerves.

All the conventions were duly honoured. The teams on making their appearance (after being photographed) indulged in 'shooting in', and the rival captains, before tossing the coin for choice of ends, shook hands in the approved manner. At first the spectators were inclined to treat the game with a little too much levity, and they found amusement in almost everything from the pace, which until they got used to it, has the same effect as a slow moving Kinema-picture, to the 'how dare you' expression of a player when she was pushed by an opponent.

But when they saw that the ladies meant business, and were 'playing the game', they readily took up the correct attitude and impartially cheered and encouraged each side. Within five minutes Dick, Kerr's had scored through Miss Whittle, and before half time they added further goals by Miss Birkins, a fine shot from 15 yards out, just under the bar, and Miss Rance.

Coulthards, who were quite out of the picture in the first half, 'bucked up' after the interval, and quite

deserved a goal, but it was denied them, much to the disappointment of the spectators. They had a rare opportunity from a penalty in the last few minutes, but the ball was kicked straight at the keeper. On the other hand, Dick, Kerr's added to their score, Miss Rance running through and netting whilst the backs were 'arguing' about some alleged offence, a natural touch which greatly delighted the on-lookers.

Mr John Lewis plied the whistle with discretion, whilst keeping within the four corners of the law, though he was clearly in a dilemma, probably for the first time in his career, when one of the players was 'winded' by the ball.

Two points stand out from this report. The first is that there is no mention of what the players were wearing, in complete contrast to the obsessive interest of journalists in the outfits worn by the British Ladies' team two decades earlier. The second is that it describes the action much as a men's match would have been reported – for the first time women's football was viewed as just that.

The match receipts totalled more than £600, the equivalent of at least £40,000 today. This was to be handed over to the Moor Park VAD Hospital which would use it to improve the lot of injured soldiers brought there from the trenches. But there was a slightly odd, and never explained, confusion between Preston North End and Dick, Kerr's Ladies about at least some of that gate money. Six days after the game, the club's board of directors met and recorded in the minutes of the meeting the following resolution: '... that the collection of £12 12s and 3d, taken in error by Mr Dougal on Christmas Day, be handed over to the committee of the ladies football match played on that day.'

GIRLS WITH BALLS

In this brief, and largely overlooked, resolution would lie the seeds of a suspicion within football's official guardians that not all was as financially rosy as it might seem. It was a suspicion which would come back to haunt Dick, Kerr's Ladies and the entire women's game. But as 1917 ended, the future of football – as least for the duration of the war – looked to be feminine.

CHAPTER EIGHT

*'We made munitions during the day and devoted our
spare time to football. We had a large following.'*
— BELLA METCALFE, MUNITIONETTE

On Friday, 7 June 1918, Alfred Frankland sat at his desk in
No 6 Department of Dick, Kerr's Munitions Factory in
Preston, and dictated a round robin letter to be typed and sent
out that evening.

> I am writing at the suggestion of a few Lancashire
> Secretaries and our own Ladies' Football Committee, to
> ask your opinion on the advisability of forming a Ladies'
> Football League in the county, to commence next season.
> If the majority of replies are satisfactory I will call a
> meeting of representatives from various clubs to discuss
> the matter at an early date in this town, Preston being, as
> you are aware, the most central for all. Thanking you in
> advance in anticipation of an early and favourable reply.

Alfred Frankland, 35, was a manager at Dick, Kerr's factory.
Under the directives of the Munitions Act the company had

abandoned its pre-war output of locomotives in favour of cable drums, pontoon bridges, cartridge boxes and artillery rounds. At the time Frankland sat down to dictate his letter it was producing 30,000 shells per week and its workforce was substantially female.

In late 1917, Frankland had watched from his window as, during their 15-minute lunch break, women workers played football against the remaining men in the factory yard. Sensing something, Frankland had suggested to Grace Sibbert the idea of forming a women's team. In that moment the seeds of what would go on to become the most famous women's team ever were planted. Though Frankland could not have known it, his idea would lead to a memorable era for the game – an era of innovation and ambition. And it would lead to those working class factory girl footballers becoming international celebrities – the David Beckhams of their day. But ironically it would also lead to the deliberate and lasting suppression of women's football.

At the beginning, neither Frankland's idea nor Dick, Kerr's Ladies were unique. Throughout 1917 'ladies' football teams – as they continued to be known – had sprung up in munitions factories across northern England. The universal aim was to raise money for war charities, which had mushroomed as the industrialised carnage of the Western Front created mass physical and financial hardship. But what began as casual novelty exhibitions quickly changed into something far more serious and far more organised.

The first of these wartime matches to be reported in the press took place on Tyneside – then at the heart of Britain's military industrial powerhouse. On Saturday, 3 February 1917 – the day that the United States broke off diplomatic relations with

Germany after the Kaiser had announced a policy of unrestricted submarine warfare – a women's team from the Wallsend Slipway and Engineering Company took on rivals from North-East Marine Engineering Company at the ground of Wallsend Football Club. Gate receipts were to be given to the Queen Mary Needlework Guild, a royal charity which cut, sewed and stitched hundreds of thousands of garments to be sent to British troops in France. In what would become a familiar trope of these early fixtures, a local worthy – in this case the wife of the managing director of the Northumberland Shipbuilding Company – was drafted in to take the initial kick-off, and a high profile male footballer, the former Newcastle United and Northern Ireland defender Billy McCracken, was retained as the referee.

There was also, in this inaugural game, a hint of the popularity which women's football would attract: 2,000 spectators turned out, each handing over the entrance price of a couple of pennies. Within two months, dozens women's teams had formed throughout the industrialised heartland of the north-east and north-west of England. Tyneside could boast nine, Teesside eleven, and sides sprang up in the less concentrated munitions region of Cumbria. Some of the matches played were still very clearly novelty knockabouts, often involving 'comic costumes' or male versus female teams (in which the men would be handicapped by having their arms tied behind their backs).

One, in November 1917, pitted a side made up of eight one-legged and two one-armed ex-servicemen (there is no record of whether the goalkeeper was able-bodied) against 11 munitionettes from Armstrong-Whitworth's No 43 factory in the Elswick district of Newcastle upon Tyne. But gradually these absurd, if well-meaning, fixtures were replaced by a succession of more serious matches between teams of rival factory girls. Most played under the patronage, and indeed the name, of the company where the women worked. But in August 1917, the first of a new breed of women's football club appeared on the Tyne. Blyth Spartans Munitions Ladies Football Club was formed under the protective wing of an established pre-war semi-professional side, Blyth Spartans FC. The men's club had been put into mothballs at the end of the 1915 season, but what remained of its membership was quick to adopt and nurture a new women's side.

The women worked in Blyth's South Docks, loading ships with ammunition to be carried to the Western Front, and unloading unceasing shipments of spent shells which were then transported for refilling. When they weren't manhandling munitions, the women played soccer on the sands, under the approving gaze of Royal Navy seamen. The sailors began coaching the munitionettes in the finer arts of the game, and on 4 August 1917, played them in an exhibition match at Blyth Spartans' Croft Park ground, and the men's club donated a set of green and white football jerseys. That this was not intended as a serious match was clear: the centre forward of the 'Jack Tarr's' men's team set the tone by giving an impersonation of Charlie Chaplin on the centre spot before kick-off.

But there must have been enough in the spectacle to inspire other women. Four days later a second team was established in the town – Blyth United Munitions Ladies – and a derby game between them and the Blyth Spartans Ladies was arranged for Saturday, 18 August, with gate receipts going to the Crofton Workman's Patriotic Fund. Spartans promptly thrashed United 10-nil, a result which appears to have ensured that the latter never again played a competitive match.

Competition – serious fixtures played by women, against

women – was now developing rapidly. Two days after Blyth Spartans' emphatic trouncing of Blyth United, the *Newcastle Daily Chronicle* reported that a Munitions Girls' Challenge Cup was to be held in the autumn. This was to be a knock-out competition between teams of munitionettes, and a solid silver trophy had been donated, presumably by local employers, which would be awarded to winners.

The aim of the competition was, in addition to being a serious new football fixture, to raise money for war benevolent funds. Charitable organisations such as Soldiers' Welcome Home Funds, Prisoner of War Funds, Aged Miners' Homes, Soldiers' and Sailors' Orphans Funds were to apply for one of the cup-tie matches to be allocated for their benefit: in return for booking the pitch and providing officials, they would receive the gate money. The Munitionettes' Cup – the first-ever women's football competition – was born.

By 21 September 1917, 14 teams had registered for the Cup, and a framework was announced of three rounds of pool matches, followed by quarter, semi and final knock-out games. Bearing in mind that all the players were full-time munitions workers, with limited free time, the fixtures were to be played throughout the 1917-1918 season, and the grand final would take place in May 1918.

Looking back with benefit of 100 years hindsight, it's clear that this was the first evidence of serious intent – a harbinger of a new era when women could play competitive football. And at least some of the press recognised this at the time. On 13 October 1917, the *Middlesbrough Herald* informed its readers that, 'Female teams are springing up rapidly, and show they can play a "gentlemanly" game. Shall we see mixed teams before the close of the season?'

Certainly, the young working class women, while juggling the demands of heavy and exhausting manual labour with the needs of families, often without the support of fathers, brothers or husbands, took their football seriously. When Blyth Spartan's regular left-winger Jennie Nuttall was married at St Cuthbert's Church on the morning of Saturday, 13 October, she dashed from the ceremony to the football pitch, in time to play and score two goals against a rival side. But there would be hints, too, of the trouble which had dogged previous attempts to promote women's football – and which would come to haunt the sport in the years to come.

The first round tie between Blyth and Aviation Athletic, fixed for 20 November, had to be postponed when the army abruptly denied the use of the proposed pitch. The local *Sporting Man* paper acidly recorded the postponement 'owing to the military authorities refusing to allow the game to proceed, although expense has been incurred'.

There is no surviving record of what reason the army gave for its refusal, though it's possible that it may simply have needed the pitch for field gun drill practice. Throughout the First World War, the War Ministry took over football grounds whenever it felt the need for large open spaces. It cheerfully erected temporary offices on the pitch at Newcastle United and turned the main stand at Tottenham Hotspur's ground into a gas-mask factory. Whatever the reason, the enforced postponement of the first round Cup Tie was an ill omen. It would not be the last time that women's teams were denied the use of football grounds.

And there were to be further warning signs that all would not go smoothly. In an uncomfortable echo of riotous scenes at women's games two decades earlier, an antagonistic atmosphere

An illustration of the first match of the British Ladies' Football Club.

Nettie Honeyball, captain of the British Ladies football team, wearing her football costume in 1895.

©*Mary Evans Picture Library*

Above: The North Team, who represented north London. *Back row (left to right)* Miss Lynn, Miss Honeyball, Miss Williams, Miss Edwards, Miss Ide. *Front row (left to right)* Miss Coupland, Miss Fenn, Miss Gilbert, Miss Smith, Miss Thiere, Miss Biggs.

Below: The South Team. *Back row, (left to right)* Miss Hicks, Miss Clarke, Miss A Hicks, Miss Edwards, Miss Clarence. *Front row, (left to right)* Miss Lewis, Miss Roberts, Miss Ellis, Miss Fenn.

Above: Night shift workers at a London munitions factory line up before a match against a team from the day shift in 1917.

Below: Playing with a specially made white chrome ball, with the pitch lit by electric lamps, Dick, Kerr Ladies (in black and white stripes) and Heys of Bradford play at the Burnley Cricket Club ground.

Above: The English and French women's football teams line up before a match in Paris in 1920. The game was watched by 12,000 people and ended in a 1-1 draw.

Below: The English women's football team in 1921.

Above: Dick, Kerr Ladies relax on a tour of Canada in 1922.

Below: Dick, Kerr Ladies take on the French ladies' international team at Herne Hill in London in 1925.

FAMOUS DICK KERR INTERNATIONAL LADIES' A.F.C., WORLD'S CHAMPIONS, 1917-25.
RAISED OVER £70,000 FOR EX-SERVICE MEN, HOSPITALS AND POOR CHILDREN.
WINNERS OF 7 SILVER CUPS AND 3 SETS OF GOLD MEDALS.

Above: The French ladies' team in 1925.

Below: Dick, Kerr Ladies pose in the goalmouth. Underneath the photograph is a list of their extensive achievements.

©*Getty Images*

Lily Parr, of Preston Ladies (formerly Dick, Kerr Ladies) practises javelin as part of her training with the team in 1938.

surrounded several of the games. In November, the entire team from Palmer's Jarrow munitions factory stalked off the pitch after arguing with the referee; a month later, a second round tie descended into chaos when the crowd invaded the pitch and pelted both players and the referee with snowballs. Then, on 5 January 1918, the third round game between Blyth Spartans and North-East Marine works was halted first by the NEM players walking off, then by a pitch invasion. As the crowd bayed for its money back, the NEM players were persuaded to return: but by then the referee had had enough and he refused to continue. Only a frantic, and ultimately successful, search for a replacement official prevented a large-scale riot.

Despite this, the Munitionettes Cup was an undoubted success – both in footballing terms and in its declared aim of raising money for war charities. The Cup Final, staged on 14 May 1918 at Ayresome Park, home to Middlesbrough FC, drew 22,000 spectators. Blyth Spartans Ladies defeated Bolckow, Vaughan Ladies 5-0. It was Blyth's 30th game since the previous August. The competition had raised more than £1,500 for the charities, the equivalent of approximately £300,000 today[20]. Women's football had proved its worth. Inevitably, so much success – and so much money, particularly in historically poor areas – attracted interest. War charities, increasingly desperate for funds to meet the demands of caring for wounded servicemen or supporting their widows and children, began to recognise women's football as a vital lifeline. But others with, perhaps, more entrepreneurial instincts spotted a potential cash cow.

The idea for an 'international' match seems to have come from Billy McCracken. A former professional player, for Newcastle United and Ireland, McCracken was, by 1917, working in a munitions factory. A dedicated and open-minded man, he had organised charity fixtures for both men and women, and was a strong supporter of the Munitionettes Cup. In late 1917, he suggested a one-off game against a representative English side (drawn, however, only from the north-east) against a team representing Ireland. The fixture was to be played at Grosvenor Park, home ground of Belfast Distillery FC, on Boxing Day – the day after Dick, Kerr's Ladies played their inaugural match in Preston.

By the time the English team left Newcastle Central train station at 4am on Christmas Eve, the organising team had been augmented with a nurse to ensure the women's welfare (which, given the routine suspicion and supervision of female munitions workers, probably translated as their moral welfare) and a manager, David Brooks, from the Newcastle satellite town of Wallsend.

For a group of working class women, unlikely ever to have left their hometown let alone their homeland, the journey to Belfast would have been daunting enough. But the passage across the Irish Sea was particularly hazardous. Since the Kaiser had declared unrestricted submarine warfare 10 months earlier, U Boats had sunk nearly 900,000 tons of British shipping.

Worse, one particular U Boat captain, *Oberleutnant zur See* Wilhelm Werner, who was known to be operating in the area, had earned a reputation for war crimes. His U 55 had recently torpedoed two British ships, *SS Torrington* and *SS Belgian Prince*, the latter an unarmed merchant vessel. On both occasions, Werner had captured the crew, smashed their lifeboats and then made them stand on the deck of his U boat while he took it beneath the sea. All were drowned.

Unsurprisingly, the women footballers were nervous. But if they had hoped to look to their manager for support they would have looked in vain. David Brooks spent the entire crossing blind drunk and locked himself in a toilet whilst singing at the top of his voice 'Waiter, waiter, bring me some paper to wipe me bumbelator'. This may have been Mr Brooks' loudest contribution to the cause of women's football, but it would not be his last.

In the event, the English team, plus nurse and intoxicated manager, landed in Belfast without attracting the attentions of the German Imperial Navy. (On the return journey, however, reports of a U Boat in the Irish Sea caused the team severe anxiety. Whether this led David Brooks to reacquaint himself with a bottle and the ship's toilet is not recorded.) They spent Christmas Day watching a men's football match, before playing their own fixture the next day. It is measure of how popular women's football had become that 20,000 spectators paid to watch this very first all-women's international[21]. It was a sign of things to come.

By the start of 1918, women's football was embedded in the working class munitions heartlands of northern England. The Munitionettes Cup was drawing large crowds on the Tyne and Tees, with planning for the 1918-19 season competition underway before the inaugural season's matches were over. Two further internationals were planned for the summer: North of England v West of Scotland and the return fixture of England v Ireland.

Meanwhile, on the other side of the country, possibly inspired by the success of Dick, Kerr's Christmas Day match, women's teams were springing up across the Lancashire industrial belt. It was only a matter of time before they, too, built a solid structure for their game and began to attract regular sizeable crowds. And, as in most emerging sports, one team would come to both dominate and embody women's football: Dick, Kerr's Ladies.

Alfred Frankland was, unquestionably, the driving force. Even a hundred years on, his vision and the innovations he would introduce mark him out as the founding father of women's football. That word, 'father' is apposite. The nature of British society meant that almost all women's teams would be managed and organised by men, but it is also clear from surviving accounts by the players themselves that they had genuine affection and respect for Frankland. He came from a solid, upper working class background. His father was a mechanic in Lancashire's still-important cotton industry; his elder brother had begun his working life as a storekeeper with Dick, Kerr and was now one of the company's semi-management senior clerks. His younger brother worked in a solicitor's office, and his sister had re-trained as a nurse after starting work as a cotton weaver.

Frankland himself had previously worked in the menswear trade. After leaving school he began work as a retail assistant in a gentleman's outfitters and had risen to become one of its managers. With the introduction of the Munitions Act he had been drafted in to apply his skills as a manager at Dick, Kerr. By all accounts, his experience in retail clothing had taught him the importance of rigorous organisation – and left him with a showman's appreciation of the importance of appearance over reality. It was a lesson he took to heart, both in his personal life – he was, in the phrase of the time 'a natty dresser', always to be seen with a fob watch draped across his waistcoat, an alpaca overcoat and bowler hat signalling that he was a man of the emerging lower middle classes. His manners and his voice, too, signified a man who had come up in the world: not for him the coarse language of the Lancashire streets.

That January in 1918, Alfred Frankland looked hard at the result of the Christmas Day match and decided that it held promise. He immediately booked Preston North End's Deepdale ground for a further three women's games, to be held in February and March. This, itself, was no small beer: Deepdale charged £20 to hire out its pitch, the equivalent of £4,000 per game today. Frankland's fixtures would need to draw the size of crowd attracted on Christmas Day if they were to yield much in the way of funds for war charities.

Nor were overheads his only concern. In 1916, the government had imposed a tax on all forms of entertainment as a contribution to funding the war effort. (This Entertainment Tax, officially known as Excise Revenue, should have been repealed in 1919. In fact it was not lifted until 1960.) Football matches, with crowds in the tens of thousands, were a rich stream of revenue. Clubs were strictly required to buy 1d or 2d tax stamps from the Post Office and stick one on the back of every admission ticket, and the cost of these was deducted from gate receipts.

But Frankland was an astute judge of the country's mood. He saw that with the national game in mothballs (except for non-league friendlies) there was a very real public appetite for new football exhibitions. The Christmas Day fixture had showed just how sharp that appetite was: and so he not only booked Deepdale for the next three fixtures, but for once-a-week training sessions as well. The contract for the 1918 fixtures, approved by Preston North End's board of directors, recorded that: 'We [Preston North End] take charge of the Gate and pay over to Dick, Kerr & Co 80% of the net gate, that is after all expenses incidental to the match are paid.'

On Monday, 23 February 1918, Dick, Kerr's Ladies turned out for their next match at Deepdale. A crowd of 5,000 watched them draw 1-1 with Lancashire Ladies. A fortnight later the gate was down to 2,000 for a Sunday fixture against Barrow. But on Monday, 29 March, 6,000 spectators passed through the Deepdale turnstile to watch Dick, Kerr beat Bolton 5-1. No record exists of the receipts for the first two games, but this final match of the season apparently yielded £200. And these figures would come back to haunt Alfred Frankland.

Surviving records unearthed by Dick, Kerr's most diligent historian, Gail Newsham[22], reveal that by the end of the season Alfred Frankland felt sufficiently confident to renegotiate the contract with Preston North End. In May he signed a new deal which reduced the cost of hiring Deepdale for matches to £12. It also shows that he had increased training from one weekly session to three – to take place during the working day on Tuesdays, Wednesdays and Thursdays.

This was remarkable. Not merely had he convinced Dick, Kerr & Co Ltd to foot the £3 per week bill, but somehow to release the women footballers from the factory during working hours. Since the Munitions Act imposed strict controls to ensure that all workers put in their required shifts, Frankland must have convinced the company either to turn a blind eye or to somehow square the release with the Ministry of Munitions.

In this, as in so much else, he was ahead of his time. This was an era long before commercial endorsements in sport. Sponsorship of professional men's clubs was many decades in the future, but Frankland clearly recognised – and convinced his board of directors – that having its own successful women's football team would bring prestige and publicity to Dick, Kerr & Co Ltd.

On the other side of the country, this level of support would, had they known of it, been envied by the munitionettes of

Tyneside and Teesside. The players who competed in the Munitionettes Cup were very definitely working women whose free time was limited to Saturday afternoons and the still sacrosanct Sabbath Day. As Bella Metcalfe, the captain of the Cup-winning side Blyth Spartans Ladies later recalled: 'We made munitions during the day and devoted our spare time to football.'

In Preston, Alfred Frankland had few such concerns. Within three months of renegotiating the Deepdale contract he had gone back to the board of Preston North End and driven down the price of his team's thrice-weekly training from £3 to £1. And he – or rather the directors of Dick, Kerr & Co Ltd – had signed an additional agreement to play 10 Saturday fixtures at the ground in the 1918-19 season. As the close season (still rigidly enforced by the Football Association) wore on he sat down to compose his round robin invitation for fixtures.

He was also hard at work on his team's accounts. On Saturday, 31 August 1918, the *Lancashire Daily Post* reported that Mr A Frankland had submitted a balance sheet for the Dick, Kerr's Ladies, showing:

> ... the fine sum of £804 10s 5d was raised from last season's activities, and after amusement [sic] tax of £105 4s 7d and rent of ground amounting to £61 4s 1d had been paid, together with general expenses that are eminently moderate, a net balance of £533 17s 1d [roughly the equivalent of £106,000 today] remained.

A fine balance indeed. But there was something odd about Frankland's figures. The inaugural Dick, Kerr's Ladies match on Christmas Day 1917 was said to have raised £600, and the final fixture of the season, against Bolton Ladies, a further

£200, adding up to almost the entire total income declared. Yet in between there were two games played in front of crowds totalling 7,000: could these only have yielded the remaining £4 10s 5d?

It was, at the very least, an anomaly. It would, in the years to come, provoke deep suspicion in the minds of the men who ran the Football Association. But, as summer turned to autumn and the 1918-19 football season opened, the on-field future for Dick, Kerr's Ladies, standard bearers for women's' football, looked entirely positive. They could hardly have foreseen the gathering international clouds which they would shortly have to face.

CHAPTER NINE

'When at last we came home, were demobilised and
doffed our uniforms, we realised how much our welcome had
depended on the glamour of our clothes... In mufti we were
no longer heroes, we were simply "unemployed",
an unpleasant problem.'

The morning of Monday, 11 November 1918 was bitterly cold. A hard white frost covered the churned and bloodied mud of the battlefields across the Western Front. In Picardy, Sergeant Walter Sweet of the Monmouthshire Regiment marched his platoon from the trenches to a village in the rear, where he was billeting them in a barn, when a colonel walked smartly in. He wished the men good day, looked at his watch and declared: 'It is 10am. Men, I am pleased to tell you that in one hour the Armistice comes into force and you will all be able to return to your homes.'

Two hours later, wartime prime minister David Lloyd George stood up in the House of Commons to make an announcement: 'The Armistice was signed at 5am this morning. War ceased at eleven o'clock this morning.' That afternoon he stood on doorstep of 10 Downing Street and told a cheering crowd: 'The sons and daughters of the people have done it. They have won this hour of gladness and the whole country has done its duty.'

Up and down the length of Britain, cities, towns and villages reacted with relief and jubilation, overshadowed by the hardships they had endured and, above all, the tragedy of so many lives lost. The people of London, in particular, took to the streets. On Tuesday, 12 November, the *Daily Mirror* carried lengthy reports of the capital's celebrations.

Wonderful Scenes of Enthusiasm Everywhere – City Given Up to Rejoicings

London went wild with delight when the great news came through yesterday. Bells burst forth into joyful chimes, maroons[23] were exploded, bands paraded the streets followed by cheering crowds of soldiers and civilians and London generally gave itself up whole-heartedly to rejoicing.

The most wonderful scene of enthusiastic rejoicing took place before Buckingham Palace. Dense crowds collected before the Palace gates, processions of cheering, be-flagged civilians and fighting men marched down the Mall.

'We want the King!' went up the shout every few minutes and at last, greeted by a thunderous cheer, the King in the uniform of an admiral, the Queen and Princess Mary and the Duke of Connaught appeared on the balcony.

'With you I rejoice and thank God for the victories which the Allied arms have won, bringing hostilities to an end and peace within sight.'

But what would peace mean? What sort of country was Britain after four long years of slaughter? And what would happen to the men and the women whose courage, strength and endurance had achieved victory?

On Saturday, 23 November, less than two weeks after peace broke out, Lloyd George set out his answer in a speech at Wolverhampton, as reported in *The Times*: 'What is our task? To make Britain a fit country for heroes to live in.' The problem was how to turn fine words into reality. The war had left the once-mighty British Empire financially as well as physically exhausted. Britain had incurred debts equivalent to 136 per cent of its gross national product, mostly to the United States, and what had been the world's strongest economy now faced huge challenges. Some of these were physical: Britain was still a nation of squalid Victorian slums and 'rookeries'. The population was, by any modern standard, supremely unhealthy (not having been helped by the introduction of food rationing early in 1918). It was a problem that had been officially recognised the year before. In August 1917, the government had created a new Ministry of Reconstruction, tasked with ensuring the rebuilding of 'the national life on a better and more durable foundation' once the Great War was over. It had set up a plethora of committees which investigated all aspects of life in Britain – from housing to local government, from labour relations to the structure of the post-war economy itself. But Britain lacked the one thing to turn its hopes and promises into 'a fit country for heroes': money.

What it didn't lack, despite the enormous death toll of the war, was manpower. Spread across all the theatres of war was a vast army of largely conscripted soldiers. In November 1918, the British army numbered almost 3.8m men. The overwhelming majority of them would need to be de-mobilised and returned home, and the government feared the industrial, financial and personal consequences.

GIRLS WITH BALLS

In 1917, it had begun planning demobilisation and within weeks of the Armistice had begun to ship men home. In a speech relayed to British troops in December 1918, the Secretary of War, Lord Alfred Milner, laid out the government's plans, and the challenges it faced:

> To put back an army of millions of men, scattered over three continents, into civil life is just as difficult as it was to raise that giant army. In fact, in some ways it is more difficult. It involves – quite inevitably – just as many complications, hardships, inequalities.
>
> Remember that, although the fighting may have ceased, all is not yet over. Impatience and over haste might yet rob us of all that four long years of unexampled struggle and sacrifice have won. We have yet to make a just, strong and enduring peace.... Our guiding principle was to demobilise in the way most likely to lead to the steady resumption of industry, and to minimise the danger of unemployment.

Unfortunately, though the process of demobilisation proved relatively unproblematic (by the end of 1919, Britain's 3.2m army had been reduced to less than 900,000, and by the time demobilisation was fully completed in 1922, there were just 230,000 servicemen) the end of the war did not witness a swift return to pre-war normality for the British economy; there simply weren't jobs for the ex-soldiers to walk into.

The resulting high levels of unemployment brought into stark reality the serious social tensions and cracks in British society which had been papered over, or sometimes widened, by the war. These started to appear in the spring of 1919, in camps holding demobilised soldiers from Britain's Dominions. In March, Canadian troops who had been waiting for months

for a ship to take them home, mutinied at their camp in Rhyl, North Wales. The revolt was only ended after a number of men were killed. Within months, rampaging Canadian soldiers broke into a police station in Epsom, Surrey, killing one policeman and causing a major riot.

Demobilisation also exacerbated simmering social tensions in British ports. A series of ugly race riots took place in Liverpool during June 1919, as the local white population clashed with black workers and seamen, many of whom were left unemployed at the end of the war. That same month in Cardiff, white ex-servicemen including Australians stationed in the area headed lynch mobs that terrorised the city's black community during a week of violence which left three men dead and dozens more injured.

Official papers from the period show that the government was seriously worried that unemployment among the millions of demobilised servicemen would cause widespread labour unrest and a potential Bolshevik takeover. In the former, their fears were born out. During 1919, 2.4m British workers were involved in strike action – substantially more even than in Germany, then in tatters and widely assumed to be the likeliest place to which the new Russian Communism would spread. (Although Bolshevik influence in Britain was, in fact, negligible, in January 1920 army chiefs were still working on a plan 'in the event of Soviet government at Liverpool'.)

There was an obvious focus for much of the anger amongst demobilised servicemen on women doing 'their' jobs, in 'their' factories. The war had required that nearly all women, single or married, were viewed as vital to industrial production, but now, the returning male workers wanted their jobs back. In particular, they felt that married women should revert to their previous occupations 'in the home'.

One of numerous government committees, the Hills Committee, accepted that married women would continue to work and that they should not be prevented from doing so, although they added that women should be discouraged from doing work injurious to health, on the grounds that: 'The primary function of women in the state must be regarded, it is not enough to interfere with her service in bearing children... but she must be safeguarded as home-maker for the nation.'

But many of the new working women had mixed feelings about stepping out of the factory and back into the home. During the war they had demonstrated that they could do what had traditionally been seen as men's work. They had heaved coal, driven trams; a group of women navvies had even built a shipyard. Women still formed the majority of the workforce in munitions, and a glimpse of the only apparent ambivalence they had towards this work can be found in an essay written by a munitionette and published in a factory magazine: 'Only the fact that I am using my life's energy to destroy human souls gets on my nerves. Yet on the other hand, I'm doing what I can to bring this horrible affair to an end. But once the War is over, never in creation will I do the same thing again.'

But eventually, the demands of ex-servicemen, and the moral claim to employment, earned in the filth of death-filled trenches, proved too strong. In 1919, the government passed the Restoration of Pre-War Practices Act which bluntly ordered women to vacate wartime jobs for returning men. In effect, this was a double rebuff for the women who had risked their health and, in some cases their lives, in the munitions factories.

The government had finally extended the right to vote, but the new suffrage bill enfranchised only women over 30 years of age and who met a strict minimum property ownership test. This deliberately excluded the hundreds of thousands of working class women who had toiled in munitions work and who were now being ungratefully shown the door. And what of football? Somewhere in that vast army of the demobilised were not just the game's traditional supporters but former professional players.

The Armistice came too late for either the Football League or the Football Association to take professional football out of mothballs and re-start competitions. The FA was, in any case, much exercised by the thorny question of what wages should be paid to players who re-joined their former clubs. The league and cup season would therefore have to wait until autumn 1919 before re-starting.

Women's football, by contrast, was rapidly gaining strength. In the north-east of England a second Munitionettes Cup competition began at the start of the 1918-19 season, and in Cumbria the proliferation of women's teams had created a Ladies Cup tournament for the north-west. But the emerging powerhouse of the women's game was undoubtedly to be found in Dick, Kerr's factories in Preston. Although the company was no longer called Dick, Kerr, having changed its name to English Electric, and was re-tooling to return to its pre-war production of railway carriages, Alfred Frankland appears to have convinced the board of directors that Dick, Kerr's Ladies should not just continue but expand.

There was unquestionably a need for them. Whilst the artillery had fallen silent in France, the demands on war charities were growing, not diminishing. Britain was clearly losing the peace and the effects were starkly felt. Money to support unemployed and often destitute ex-soldiers and their families was desperately needed. Frankland saw this as an opportunity: in addition to winning the backing of his board, he also enlisted the vital local political support of powerful aldermen. Whatever might happen to other munitionette teams, the Dick, Kerr's Ladies were not about to hang up their boots just because Germany had laid down its guns.

Frankland was also sharp to spot that the rapid de-mobilisation of women munitions workers might offer an opportunity to strengthen his team. As other ladies teams folded, he would have the pick of their talent. And so the first transfer market for women footballers came into being. It had begun in September 1918, when he persuaded Molly Walker to switch from Lancaster Ladies to the Dick, Kerr's side.

Two months later, on Saturday, 21 December, she appeared in Dick, Kerr's Ladies' second match of the season at Deepdale, against her former club. The result, 1-0 to the visitors, was only the second defeat for the Preston side, and watching the game, Frankland saw that four of the Lancaster team were exceptional players. Within days he had signed three of them – striker Jennie Harris, centre-half Jessie Walmsley and goalkeeper Annie Hastie. On Christmas Day, exactly a year after Dick, Kerr's Ladies inaugural match, the three players lined up with their new team for a fixture against Bolton Ladies. Eight thousand spectators turned out to watch the action.

How was Frankland able to poach these nascent stars? Lancaster was a very strong team in its own right and its record against Dick, Kerr's was a very respectable one win, one draw and one defeat. Moreover, it had been the only side to beat Cumbria's strongest outfit, Whitehaven Ladies, in the previous season. What was it that made them sign up with Dick, Kerr's?

The answer was, inevitably, money. Not only was Frankland able to promise them steady employment, but he was also backed by a sizeable company chequebook for paying their footballing wages. His deal with Molly Walker was typical of

those with rest of his team: she received 10 shillings (the equivalent of £100 today) for every game she played.

But there was another far more serious factor at play, one that not only threatened the poverty-ridden industrial British heartland but which was rapidly tearing apart the very fabric of society worldwide. In the summer of 1918, children across Britain could be heard signing a new skipping rhyme:

> I had a little bird
> Its name was Enza,
> I opened the window
> And in-flew Enza

The influenza pandemic of 1918-19 claimed the lives of between 20m and 40m people around the world, at least three times the number killed in the war. More died in a single year than were killed in the four years of the Black Death from 1347 to 1351. In the spring of 1918, soldiers in a British military field hospital at Étaples in northern France became ill with what was then termed *la grippe* (now the universal term in French for influenza). They complained of sore throats, headaches and a loss of appetite. Although the illness was highly infectious, and the primitive, crowded conditions made rapid spread inevitable, recovery was initially swift and doctors dismissed it as no more than a three-day fever. But then, just as suddenly as they had seemed to recover, many of the men fell ill and very quickly died.

Those who recovered, as well as those who had been in the camp but not displayed symptoms, were often sent back to Britain on home leave, bringing the virus with them. In May 1918, Glasgow was the first British city to be affected and within weeks the illness had spread south, reaching London by

June. During the next few months, 228,000 people died across Britain. About a fifth of those infected developed pneumonia or septicaemia. Often this progressed to heliotrope cyanosis, a lavender hue of the skin that signalled shortage of oxygen and imminent death. Onset was devastatingly quick. Entire families could be perfectly at breakfast, but dead by tea-time. Often, they died choking on a thick scarlet jelly-like substance which suddenly clogged the lungs. On 29 September 1918, Glasgow physician Professor Roy Grist described the deadly impact of the infection in the *British Medical Journal*:

> It starts with what appears to be an ordinary attack of *la grippe*. When brought to the hospital, [patients] very rapidly develop the most vicious type of pneumonia that has ever been seen. Two hours after admission, they have mahogany spots over the cheek bones, and a few hours later you can begin to see the cyanosis [blueness due to lack of oxygen] extending from their ears and spreading all over the face. It is only a matter of a few hours then until death comes and it is simply a struggle for air until they suffocate. It is horrible.

The epidemic was quickly (and with predictable distrust for anything foreign) dubbed 'Spanish flu'[24]. British cities, crowded and insanitary were ill-equipped to cope with the epidemic. The war had cost the country most of its finances, industry was disrupted, there was damage to public services and millions were dead, missing or wounded. Meanwhile, ships continued to bring soldiers back from the front carrying the virus to their homes and communities.

Hospitals were overwhelmed, and an unequal army of doctors and nurses worked to breaking point. Most British doctors were still out at the front treating war casualties, and with them the majority of nurses, both paid and voluntary. In some cities at home, an estimated three nurses were available per million of population. There was, in any event, little they could do. There were no treatments for influenza and no antibiotics to treat ensuing complications such as pneumonia. All the medics could do was watch as patients died by the thousand. The best advice was printed in the *News of the World*. On 3 November, it suggested ways to combat the epidemic: 'Wash inside nose with soap and water each night and morning; force yourself to sneeze night and morning, then breathe deeply. Do not wear a muffler; take sharp walks regularly and walk home from work; eat plenty of porridge.' (Oddly, this was remarkably good advice, and holds good for the modern variant of Spanish flu, bird flu. The porridge, though, is optional.)

The government and local authorities also struggled as the epidemic gripped the country. In London, nearly 1,500 policemen, a third of the force, reported sick simultaneously. Council office workers shed suits and ties to dig graves. Coffins that had been stockpiled during the war (a wartime agreement had been made that no bodies would be brought back from the battle lines) were suddenly in short supply. Railway workshops turned to coffin manufacturing and Red Cross ambulances became hearses.

Armistice Day on 11 November, triggered a second wave of infection. As people gathered to celebrate the end of the war and to remember the dead, the virus swept through them. Parties and parades turned to disaster. Nor was Britain alone. Spanish flu swept across every continent (although Australia, which imposed strict quarantine conditions, suffered the least effects) and populations in country after country were decimated.

In Manchester, the Medical Officer of Health, a Scottish

surgeon called James Niven, realised that the virus was an airborne infection spread by the inhalation of infected droplets from coughs or sneezes. Niven took drastic and previously unheard-of action. With the alarming motto 'spit kills', he ordered Manchester businesses and schools to close. His advice, at a time when the city's industrial production was returning to its pre-war heights, and people were trying to get their lives back to normal, was far from welcome. But it undoubtedly prevented the city from suffering an even higher death toll. Gradually, others followed his advice across the nation.

Medical schools closed their third- and fourth-year classes (with students helping out in hospital wards). Councils instructed cinemas to be cleared every four hours and windows opened to aerate the auditoriums, while theatres, dance halls, churches and many other public gathering places were simply shut, some for many months. Streets were sprayed with chemicals and people wore anti-germ masks. Some factories relaxed no-smoking rules believing that cigarettes would help prevent infection.

What made the worldwide pandemic even more alarming was its choice of fatal victims. Previous flu epidemics in Britain had killed the old, the infirm or the new-born. The 1918 Spanish flu attacked the young and healthy, typically aged 15 to 40, to lethal effect. It would take until December 1920 for the disease to disappear, almost as quickly as it had arrived. Worldwide, the pandemic claimed between 40m and 100m lives. The death rate was 25 times higher than in a normal flu epidemic and may have killed more than the medieval Black Death.

Oddly, football not only carried on throughout the worst of the pandemic, but in England made its post-war professional debut. The 45th season of competitive men's football opened in

September 1919, with the Football League First Division actually increasing in size from 20 clubs to 22. The FA Cup competition also re-started, and (perhaps giving an indication of the widespread ignorance of how to combat Spanish flu) crowds flocked to all the fixtures.

The situation regarding women's football was more complex. In the north-east, although the Munitionettes Cup competition got under way, the strength of the teams was beginning to ebb away. Munitions factories were shutting down production lines, overtime was ended and workers were moved from the more lucrative piece rates to a simple but less rewarding wage based on the time they spent working. There was no general discharge of the munitionettes who had been drafted by law into the armaments works, but the regulations preventing workers from leaving without a government permit were abandoned. The plan, plainly, was to downsize by natural wastage. There was also a more ominous sign of the times in the response to a new scheme of unemployment benefit. Under this, men would receive 24 shillings a week, while women were entitled to 20 shillings. When the scheme was launched on 25 November, 1918, newspapers across Tyneside reported a large female registration but very few men. As the *Newcastle Daily Chronicle* noted: 'It is thought that in this district there will little difficulty in finding employment for the men, but a great problem is presented in the case of the women workers.'

Since, with the possible exception of Blyth Spartans Ladies, all the women's teams were entirely based on the munitions factories which employed them, the future looked anything but bright. Despite this, another international match was arranged. Billed as a return fixture, it pitted Ireland Ladies against a team of north-east munitionettes, drawn from several of the local teams.

The organising committee booked St James' Park, home to Newcastle United, and added a tug-of-war contest and a penalty-kicking competition to the activities. But match day, 21 September, 1918, attracted just 2,000 spectators – a fraction of the crowds who had flocked to games in the previous season. The most likely explanation for this drop in attendance was Spanish flu. Certainly, it took its toll on the Munitionettes Cup the following month. A second round tie between North-East Marine Works and Armstrong-Whitworth's 58 Shop Ladies on 16 November, again staged at St James' Park, turned into something of a farce. Nine of Armstrong-Whitworth's team had been struck down with flu and just two turned up. The game went ahead, but only after six munitionettes were pulled from the crowd and persuaded to play. In the end, an absurdly unrepresentative nine-a-side match was played. The 1918-19 Munitionettes Cup would be the last ever held.

There were worrying auguries off the field as well. Three days after the make-shift fixture at St James' Park, the secretary of the Munitionettes Competition was hauled before Middlesbrough Magistrates. Francis Taylor was accused of failing to provide proper accounts relating a significant number of Entertainment Tax tickets. The court ultimately accepted his defence that the missing documentation was held somewhere inside the organisation, and let him off. But it was a worrying reminder that little or no monitoring of women's football finances was being exercised.

Over in Preston, however, the picture was altogether better. Alfred Frankland was busily building his Dick, Kerr's Ladies into a formidable outfit. He had continued his deliberate poaching of the best players from other teams and steadily increased the team's profile. Increasingly large crowds were now drawn to any game involving Dick, Kerr's Ladies. When they played an away fixture against Newcastle United Ladies at the start of 1919 -20 season, 35,000 spectators passed through the turnstiles at St James' Park.

But as the deadly combination of Spanish flu and redundancy steadily eroded the number of munitionette teams, Frankland saw that he would need to find a new outlet for his increasingly popular charges: and that meant looking much further afield.

CHAPTER TEN

'Soccer by Searchlight! Novel game played for ex-service
unemployed fund won by Dick, Kerr Ladies' football team.'
– Pathé Newsreel report, December 1920

arly in March 1920, Alfred Frankland sat down at his desk
to compose a letter which would, with typical bravado,
put women's football back on the front pages – and ensure that
Dick, Kerr's Ladies dominated the headlines. The person he
would write to had become a controversial campaigner for
female sports and had founded, a year earlier, a national
organisation to champion them. Her name was Alice Milliat
and she lived in Paris. Frankland's proposal was the first-ever
genuinely international women's football match.

Frankland had heard that the English Amateur Football
Association, still resolutely male and determinedly
unreconciled to either professionalism or the FA, planned to
cross the channel in April for a game against their French
counterparts. England's amateur men's team was a pioneer of
international fixtures, having played the first-ever game against
France in 1906 and following that with a series of fixtures

against European and Scandinavian teams. By contrast, the FA's professional side only played its first international (again against France) in 1923. Ever conscious of the power of publicity, Frankland decided to go one better.

Women's football in France was then in its infancy. There were only two teams, both located in Paris, and both were struggling to overcome the prevailing belief that sport and women should never mix. This was not simply a matter of public opinion. The most powerful figure in French sport was Baron Pierre de Coubertin, the man who, in the 1890s had been responsible for creating the first modern Olympic Games. He was a tireless, if somewhat puritanical, campaigner for what he saw as the Athenian ideals of amateurism and gentlemanly conduct.

He was also vehemently opposed to female athletes, declaring memorably that women's only role in sport was to 'place laurels on the heads of the victors'. By 1920, he was both the president of the International Olympic Committee and the driving force behind the chief national sports association in France, *L'Union de Sociétés Françaises de Sports Athlétiques*. Not surprisingly, then, when the French Football Federation (FFF) was formed in 1919, it specifically excluded women from membership.

But neither the FFF nor Coubertin had appreciated the force of nature which was Alice Milliat. Born in the western French provincial town of Nantes in 1884, she grew up to become an excellent athlete. Her favourite sport was rowing and she was the first woman to be awarded the *Audax* long distance rowing certificate for covering several dozen kilometres in a skiff within a given time limit. She was also a very professional organiser, first tasting the power of sports administration with the Parisian multi-sports club *Fémina Sport*. This was France's oldest sporting organisation for women, founded in 1912, and Milliat took over its presidency three years later.

Despite the carnage on the Western Front, elsewhere in France women's athletics events grew in popularity and regularity during the First World War. By 1917, enough clubs existed for Milliat to organise an interclub tournament, to which crowds, and just as importantly, the press, flocked. Buoyed by this success, Milliat was able to set up the *Federation des Sociétés Féminines de France* (French Federation of Women's Clubs) and on 10 March 1919, she became its president. A year later, at around the time that Alfred Frankland's letter was delivered to the Federation's door, major periodicals including *Le Soldat de Demain* and *L'Auto*, began publishing articles by her in which she championed women's football.

Writing in *Le Football Feminin*, she declared: 'In my opinion, football is not wrong for women. Most of these girls are beautiful Grecian dancers. I do not think it is unwomanly to play football as they do not play like men, they play fast, but not vigorous, football.' Milliat's seemingly idealised description of women footballers bore little relation to the reality either of Dick, Kerr's Ladies or their style of play. But it had been well-chosen: orthodox French female athletes were exclusively middle or upper class, and tended to embrace a feminine version of Coubertin's admiration for the (entirely mythical) sporting values of Ancient Greece, and variously hurled javelins, threw the discus and leapt obstacles in an unintentionally comic parody of how they imagined their heroines to have behaved. Sometimes they wore long flowing white robes, the better to imitate their forebears.

On the face of it, an invitation from a lower middle class factory clerk in an unpromising northern industrial town should have seemed utterly incongruous. But in Alfred Frankland, Alice Milliat had a fellow traveller on the path towards female sporting equality: theirs was a mission both shared and self-evidently righteous. His invitation was graciously accepted.

Frankland had, by 1920, firmly cemented his place in Dick, Kerr (or, more accurately, English Electric, as it was now known[25]) and in local society. Although the war draft which had brought him to the company had ended, the directors had retained him as a manager – the only one of his Munitions Act comrades to have been kept on. In part, this was undoubtedly due to the publicity his ladies football team was generating; but he had also worked tirelessly to raise hundreds of pounds for the regeneration of Preston, thus earning him the gratitude and the ear of the town's great and good.

He had also persuaded the company to invest in sporting facilities. The Dick, Kerr factory had originally been erected on waste ground which had served as a sports field for Preston. Early in 1920, and prompted by Frankland, Dick, Kerr bought Ashton Park as a recreation ground for company staff, complete with a tennis court, a cricket pitch and a war memorial to honour the men from its works who had been killed in the Great War. It also boasted a purpose-built football pitch.

Between them, Frankland and Milliat agreed that there should not one, but four matches. These were all to be played within the space of one week and would take the structure of a tour, although the first game would be staged at Preston North End's Deepdale ground, the others would be held in Stockport, Manchester and London.

Frankland does not appear to have scheduled any warm-up fixtures for Dick, Kerr's Ladies. In fact, the only match they played before the scheduled internationals had already taken place in February. On the other side of the channel, Mme Milliat took a rather more professional approach, organising trials and practice games to select her best squad. This was, perhaps, also recognition of the differences between English women's football and the French version. In France, a code of rules, set out in 1918, defined the game as *educolore, dénicotisé* – loosely translated as 'sweetened and sanitised'. Women played on a shorter pitch and for a shorter time (60 rather than 90 minutes).

Milliat also worked to ensure the matches attracted as much publicity as possible, contacting the *Daily Mirror*'s Paris correspondent, John Bell. Over the ensuing weeks she drip-fed him details to tantalise a British readership – chiefly the colour of the French ladies team strip (horizon blue shirts with a red white and blue cockade on the breast, navy shorts, black socks and a stereotypical black beret to top it off).

On Monday, 26 April 1920, 17 young Frenchwomen – 16 players plus Alice Milliat as their manager – disembarked from the ferry at Dover and took the train to London. They were met at Victoria Station by the customarily boisterous British press corps. Alfred Frankland was on the platform to greet them, but had trouble pushing his way through the throng of reporters and photographers. Milliat, ever-aware of the importance of good publicity, ensured Fleet Street had full access. The French captain was interviewed about losing her hat overboard during the crossing, while the manager pronounced, in perfect English: 'We are very happy to be here and we are looking forward to a most pleasant visit. Of course, the girls are all very excited and full of it.' The girls themselves were uniformly *petites bourgeoisies*. Milliat was a professional interpreter (hence the perfect English), and her squad included three shorthand typists, two dressmakers, one bookkeeper, a trainee dentist and a philosophy student. They lived in respectable middle class

Paris *arondissements*. They were shortly to confront the rather less pleasant reality of northern industrial England.

Two days after their arrival in London, Milliat's squad left the capital on a train bound for Preston. It arrived at 6pm and was met by another swarm of pressmen, Alfred Frankland, and the Dick, Kerr brass band which struck up a rendition of *La Marseillaise*. The culture shock which the French women were about to encounter was not one-sided: the young women who stepped onto the platform were petite, and impossibly chic. They wore smart, closely-tailored dark coats, emphasising their slender figures, fashionable waistless dresses which seemed to float on slim and beautifully toned shoulders, and shod in pretty high-heeled shoes. Beneath cloche hats, their hair was bobbed. They looked what Britain would come to term 'flappers'. And Preston had never seen their like.

They must have realised how different – alien, almost – they appeared. Madeleine Bracquemonde (the captain who had lost her bonnet on the ship) enquired of one of the reporters: 'Tell me about the Lancashire girls. They are big, strong and powerful, *n'est-ce pas?*' In that, Mademoiselle Bracquemonde was undoubtedly correct. Unlike the resolutely middle class French players, Dick, Kerr's side was made up of working class women who had been born to labour in the mills and factories of north-west England, the products of a working class culture based on hard work and muscular Christianity. Compared to the French ladies they were Amazons.

So who were they, these 'big, strong and powerful' women? For a start they were not all, originally at least, Dick, Kerr's Ladies. By April 1920, Alfred Frankland had been assiduously seeking out the best talent from across the north-west and, company cheque book in hand, had bought in players from rival teams. One of his first signings was Alice Woods, the product of a transfer raid on St Helens Ladies, and already a pioneering athlete. She had been born in 1899, one of seven children. Her father, Jem Woods, died when Alice was three leaving her mother, Margaret, then 51, to bring up the family in the grimy and polluted streets of St Helens. The Woods were a family of miners, and Alice's elder brothers worked in the Lancashire coalfields which, together with town's concentration of chemical works, belched a noxious blend of coal-dust and industrial toxins into the foul-smelling air and the rancid canal.

But the Woods brothers were also keen sportsmen (one, Jack, played centre forward for Halifax Town FC) and encouraged in their kid sister a passion for athletics and football, marking out a rough and ready pitch as well as a 200-yard running track, built on waste ground near the family's three-bedroom terraced home with cinders from domestic and industrial fires. Alice was barely a teenager when she began competing at pre-war athletics meetings, and she regularly won the 80-yard sprint event. She was growing into a tall young woman, at least for the time and the place, close to 5' 6" (1.68 metres) with a slim, muscular body.

When the Great War interrupted sporting fixtures, Jack Woods swapped his football boots for the hobnails and puttees of a Tommy's uniform. At the age of 17, Alice was herself drafted into the war effort, called up as a munitionette at the Sutton Glass Works, a few steps from her home, but light years away from her previous sporting life. Here she was issued a long drab overall, buttoned down the front and pulled in at the waist, with a matching mob cap under which she was required to stuff her long and unruly curls. A series of badges – to be worn at all times in the factory, and stating her name, her status (single) and that she worked in the shells department – were pinned to the front of her uniform.

GIRLS WITH BALLS

Whilst welfare patrols, made up of older and presumably unimpeachably respectable ladies, were employed to ensure the moral health of their charges (and indeed to root out all improper after-hours mixing of the sexes in the grimy backstreets of St Helens), the factory would have been spartan at best, filthy at worst. There were no regulations on levels of pollution. Toilets – if they existed at all – would have been designed for the rather simpler requirements of the pre-war male workforce; and the already foul air would have been blue with the ripest of language.

Alice Woods may have been working class, but the family was solidly respectable. Their house was in a decent part of town, its front step rigorously scrubbed clean. There were two types of poverty in squalor of these rutted streets: honest and feckless. Alice's family was the former, and the mark of their pride was a well-scrubbed front step.

Munitions workers at the Sutton Glass Works kicked a football about during their mid-day break – like at Dick, Kerr's in Preston – and it was here that Alice Woods began to take the game seriously, so when a ladies team was formed to play matches for charity, her natural athleticism made her an obvious candidate. Family lore has it that her mum, Margaret, was not impressed: football, she insisted, was not a game for women and most certainly not for Alice. But her brothers were more supportive; Jack, home on leave, apparently encouraged his sister with the words 'there's no need for Mum to know', and marked out the players' positions on a blackboard. He also taught her how to kick, trap and dribble the ball, and how to head it. In this, he and Alice were ahead of their time. Few women footballers made any use of their heads – hardly surprising, given the rigorously-enforced requirement of wearing caps during matches.

By September 1918, with the end of the war in sight, Alice

had returned to athletics. That month she took part in the first women's race meet to be held under the laws of the Amateur Athletic Association, beating her long-time rival Miss Elaine Burton, from Harrogate, at 80 yards but losing to her after falling in the 100 yards. It was clearly a defeat which rankled. When, the following year, Miss Burton's father declared in *All Sports Weekly* that his daughter was the 100-yard World Champion, Alice Woods sent an angry letter to the magazine, pointing out that she had beaten Burton on many occasions. She also challenged her rival to a new race for a prize of £25 – the equivalent of £5,000 today.

The offer seems not to have been taken up: there is no reference to any re-match, much less such lavish prize-money. Which is possibly just as well. At the Salford Harriers Sports event in Manchester on 24 May, Burton beat Alice Woods in a race advertised as the North of England 100 yards Women's Championships. Her winning time of 13.0sec was greeted as an inaugural British best performance. Three weeks later, at the same ground, the women's 100 yards was again advertised as the North of England Championships and Woods came in second, though she did beat her arch-rival who came third. (Elaine Burton would go on to become a member of parliament and was eventually elevated to the peerage.)

By then, football awards had an equal place, with the athletics trophies standing proudly on the sideboard in Alice Woods' house. St Helens' Ladies had ceased to be a factory team when the war ended and women were eased out of the munitions works. But the women had carried on playing as representatives of their town, and their second formal fixture was a game against Dick, Kerr's Ladies. The scoreline – 6-1 to the Preston side – was hardly flattering; but Alfred Frankland spotted the two players in the St Helens XI who would be a worthy addition to his growing football enterprise. After the final whistle he calmly walked up to Alice Woods and introduced himself. Would she, he enquired, join Dick, Kerr's? And would she also use her good offices to ensure that the powerful outside left from her team signed up as well?

The winger in question was a 14-year-old girl called Lily Parr. She would, in time, play more matches and score more goals than any other woman. She would go on to become the most famous woman footballer the world over, and long after her death would be immortalised into the Football Hall of Fame at the National Football Museum. But she would also play a role in the suppression of women's football – a part which, on that day in 1920, she could never have anticipated.

Gerrard's Bridge was a small corner one of St Helens' less salubrious neighbourhoods known as Windle. Unlike Sutton, where Alice Woods lived and her family had grown up in a strong and proud mining community, Gerrard's Bridge was a rough and sometimes violent area, home to a largely unskilled population. In the years during and after the Great Potato Famine in Ireland, impoverished immigrants from across the water had settled here, rapidly acquiring a well-deserved reputation for drinking and fighting. This was a very different kind of poverty to the one into which Alice Woods had been born. The two communities shared the same unequal struggle with hardship, but – in the unyielding strata of the English class system, the miners of Sutton habitually looked down on the 'undeserving' poor of Gerrard's Bridge.

Lily Parr was born on 26 April 1905 in a rented house on Union Street, at the shabby heart of Gerrard's Bridge. She was the fourth child of George, a labourer, and Sarah, a maid in service universally known as Sal. When times were hard, as they often were, if George was out of work, Sal took on a coal round, heaving heavy sacks from a cart and delivering them to backyards across the neighbourhood. Their home, an end terrace formerly a local shop, had a back yard and stable behind it. Sal and George kept a family of pigs in the former, and let out the latter to local carters. The house also had an attic which was rented to an Irish immigrant down on his luck. Given that his nickname was Smelly Kelly, the small Union Street house must have been both crowded and almost as noxious as the fumes which choked the air outside.

Lily's brothers, John and Bob, were keen footballers, signifying something unusual about the Parr family because St Helens – and particularly Gerrard's Bridge – had a dominant tradition of rugby. This was not the elevated and privileged game of the public school elite. In 1895 rugby had endured a schism between amateurs and paid players greater even that than which had caused such strife within Association Football.

Northern clubs were resolutely working class and recognised that players needed to be compensated for time off work. What started out as the Northern Union, playing under traditional rugby rules, gradually morphed into a different and resolutely professional game of its own. Thus, rugby league was born and offered the opportunity for a living to be made on its turf. St Helens became a bedrock of the game.

Nonetheless, John and Bob Parr cleaved to soccer rather than rugby. Pick-up games, often with a mass of players and indeterminate rules and timing, and thus a throwback to the old traditions of folk football, were a nightly feature in the streets around their terraced home. A barren patch of gravel behind Chessie's, the local pub, saw slightly more organised matches, with teams of married men pitched against sides of single players.

GIRLS WITH BALLS

John and Bob were regulars in the unmarried men's sides, and by the time she was on the cusp of becoming a teenager, so was Lily. Photographs show a strikingly tall and strong girl – almost six feet (1.82 metres) – with a tough and handsome face from which a shock of unruly jet black hair was brushed straight back. But as much as her physical stature, it was her nature that enabled this unconventional teenager to fit in with the footballing men of Gerrard's Bridge. By the age of 14, Lily reputedly smoked, swore and spat as fluently as any man.

But she was also, quite evidently, a natural and powerful player. Left-footed and agile despite her size, she had worked endlessly on her kicking technique with the result that her shot was – even by male standards – remarkably mighty. In 1919, playing for St Helens Ladies at Chorley, a male professional goalkeeper was dismissive of the strength of her shot and challenged her to put the ball past him. Lily lined up the kick, belted it... and the force of the shot broke the goalkeeper's arm. This, then, was the young winger that Alfred Frankland asked Alice Woods to bring with her to Dick, Kerr's Ladies.

Alice made the trip across town to Gerrard's Bridge with her young sister, Jane, in tow. She arrived in the evening, when Union Street's flickering gas street lamps made the area, already populated by drunks and pick-pockets tramps and punctuated by bouts of shouting and fighting, even more daunting to a respectable young woman from Sutton. According to Barbara Jacobs, one of the two biographers of Dick, Kerr's Ladies[26], before she found the Parr's end terrace house, Woods was drawn to the sound of a football being kicked – regularly and powerfully – against one of the iron lamp posts. In its fitful light she found Lily Parr practising her shots, a Woodbine cigarette glued to her adolescent lips.

172

When Alice stated her business, Lily Parr flicked the smouldering butt at her and indicated that she would need to consult her mum, Sal. They traipsed over to the overcrowded little house. Inside, there was an overpowering stench, a toxic blend of pigs, children, soot from the fire and the smoke of George's cigarettes: the smell of true poverty. Sal Parr was, by this time, struggling with the unequal task of matriarch, mother and being pregnant once again. She had her hands full, not least with the rebellious and headstrong Lily. Despairing of her daughter, Sal had turned over what passed, in these streets, for her education to local nuns. It had not proved a particularly noteworthy success.

And so, when Alice Woods asked Sal's permission for Lily to leave home and join Dick, Kerr's – both as a worker in its Preston factory and a footballer in Alfred Frankland's team – Sal had only one condition. Alice, an evidently sensible and level headed young woman, would have to promise to go with her and take charge of the 14-year-old. There was just one problem. Whilst Margaret Woods was prepared to allow her talented athlete daughter to join the most obviously ambitious women's football team, she was adamantly opposed to Alice leaving St Helens and – just as importantly, given Margaret's need for Alice to help look after the family – to leave home. But Sal was adamant: if Alice wasn't moving to Preston, then neither was Lily. Dick, Kerr's was not, it seemed, about to make two new signings.

But neither Sal Parr nor Margaret Woods had factored Alfred Frankland into their reckoning. Frankland was a determined, almost driven, man. If sending Alice as his emissary had failed, he would have to travel to St Helens and make his case in person. He went first to Union Street. Amid the mess and chaos of the Parr family house he told Sal that Lily was the best footballer he'd ever seen and that she was crucial to the success of Dick, Kerr's. If Sal would agree, he would arrange a job for her daughter at the factory and lodgings at the home of one of the team's other players, a decent and hard-working family. Lily would also be paid 10 shillings per match to play – a clear indication that Frankland was well down the road to creating a semi-professional side. Sal, apparently, was torn.

With another baby on the way, Lily, despite her tomboy nature, would have been useful as a helper in the home. Equally, though, football was the only thing that Lily showed any real interest in, and anyway, it was high time she began work. Sal had gone into service when she was just 12. In the end she agreed. But if Sal Parr had underestimated Alfred Frankland, he was guilty of the same offence with Lily. With her mother's agreement secured, she now imposed a condition of her own. She would only agree to move to Preston if she was given her own room in her new lodgings. It was a remarkably forward demand: children in working class homes in Lancashire counted themselves lucky if they had their own bed, never mind a room all to themselves. And given the overcrowding in the little house in Union Street, Lily could hardly claim to have been used such privilege. But she stood her ground. It was her own room, or the move was off. Frankland knew he had been outflanked; with no certainty of being able to deliver on the promise, he agreed to Lily's terms.

Margaret Woods, meanwhile, proved immune to Frankland's entreaties. She obstinately refused to allow Alice to leave St Helens. Reluctantly, Dick, Kerr's manager agreed to a compromise. Alice would join the team, but would remain at her old job at Suttons Glass Works, and continue to live at home. Oddly, given Frankland's unconcealed conviction that he needed both Alice Woods and Lily Parr to make his side the best in England, he doesn't appear to have included the 15-year-old in the team he drew up to play against the French XI. Records of the first three International matches that April – played at Deepdale in front of 22,000 spectators, Stockport before a crowd of 15,000 and Hyde Road, Manchester where the strangely smaller number of 3,000 people passed through the turnstiles – do not include a full team sheet. But they do reveal that Dick, Kerr's won the first two games 2-0 and 5-2 respectively; that centre forward Florrie Redford scored in both matches (along with fellow striker Jennie Harris and the French captain Mlle Bracquemonde); and that the third fixture ended in 1-1 draw.

Not until the fourth, and final, match in the series – played at Stamford Bridge, home ground of London's Chelsea Football Club on 6 May 1920 – do we find a listing of the players. It shows that Alice Woods was now in the team, playing in the forward line with Florrie Redford and Jennie Harris. But there is no mention of the teenage wunderkind, Lily Parr. If Frankland saw in her the vital ingredient for the future of his side, that future was evidently still a little way off. The present, however, was remarkable enough.

Despite the steady progress of modern travel, with the Victorian railway network by now at its peak and motorised vehicles were no longer a source of wonder and surprise, the only time working class people had travelled beyond the borders of their county had been when men were conscripted into the war-time army. London, for most, was as impossibly distant as another planet. Its fashions and politics, low-life criminals and high-living aristocracy were read about in newspapers, to be sure, but they were glimpsed only in the new craze for celluloid newsreels, shown in the ever-mushrooming

Kinemas. To travel to London, then was, for the Dick, Kerr's Ladies, to travel to another world.

But if London was glamorous and exotic to these northern factory girls, the capital returned the compliment. Not since the days of Lady Florence Dixie (who died in 1905, and so would never have seen the realisation of her dream for women to play competitive football) and the enigmatic so-called Nettie Honeyball nearly 25 years before, had women been seen to set foot on the hallowed men's turf of a football pitch. Ten thousand spectators paid the entry price and crowded the terraces, but more significantly, Pathé News, the originator and European innovator in newsreel technology, sent along a camera team to record the match.

It would be the start of an enduring relationship between the Kinemas and the Dick, Kerr's Ladies, and one which would spread the gospel of women's football across the land. For the first time 'lady footballers' would be treated not as objects of patronising amusement or misogynistic scorn but as serious sporting players. In that first 54-second newsreel, preceded by the trademark Pathé logo of a crowing rooster, lay the seeds of a nationwide flourishing of the women's game – and of the very masculine determination to suppress it.

Watching the flickering footage today (it is available to view on-line at www.britishpathé.com) is a remarkable and telling glimpse into the dream of women's football. The cameras, on that spring day in 1920, capture the Dick, Kerr's Ladies walking out on to the pitch through the crowds, clad in their customary strip of black-and-white striped shirts, baggy black shorts and hooped caps, and the leading player (probably the captain, Alice Kell) kicks the brown leather ball high into the air.

The team runs past the camera lens, followed by the French XI. They march in neat formation from the players' dressing room, each wearing a light-coloured shirt bearing the French national emblem (the same cockerel as adopted by Pathé) and black beret; each player was also kitted out in gloves. Their shorts, shorter and tighter than the British version, would subsequently cause much excitement among the gentlemen of the press. Under the heading 'Shorts – Very Short: exclusive' and a photograph of a French player next to one from Dick, Kerr's, one newspaper breathlessly informed its readers: 'It was noticed in the Anglo-French ladies' football match at Stamford Bridge that many wore knickers so scanty as would be frowned upon by the F.A. if worn by men.'

A few seconds of the match itself were captured on Pathé's revolutionary celluloid showing little more than a goal-mouth scramble. And perhaps that is all the play merited. With the exception of a decidedly un-English kiss on the cheek from the French to the English captain, and striker Jennie Harris being knocked unconscious early in the first half (Dick, Kerr's therefore playing the majority of the game one woman short) the action itself was hardly memorable. The match ended with a 2-1 win to France, the deciding score being an own goal.

But its significance was far greater than the sum of its play. This was a match that not only brought women's football out of the industrialised working class north and into the opinion-making heart of Britain's empire, it was also the game that began turning ordinary English factory girls into the equivalent of international film stars. In this it reflected a new and gathering force in the country: it was both the product of and an accelerator for, women's rights. And it was also a warning, the sounding of a long-overdue alarm bell which signalled the rise of the working class as a power base to be recognised and, in time, respected.

Whether in May 1920 the Dick, Kerr's Ladies would have

seen it this way is debatable, but as they prepared to leave London they were witness to another sign of the restless times. After waving *adieu* to Mme Milliat's French squad at Waterloo they crossed London for the steam train which would carry them home from Euston to Preston. En route they ran into a women's demonstration: shopgirls employed by the John Lewis department store had gone on strike to protest against the company's requirement that they, unlike their male counterparts, must live in the shop's own hostels. Industrial unrest was far from uncommon in 1920, and would shortly get much worse. But for working women to withdraw their labour was unprecedented. Before and during the Great War it would have been, quite literally, unthinkable. In peacetime, this first-ever female strike was a sure sign that the old and rigidly-male order was under threat.

Back in the world of football, for Alfred Frankland the inaugural international matches were the start of a new era for the team he was building. They brought to a close the 1919-1920 season, a season in which his nascent stars had played seven games in front of at least 100,000 spectators, and in which they raised both the company's profile and a very tidy sum for charity. The French team had hardly arrived back in Paris before Frankland suggested return fixtures near the opening of the following season.

Did Frankland know what he was starting? The man left remarkably few documents or letters, and what little there was appears to have been burned, on his instructions, after his death. But with benefit of hindsight, and with the accounts of others clearly pointing to a man with both vision and insight, it's hard to resist the conclusion that this otherwise unremarkable provincial factory manager was deliberately casting a sizeable rock into the sluggish and complacent waters of the British football pond. Certainly, the impact of the French matches began to ripple out across the country. As the previous northern munitionette teams fell by the wayside, new sides sprang up to replace them, and to do so in the previously untapped regions (for women, at least) of London and the south-west.

In the 1920s, J Lyons & Co owned the dominant restaurant chain in the capital. Founded in 1887 as a spin-off to a tobacco business, it had long been a major food manufacturer. In 1894 it opened the first of a series of innovative and pioneering teashops, and within 10 years this modest venture had been transformed into a nationally famous chain of restaurants. Lyons Corner Houses (so-called because they were situated on or near the corners of the Strand, Tottenham Court Road and Coventry Street – all in the heart of London's fashionable West End) were colourful and bustling, with bright lights and ingenious window displays. Each boasted four or five floors. At street level was a lavish food hall with counters for delicatessen, sweets and chocolates, cakes, fruit and flowers. On the upper floors were hairdressing salons, telephone booths, theatre booking agencies and – for a time at least – a twice-a-daily food delivery service. There were also several restaurants, per establishment, each with a different theme and all with their own musicians. By 1920, Corner Houses were open 24 hours a day, and employed 400 staff – the majority of them women.

Waitresses in a Lyons Corner House were issued with a distinctive maid-like uniform, a matching hat, and an instantly recognisable name – Nippies. (Originally, the company had decided to call all its waitresses 'Gladys'. Not surprisingly perhaps the name failed to catch the public's enthusiasm.) In this, as in much else, Lyons was ahead of its competition. By the 1920s it was standard practice in advertising to use attractive female models to market products. Lyons ensured that Nippies appeared in all manner of advertising, on product packages, and on promotional items. The Nippy soon became a national icon, perhaps because, unlike other endorsements of the period which often took the form of popular celebrities or cartoon characters, a Nippy was comfortingly accessible and reassuring. A Nippy was, after all, a real-life figure who could be seen and interacted with every day for the price of a cup of tea.

Lyons was extremely careful to maintain the image of a Nippy as wholesome and proper, and yet still (potentially, at least) sexually available, and prior to the Second World War the company would not hire married women as Nippies. But it was the uniform which truly enshrined the Nippy, and therefore Lyons, in the affections of the public. A photograph from the time, captioned 'The Perfect Nippy' and listing the company's requirements, makes abundantly clear the standards Lyons expected of its waitresses.

Cap correctly worn, monogram in centre
Ribbon clean and pressed
Teeth well cared for
No conspicuous use of make up
All buttons sewn on with red cotton
Plain black stockings
Dress correct length

So popular was this image that miniature Nippy outfits were purchased (by middle class parents, at least) for children to dress up and wear to garden fêtes and other suitably prim events.

Whether the decision to form a Lyons women's football team came from the management or the workers themselves – and given the company's sharp-eye for a marketing gimmick, the former is more likely – by the time the 1920-21 football season approached, there were at least four Corner House Ladies Teams, and one from its other main restaurant on the Strand. The company clearly knew the value to its business of these sides; it supported them with a training ground and changing facilities in the north London suburb of Sudbury. Not only were these far in advance of anything which even Dick, Kerr's could provide, they were the envy of many long-established male football clubs.

Outside the capital, two cities in the south-west of England established teams to carry forward the banner of women's football. In genteel Bath, the local professional (male) team helped establish a ladies side, with one of Bath AFC's committee serving as the women's team manager, and the two-year-old daughter of the club chairman being kitted out as a mascot to accompany the team to every match. In Plymouth, the new women's team brought in a professional coach, although it is not clear whether he was paid for his services. Frank Zanazzi was a former army physical training instructor and successful athlete. Under his tuition, Plymouth Ladies trained regularly – often in non-traditional football disciplines such as hurdling, shot-put and javelin – to improve their fitness and co-ordination. Surviving photographs show Zanazzi putting his squad through their paces on the local beach.

He also had an eye to the importance of providing a fully-rounded spectacle at women's games. Adopting pre-match routines from America, routines which were decades ahead of anything the men's game in England had to offer, Plymouth Ladies would warm up both themselves and the crowds with athletic and gymnastic exhibitions. And as the zeal for women's football spread across the country in the aftermath of the Stamford Bridge international, new teams were formed and they also began taking on experienced male trainers.

F K Selman, in charge of Coventry Ladies, was evidently determined to turn his squad of enthusiastic amateurs into a disciplined and well-ordered team. He began by calling them together for a team talk during which he identified the flaws in each individual player and then sent them out for a cross-country run, while he waited at the finishing line with a notebook and pen. As each player returned he noted down their time and the order in which they had arrived. The first five women back, and therefore the quickest runners, were told they were forwards; the next three halfbacks and the remainder were assigned as full backs or goalkeeper. That this was a much-needed exercise became clear when it emerged that until then the fastest and most adept forward amongst the women had previously been somewhat randomly chosen as goalkeeper.

Selman also realised that his players, in common with many other women's teams, were reluctant to head the ball. He quickly saw that if he could induce Coventry Ladies to overcome their fear, the team would have a distinct advantage over its rivals. According David Williamson, the first modern writer to examine women's football[27], contemporary accounts show that he settled on a training approach that was as direct as it was unusual: 'He formed the players into a wide ring, each one of them facing inwards with her head bent slightly forwards. Mr Selman then threw the ball at each player's head until they had had enough.'

But it wasn't simply the increased professionalism (at least in the sense of the team's approach to training and playing) which marked out this new wave of women's football. There was a clear indication that many of the rapidly appearing new teams were drawing their players from a middle class background. Unlike the munitionette teams of the war years – of which Dick, Kerr's was the chief survivor – these newly energised women players were not manual labourers and mill girls.

In November 1920 in Huddersfield in the heart of the West Yorkshire textile belt, a group of middle class women got together 'to provide games for the women of Huddersfield, to foster a sporting spirit, and a love of honour among its members'. The name chosen for this venture was The Atalanta Sports Club, indicating the educated background of the founders. Atalanta was a strong female character from Greek mythology, and therefore a suitable role model. She was abandoned at birth and reared by a bear, growing up to be a mighty huntress with an alarmingly direct response to anyone bold enough to seek her hand in marriage. She would challenge them to a race, and if they beat her they would win her; if, however, they lost, Atalanta would kill them.

The resolutely bourgeois nature of Huddersfield Atalanta was recorded by one of the few working class women to join up at the outset. Ada Beaumont was a mill girl when she read in the pages of the *Huddersfield Examiner* that a women's football team was being formed. She offered this insider's view:

> In the beginning they were mostly teachers, secretaries, young women who thought they were something, you know. A very high opinion of their own capacity and all that sort of thing. Well, that didn't go down very well with me. I never liked the show-off in anything.
>
> There weren't a right lot of us in the club who were what you might call manual workers, but we were the ones who played the football, you see, because we were

used to hard knocks in life. What you might call the rough 'eads.[28]

In this middle class trend, women's football was both reverting to the era of Lady Florence Dixie and the British Ladies' Football Club, and going in the opposite direction to the men's game. By 1920, professional football had shed the last threads of the old public school tie and had become recognisably the people's game. Yet, whilst male footballers were almost universally working class (the snobbish and self-satisfied Amateur Football Association still limped on with its cast of gentlemen) the administration of the game was still unquestionably the burden of the great and the good. The FA demanded continual obeisance to its laws and mandate – and the reins of that power were gripped tightly by the upwardly-mobile merchant class. This, perhaps, would play into the hostility which would, within a year, come to characterise the FA's attitude to women's football.

But, that autumn of 1920, there was no doubting the public appetite for lady footballers. Not merely did crowds flock in their thousands to each fixture, but charities, too, competed for the favours and beneficence of the women's game. The 'land fit for heroes', promised by Lloyd George two years earlier, had failed to materialise. Hundreds of thousands of wounded soldiers were still dependent on charitable handout – and this at a time when unemployment was steadily rising. The government's unemployment insurance scheme, set up originally in 1911, had been expanded during the Great War and, by 1920, in theory covered the majority of manual workers over the age of 16 (as well as white collar workers who had earned less than £250 a year).

But there were huge gaps. Those previously employed in

agriculture, forestry and domestic service, as well as teachers, nurses, policemen, railway workers and, most crucially, the military – were all excluded from its protection. The result was an ever-increasing reliance on private charity. Women's football teams, specifically established to generate this much-needed revenue, were at the forefront of the effort. And none more so than Dick, Kerr's.

The international matches against France had cemented their place in the public imagination, and as 1920 progressed they were clearly on their way to being a semi-professional side. Their fixture list, with each game being played for charity, was growing faster than new opposition could be located. A snapshot of one month – March 1920 – drawn from the personal diary of Alice Woods, shows both the range and the popularity of Alfred Frankland's team.

> Tuesday 1st. Glasgow. 6,000 spectators. DK 9,
> Scotland 0
> Wednesday 2nd. Edinburgh. 23,000 spectators. DK 13,
> Scotland 0
> Saturday 19th. Hull. 20,000 spectators. DK 4,
> Hull Ladies 1
> Tuesday 29th. Cardiff. 18,000 spectators. DK 4,
> Cardiff 0

In that one year alone, Dick, Kerr's Ladies would play 30 matches: far more than any professional men's team of the time. (They would win 25 of these, drawing two and losing just three with the remarkable statistic of scoring 133 goals whilst conceding just 15). Frankland was plainly conscious of maintaining, and enhancing, the value of his 'brand'. The internationals which had proved so influential for Dick, Kerr's and the women's game in general, were to be repeated, but this time his team would make the trip across the Channel.

A manager as astute as Frankland must have known that this would be a pointed reminder that, for all its airs and graces, the FA had yet to arrange a professional men's international in Europe.

In October, with the plans already firmly in place, he wrote to Mme Milliat outlining Dick, Kerr's hopes for the tour. The letter was subsequently translated and published in French newspapers.

> We come to France with feelings of friendship towards France unsurpassed by any sporting organisation which has yet visited your shores. To many of us there will be a touch of sadness in our visit, insomuch as many of those near and dear to us are taking their last long sleep along the various fronts we shall visit.
>
> We feel we are doing something to cement the good relationship existing between our two countries. Needless to say we are out to win all our matches in France. We recognise the splendid athletic qualities of our opponents, but at the same time we remember our strength in different directions.
>
> The public will see really good football played in Paris, Roubaix, [Le] Havre and Rouen. We shall also have the honour of playing under the patronage of His Excellency the Earl of Derby (British Ambassador to France) amongst others.
>
> We shall take the field wearing our usual colours – black and white striped jerseys, wearing a small Union Jack on our left breasts. The sporting public of this

country look forward to the results of our matches with great keenness.

The wonderful reception which the French party received here proved the splendid feelings towards our brave French allies. We claim that these international sporting events are a big help to the League of Nations, helping the people to understand each other better.

A. Frankland – Dick, Kerr's Ladies' Football Team

Whether from genuine belief, hubris or a shrewd sense of marketing, Frankland was deliberately setting the bar high. He had secured serious political patronage: Edward George Villiers Stanley, 17th Earl of Derby (Knight of the Garter, Knight Grand Cross of the Order of Bath, Knight of the Royal Victorian Order, Knight of the Venerable Order of St John, Privy Councillor and Justice of the Peace) was about as close to British royalty as it was possible to be without sharing the late Queen Victoria's bloodline. The Earl had also managed to fit into his busy life, careers as a soldier, a politician and – at the time he agreed to become patron of the French tour – was honorary President of the Rugby Football League.

And Frankland's declared ambitions for the trip were no less lofty. The League of Nations had been founded the year before at the Paris Peace Conference which formally ended the Great War. Its primary goals, as set out in its founding Covenant, included the prevention of future wars and settling international disputes through negotiation and/or arbitration. For good measure the founders tacked on to the inaugural Covenant a series of related treaties including labour conditions, just treatment of native inhabitants, human and drug trafficking, arms trade, global health, prisoners of war, and protection of minorities across Europe[29].

GIRLS WITH BALLS

By deliberately hitching his team of Lancashire factory girls to the international star of the League of Nations, Frankland was, whether he realised it or not, rubbing further salt into the wounds of football's self-appointed rulers. It was a slight that would, before very much longer, come back to haunt not just Dick, Kerr's but the entire women's game.

But before the tour could get under way, Dick, Kerr's Ladies had to apply for passports. In 1920 these were largely unknown, even for middle class men, let alone working class women. They were also strikingly different to a modern passport, being a single sheet of A4 paper, folded into eight squares, and requiring the applicant to give accurate descriptions of hair colour, facial shape, size and classification of the nose, mouth and chin. Even for a relatively well educated young woman like Alice Woods it would have been an intimidating document. For a young and decidedly rough girl such as Lily Parr it was the first real taste of the seriousness of women's football.

Lily, by then lodging in the neat and unmistakably respectable Preston home of Alice Norris (a house with no pigs and squalling babies, and with firm rules about appropriate behaviour) was already earning a reputation. Her appetite was prodigious, as was her consumption of cigarettes, a habit which severely tested her landlady's patience, not least because she insisted on stubbing out her butts on the family's furniture. She was also not averse to light-fingered pilfering, including the regular appropriation of match day footballs, which she appears to have then sold on at 6d a time.

Outside the confines – and Lily most definitely saw herself as confined – of Preston, national newspapers were also beginning to take interest in this teenage prodigy. Under the headline '15-year-old with a kick like Division 1 back', the *Daily News* reported that Lily 'is said to kick like a First Division man'. Just as the press had, 25 years earlier, adopted 'Tommy' as the adolescent star of the British Ladies' Football Team, Lily Parr was now bathed in the media spotlight. The French tour was guaranteed to increase reporters' attention. On the eve of the team's departure, newspapers across Britain carried an interview with Dick, Kerr's Ladies captain, Alice Kell.

> We intend showing the people of France what fine sportswomen the English women are, and we shall not allow sentiment to creep in as much as we did when the French team played over here earlier this year.
>
> Of course we didn't underestimate them, or allow them to win, but we didn't put in the 'last ounce' as you might say. And we were unlucky at having more than our fair share of injuries to our players in all the matches with the French ladies. Surely we will not have the same bad luck again.

More pointedly, she re-enforced Alfred Frankland's political remarks about the diplomatic value of the trip.

> If the matches with the French ladies serve no other purpose, I feel that they will have done more to cement the good feeling between the two nations than anything which has occurred during the last 50 years, except of course the Great War.

On the evening of Wednesday, 27 October, Dick, Kerr's laid on a formal dinner with musical entertainment for the 16 women and three men (Frankland's empire having been bolstered by a club treasurer and a trainer) who would set out from Preston the next morning. To highlight that the venture was officially

blessed (as well as company-sanctioned), the Mayor and
Mayoress of Preston headed up the array of local worthies
seated at top table. But there was one, rather more telling, piece
of business to be announced at the dinner – the total sum
raised, mostly for charity, by the club since its inception nearly
three years earlier. This was proudly announced to be £8,600,
the equivalent of more than £1.7m today. It was an
extraordinary figure, and one which would be noted with some
interest by the Football Association.

The journey from Lancashire to Paris would take two days. The
squad was driven to Preston station, through streets thronged
with cheering crowds, in a motor charabanc displaying both
the Union Flag and the French Tricolore. After an overnight
stop in London they travelled on to catch the boat train at
Dover. Alice Woods had bought a small, new notebook to
record her impressions of the trip. The entries made in England
cover the small details: the 15 shilling (75p) price of the cross-
channel journey and the sea-sickness suffered by most of the
tour party. But the notes this sensible, quiet young working
class woman made of her impressions in France are much more
poignant. Between Calais and Paris, the team passed through
towns and villages whose names were burned into the minds,
and sometimes bodies, of women, men and children the length
and breadth of Britain.

En route for Paris. Saw soldiers' graves at Étaples. One
mass of beautiful flowers on Hill Gloria Jesus Christ.

This was among the first of the poignant entries in Alice
Woods' little notebook on that tour of France. It would not be
the last. The squad arrived in Paris at 7.30pm on Friday, 29

October and was met with the same enthusiasm, from officials and journalists, which had characterised their departure from Preston. Banquets, sightseeing and visits to a military academy were laid on by their hosts (though what the factory girls made of Mme Milliat's instructive lecture on 'The Analysis of Movement in Military Gymnastics Through Moving Pictures' is sadly not recorded).

The war and its political overtones were further re-enforced on the day of the first match of the four-game tour. On Sunday, 31 October, the squad was first taken to the French Military Training School at La Place de Fotenoy in the 7th *arondissement* in the very heart of Paris. Alfred Frankland wrote a note in the visitors' book:

> Dick, Kerr's Ladies Football Club desires to place on record their grateful appreciation of the splendid manner in which they have been received by the Officers of our Brave French Allies. Long live France.

From here they travelled to Vincennes, in the city's eastern suburbs, and the newly-built *Stade Pershing*. This, too, was a reminder of the war. The stadium, with a capacity for 29,000 spectators, had been constructed by the US Army on the orders of its most senior commander John 'Black Jack' Pershing. His purpose was to provide a location for the wartime allies to celebrate their victory with an annual sports tournament.

The match was kicked off by the French Minister for Aviation in front of 22,000 spectators. Contemporary reports suggest that the teams were evenly matched, with the score at 1-1 with 10 minutes remaining on the stadium clock. At this point the referee gave a corner to Dick, Kerr's and Lily Parr moved into the penalty area readying herself to head the ball towards the net. But before the kick could be taken, the French crowd, inflamed by the referee's decision, invaded the pitch. Lily Parr was knocked over in the ensuing *mêlée* and the game was abandoned. Dick, Kerr's needed a police escort to regain the safety of the changing room. It was an uncomfortable echo of the crowd troubles which had plagued the women's game a generation earlier (and would presage similar riots at French ladies matches in the years to come). The newspaper accounts of the incident were unlikely to have been missed by the Football Association back in London.

The next day, Dick, Kerr's made the 140-mile train journey from Paris to Roubaix, a small town in Nord-Pas-De-Calais, close to the north-eastern border with Belgium. Alice Woods' notebook recorded the sobering sights from the train window:

> Barbed wire entanglements... trenches full of water... woods demolished... Louvain: train bombed off rails still there... Blangy: small huts like Eskimos' live in, made of all tins picked up from the dumps.

Roubaix, the location for the second match, had been an industrial centre much like Preston or St Helens. It had also been one of the first towns to be overrun and occupied by the Germans who systematically looted it, and shot or deported to slave labour camps thousands of its citizens. In the middle of October 1918, British troops, many from Lancashire battalions, had liberated the area. Some had remained and their number had been boosted by cotton workers from across the north of England, called in to rebuild the mills which had once supported Roubaix and its surrounding villages. They, along with the remaining population of the town, lined the streets to welcome Dick, Kerr's Ladies.

After the match – a 2-0 victory to the English women, and watched by 10,000 spectators – the team paid their respects to those who had fought across these fields of Normandy. Alice Woods' notebook records this, and the subsequent tour of the region's killing fields.

> Went to cemetery Roubaix and laid a wreath for the fallen soldiers, then travelled in ammunition wagon past Tourcoing cemetery of all the British soldiers... Armentières: every house demolished...

When the team returned to Paris, their hosts laid on several days of sightseeing. Even this, though, was clouded by memories of war. After a tour of the magnificently opulent Palais de Versailles – a seventeenth-century feast of gold and velvet, Louis Quatorze architecture and vast formal gardens – Alice Woods noted: 'I have stood where peace was signed. Table on which peace was signed 28 June 1919.'

For the next week, the schedule would be the same mix of sightseeing, wreath-laying and travel, first to Le Havre where 10,000 spectators turned out to watch a 6-0 whitewash by Dick, Kerr's, and then to Rouen for the final match. Alice Woods' team won this 2-0 in front of a crowd of 14,000. The team arrived home in Preston on Tuesday, 9 November 1920. This band of working class girls had covered more than 2,000 miles, entertained 56,000 spectators, and paid a nation's respects at numerous cenotaphs and cemeteries. But above all, they had put women's football firmly on the map. Newspapers recorded Frankland's press statement that 'with the exception of slight colds, the team returned with a clean bill of health and they had been able to field the same team in every match'.

Their reception at Preston railway station was of a size and enthusiasm usually reserved for FA Cup winners. But unlike professional men's teams, there would be little time to savour their success. Not only did they have jobs to return to, but Alfred Frankland was keeping up their football schedule. On 20 November, just 11 days after they got home, Dick, Kerr's Ladies travelled to Leicester to play a match against St Helens in aid of the Leicester Fund for the Unemployed. More than 20,000 men, women and children passed through the turnstiles, raising £730 (the equivalent of £8,800 today) for the charity. 'Slight colds' or not, Alice Woods' side won 2-0.

Preston, too, needed the money that Dick, Kerr's Ladies could raise. As Christmas approached, the town's Fund for Unemployed Ex-Servicemen asked for Frankland's help. Soldiers who had fought on the very battlefields his team had so recently visited were going hungry: could Dick, Kerr's stage a match to provide cash to buy them food for the festive period? They could – at Deepdale and against a rapidly created Rest of England side. But Frankland also had another of his ideas to generate publicity, and more income.

In 1920 no sports ground had floodlights. All matches had therefore to be played during daylight hours. Frankland spotted an opportunity and, since his employer happened to be in the business of electricity, staging a game under artificial light would generate huge press interest which would help the company's marketing and attract a decent crowd. There was, though, a political problem. Whilst the engineers of English Electrics (*née* Dick, Kerr & Co Ltd) could handle the technical aspects of the wiring and generators, the company didn't own or produce lamps powerful enough to light the pitch. The only organisation which did have them was the army. It was happy to loan out two military searchlights – one to be placed at either end, and 40 carbide flares for the touchlines – for the occasion, but permission would need to be sought from Whitehall. Frankland once more dictated a letter, this time to the Secretary of State for War, Winston Churchill, at the War Office (which would become the Ministry of Defence in 1964). Whether Churchill, an astute if sometimes maverick politician, sensed the prevailing mood or simply saw no reason to object is not recorded. But on Wednesday, 15 December, the day before the match, a pair of anti-aircraft spotlights and several boxes of flares duly arrived at Preston railway station. In their wake the following day came representatives of the national, regional and local press – and a camera team from Pathé News. And with the media came spectators: 12,000 people turned out on a cold, clear night to watch Dick, Kerr's win (two goals to nil) the first-ever game of floodlit football – raising £600 (£120,000 today) for the unemployed ex-servicemen. But many times that number watched the flickering one minute and 19 seconds newsreel in Kinemas throughout Britain.

For Frankland and his team there would be just one more game to play before the end of the year. But it would be both the high-point of their extraordinary rise to public acclaim – and bear within it the seeds of their downfall.

Earlier that autumn a Liverpool businessman had written to the *Topical Times* – the newly launched and first weekly periodical devoted to football – suggesting that Frankland organise a fixture in the football-obsessed city. Such an event, he promised, would raise the sum of at least £1,000 for charitable distribution. With his habitually sharp eye for the market, Frankland set about arranging a match for Boxing Day, traditionally the best date in the footballing calendar. He approached Dick, Kerr's long-time rivals, St Helens' Ladies, and with their agreement secured, along with the rental of Everton's Goodison Park stadium, he marketed the game as a Cup Final. It was, at best, an audacious bit of cheek, since there had been no preceding rounds, much less any proper competition. More seriously it was bound to prod the slumbering lion of the FA and thus incur its ire. There was, as far as football's guardians were concerned, only one Cup competition – and they owned it.

Even Frankland's wide-ranging ambition could not have foreseen the huge interest in his self-proclaimed Cup Final. Fifty-three thousand spectators pushed their way through Goodison Park's turnstiles and 14,000 more were locked out because the ground was simply full. As they spread out through the surrounding area, the streets became blocked and police had to force a way through to enable the women's teams to get into the changing rooms. On the pitch, the crowd was entertained by Ella Retford, then one of the most popular and famous stars of the music halls and, thanks to her patriotic war-time song 'Hello There, Little Tommy Atkins', something of a national treasure. True to form, the game was another Dick, Kerr's victory – 4 goals to nil. At the final whistle the players were showered with flowers and, as they ran to the safety of the changing rooms, were pursued by a mass of autograph-seekers. Women's football had its first genuine celebrities.

A calm, cryptic note, penned in a steady hand in Alice Woods' notebook, reads:

Boxing Day match at Everton (1920). 53,000 spectators (between 10,000 – 14,000 turned away being unable to gain admission.) Gate receipts – £3,115.

It is a measure of the honest, down-to-earth character of Alice Woods and her team that this financial accounting was left to last and noted with an unassuming matter-of-factness. And yet the sum was quite extraordinary: £3,115 in 1920 equates to £623,000 today. In one match alone this remarkable group of working class women had raised more than half a million pounds.

That they had collectively become the David Beckhams of their era, more famous even than most male professional footballers, does not appear to have affected them, much less changed their routine of factory work and family commitments. Yet 200 miles south of Liverpool people were observing and noting, and were very much affected by what they saw. In the comfortable offices of the Football Association, righteous and proud men read the newspaper reports of these new sporting heroines. And they liked not what they read.

CHAPTER ELEVEN

When upon the field of play we go
Thousands come to cheer us on our way
And you will often hear them say
Who can beat Dick, Kerr's today?
– DICK, KERR'S TEAM SONG

Some years are recorded immediately in history as great ones. Others have greatness thrust upon them with the benefit of hindsight. The year 1921 has largely been overlooked in either category, yet it was a pivotal period: the bridge between two worlds, the fading glory of Victorian England and the beginnings of a new order. It was a year when the seeds of change, planted during and in the aftermath of the Great War first broke through the cracking surface of a modern Britain. Above all, it was a year in which the traditional, and largely self-perpetuating, rulers were challenged by those they assumed they governed.

In Ireland, long a restive province of the Crown, the

demand for nationhood and self-rule tipped over into violence. The conflict had been simmering, with several outbreaks of lawlessness, since 1914. But from January 1921, it burst into the flames of open warfare. In the six months between January and July at least 1,000 people, including police, British military, IRA volunteers and civilians, were killed, amounting to 70 per cent of the total casualties for what would become a three-year conflict. Additionally, 4,500 IRA personnel (or suspected sympathisers) were interned. And in March 1921, the Irish Parliament, the Dáil, formally declared war on Britain, challenging one of the most strongly-held tenets of the United Kingdom – the right of the rich and powerful London Parliament to impose the Royal will on His Majesty's Irish subjects.

More personal politics, too, began to shift. Women, so long an adjunct to men in the eyes of the law and those who made it, were starting to emerge as people of importance in their right. True, these were privileged women. On 11 March, for example, Queen Mary was awarded the first honorary degree ever conferred on a woman by Oxford University, and less than a week later Marie Stopes (the daughter of a palaeontologist and a Shakespearean scholar) opened the country's first-ever birth control clinic. But as a sign of the changing times it was what these women represented, rather than who they were which signified a shake-up of traditional, chauvinistic British society.

In Westminster, the very seat of previously-male power, the Sex Disqualification (Removal) Act, passed just before Christmas 1919, became law on the first day of the new year, and abruptly threw out several hundred years of legal discrimination against women by proclaiming that:

A person shall not be disqualified by sex or marriage from the exercise of any public function, or from being appointed to or holding any civil or judicial office or post, or from entering or assuming or carrying on any civil profession or vocation, or for admission to any incorporated society (whether incorporated by Royal Charter or otherwise)... [and a person shall not be exempted by sex or marriage from the liability to serve as a juror].

Within months Margaret Wintringham, the first woman ever to enter Parliament[30] took her seat in the House of Commons. A new and significantly more emancipated era was being ushered in. But if the blunt arithmetic of politics – set in motion by the extension of the right to vote two years earlier – meant that women's voices had to be both heard and heeded, this did not signify a sudden acceptance of feminism by Britain's great and good. There was bound to be a backlash.

Sport, as so often, was the valve by which this combination of traditional misogyny and resistance to change could safely be expressed. It had first found expression in the previously staid and stuffy All England Tennis Club. The Wimbledon championship had restarted, after suspension during the war years, in 1919. That year, a flamboyant 20-year-old French woman, Suzanne Lenglen, had caused outrage when she took to the tennis court in a daringly modern outfit. Previous women players had sported full blouses, long dresses and petticoats, covering, with proper modesty, black stockings held up by a complicated suspender-belt. Lenglen, however, appeared in a dress revealing bare forearms and which ended just above the calf, openly revealing white stockings held in place by simple garters. For good measure she also swigged brandy between sets.

Reaction was immediate and unfavourable, and by the time she returned to Wimbledon for the 1920 championship, newspapers breathlessly reported that she regularly did in broad daylight what most people only dreamed of in the dark of night. She drank, she danced, she smoked, she swore, and she had lovers – lots of them. While her supporters proclaimed her as 'La Divine', to the outraged guardians of English morality she was a dangerous Gallic personification of that post-war menace (all-too visible in Hollywood silent films showing at Kinemas the length of breadth of the country): The Vamp. Newspaper letters columns filled with righteously indignant correspondence.

Football, or at least its self-proclaimed arbiters, had also felt the first stirrings of discontent. On Thursday, 13 November 1919, the *Hull Daily Mail* informed its readers:

> At a meeting of the Surrey County Football Association last night the question of admitting ladies to the referees' qualifying examination was discussed. A lady had sent in an application form. It was decided to return this and a resolution was passed that it be an instruction to the County Referees' Society that no application from any lady be entertained.

The following day other newspapers picked up the story. The football correspondent of the *Chelmsford Chronicle* mused:

> Can a lady qualify as a football referee under the Football Association? This knotty problem arose recently at Woking when a lady from a school at Ripley presented herself

before the examining committee of the Surrey County Referees' Committee. The committee discussed the point at length, eventually declining to examine the candidate, but to request the ruling of the Football Association.

It seems to me that here is a possible solution to the referee shortage difficulty.[31] Ladies have, during the war, played football and why should they not referee? There are pros and cons, but what do my readers think about it?

What the footballing fans of Chelmsford thought about it is not recorded. But the FA was in no doubt. It banned female referees unanimously and unequivocally. But as 1921 dawned, in Preston at least the future for women's football looked entirely favourable. Dick, Kerr's Ladies had established themselves as a nationally known brand. The pioneering inventor of collectible football cards, John Baines Ltd, had included them in the wildly popular series of national football club cards – the only female side ever to feature in the 20m cards sold between 1885 and the late 1920s.

Charitable causes, too, were queuing up, begging Alfred Frankland for the team's favours. So great was the demand that Frankland booked his prodigies to play an average of two games a week – one on Wednesdays and one on a Saturday. He accepted 61 such fixtures but had to turn down double that number. For a professional men's club of the year (or indeed today) this would have been an unthinkable schedule. But for a team of amateur women, albeit they were being paid 10 shillings a match, it is extraordinary. All of the Dick, Kerr's Ladies were full-time employees, although some had lost their jobs to make way for men returning from the war. The demands on their time were beginning to prove troublesome, as Alice Norris, one of the side's youngest players later noted:

'It was sometimes hard work when we played a match during the week because we would have to work in the morning, travel to play the match, then travel home again and be up early for work the next day.'

And where the players could no longer rely on the support of the company (Florrie Redford, for example, the side's leading goal-scorer, was training to be a psychiatric nurse) the position was even more difficult. To make up for the time off for football, she worked additional night shifts, often cycling directly from them to training or matches. Anecdotal accounts suggest it took all of Frankland's considerable skills of persuasion to persuade his players, their families and their employers to get them to every game.

This tension between the traditional role of women (as well as their continuing employment) and their status as football celebrities began to attract comment. The *Football Special and Sporting Pictorial*, a weekly magazine launched a year earlier, had a column about the women's game written by 'Football Girl'. Whoever the anonymous author was, she (or quite possibly he) had strong words of advice:

> Zeal for the game one plays is a very good thing; it helps to make one a better player. But when enthusiasm is carried too far and given the rein over common sense it is apt to lead into dangerous paths, and unless some girl footballers are very careful they will find their over enthusiasm leading them into danger.
>
> An obsession is never a healthy thing, and there are a few girls who (like a great number of men to be sure) are obsessed with football. They not only play it, but when they are not playing all their spare time is spent in training for it and talking about it. Friends are sacrificed to the

demands of football, reasonable amusements and other diversions are cut out to make room for it, and everything is considered in its relation to football and its likely effect on their play.

Now, such a degree of enthusiasm is both foolish and harmful. A girl who is obsessed with one idea is not popular. Usually, she thinks she is being noble and all that sort of thing when she gives up her other pleasures for football, but as a matter of fact she is being nothing of the kind – she is simply being short-sighted and selfish.

A girl in her teens and early twenties should have many interests in life, and it is not good for her to bother with just one thing. When she is playing football let her play football with all her heart, but at other times let her put it out of her head. She will enjoy games far more if she does this.

The weekly games should be something eagerly looked forward to; they should be a refreshing change from work. If a girl is constantly playing and training she has nothing to look forward to; besides which too much training is worse than too little. Over-trained and under-trained play badly, but whereas the under-trained girl can still enjoy playing, the over-trained girl can't because she has become stale and the game has lost its freshness for her.

'Football Girl's' stern lecture is interesting for two reasons. It was the first hint that the old fears about the effect of competitive sport on women's health had not been forgotten. They would soon re-emerge more loudly and more powerfully than ever before. But more crucially, the article was clearly aimed squarely at Dick, Kerr's Ladies: a sign that their new-found celebrity would not insulate them from the prevailing mores of society.

GIRLS WITH BALLS

As the year progressed and Dick, Kerr's exhausting schedule of fixtures continued, that criticism became more open and pointed. Under the headline 'Are Dick, Kerr's So Good?', Football Girl advised her readers:

> There are rumours that Dick, Kerr's are not as good as they used to be. People who have seen them play, both this season and last, seem to be pretty unanimous in saying that their play has deteriorated. Perhaps we can't tell really, for they are still winning their matches by comfortable margins, so that it is probable that they do not exert themselves to the degree they would if they were in danger of losing. We shall perhaps see keener play when the other clubs who play fewer matches have got more into their swing.

This, too, is revealing. The side was indeed winning its games by very healthy margins. The first match of the new year saw them defeat a Rest of Lancashire side 17-0; a fortnight later they hammered Bath ladies 12-0, following that with two games against St Helens in which they scored 15 goals and conceded only one. In the return fixture against the Rest of Lancashire they didn't concede a goal and put 10 past their opposition. By the end of March the statistics read: played 15, won 15; scored 100, conceded 4.

The problem was finding sides capable of matching them. If the crowds were still to be attracted – and they came in tens of thousands to each game, raising substantial funds for the chosen charities – the play could not continue to be so one-sided. Only St Helens Ladies seemed to playing with same fluency and skill, but they still found it impossible to beat Dick, Kerr's. Frankland began casting the net wider: a short tour was organised to play a representative team from Scotland, but that too saw Dick, Kerr's crushing their opposition. He tried fixtures against county teams, whose players were drawn from the best local clubs: these, too, proved no match for the Preston side. As the spring progressed, the only slight bump in the otherwise stately progression of Frankland's side was a match at Stoke in which Lily Parr was sent off for fighting (thus earning the dubious – if inevitable, given her nature – honour of being the first woman footballer to be shown a red card).

But other clouds were gathering. By mid-January 1921, 927,000 adults of working age were unemployed. A month later that figure topped one million, and as spring headed towards summer, so unemployment rose towards 2m. The spectre of economic slump was at the door and poverty, particularly in the industrial north, was severe and endemic. Then, on 31 March, the government declared a state of emergency throughout Britain. The cause wasn't unemployment: it was coal.

In the early part of the 20th century, coal was used on a scale barely conceivable today. It drove factories and mills, locomotives and merchant ships; it was turned into coke for steel-making; was the sole form of domestic heating and the source of the gas lamps which lit the streets. It yielded a cornucopia of chemicals, some of which were crucial ingredients in the production of munitions. When Britain signed up so optimistically for the First World War, demand for coal boomed – to such an extent that mineworkers who had volunteered for the forces were shipped home and sent back to the pits. Coal was King and so vital to the war effort that the government took the radical step of seizing control of the mines. Colliers, the men risking their lives in the filth and dark of an often lethal industry, were required to work harder, produce more. In return, the new masters of the mines, the mandarins of Whitehall, added a few shillings to their wages.

When the war ended, so too did demand for coal. Internationally, coal prices dropped as Germany, Poland and the USA increased production and started to make inroads into British markets. Pit owners lobbied for their mines to be handed back and for them to be given a free hand in reducing costs. But after four years of (relatively) enlightened management – four years in which hours were controlled, wages maintained and safety improved – and with the grim toll of unemployment rising around them, miners vehemently opposed re-privatisation. Throughout 1920, tension had mounted. The government's answer was to appoint a Commission of Inquiry, led by the eminent lawyer (and member of the up and coming Labour Party) Sir John Sankey.

Whatever Prime Minister Lloyd George had expected, Sankey's commission very firmly recommended that government ownership of the coal industry should continue. Mine owners were outraged and lobbied the PM, mindful of the confluence of capitalism and politics which dictate that those with the money to organise tend to win a fight. In March 1921, he gave them what they wanted: nationalisation was ended and the pits returned to their previous masters. The outcome was as immediate as it was inevitable. Mine owners imposed swingeing pay cuts and increased working hours. Miners, the very men who had kept the home fires burning, were told they had to accept the new conditions or lose their jobs. A strike was called, and on 31 March, the day the pits legally ceased to be under government control, Number 10 declared a state of emergency.

What followed has resonant parallels with the coal strike of more than 60 years later during Margaret Thatcher's premiership. In 1921, as in 1984, miners hoped for the support of their fellow trade unionists. This failed to materialise (though, unlike the Thatcher-era dispute, this was largely the result of a painful stab in the back by railwaymen and transport workers). Violence between strikers and those still producing and selling coal (albeit on a somewhat haphazard basis) also marked the stoppage. On 29 April 1921, the *Yorkshire Evening News* carried a breathless report of a mass brawl at the brick kilns section of a colliery in South Yorkshire.

> What has already become known as the battle of the brick kilns has created a tremendous sensation in Woodlesford, Rothwell, and the surrounding district. It appears the news that 100 Woodlesford miners were working night and day at the pit hills of the Water Haigh Colliery, the property of Messrs. Henry Briggs, Son, and Company, Limited, reached Rothwell, and the miners there, after an angry discussion resolved to march to Woodlesford and stop by forcible means any further digging.
>
> Each miner carried with him a hefty stick. Reports differ as to the number of men who took part in the march, but 120 seems to be somewhere near the mark. The men marched in perfect order, looking grim and determined, until they came to a spot about half a mile from the pit-head, where the Woodlesford miners were working.
>
> Here, near the brick kilns, they encountered a number of carts and motor vehicles laden with coal. Without any hesitation they set upon the vehicles, and upset the loads. As the drivers did not show any opposition they were left untouched, but the punishment they would receive if they 'repeated the offence' was explained in the strongest possible language.

Elated by their 'victory', the Rothwell men cried out: 'Now for the Woodlesford men.' A Woodlesford pit youth told a *Yorkshire Evening News* representative today that as soon as he saw the little army of miners pull up the carts he dashed off to the pit hill and breathlessly informed his mates of the impending attack. The Woodlesford miners, numbering several hundred, ceased digging, and seizing their picks and shovels started off in a body to repel the attack. To use the words of one of the Woodlesford men who took part in the affray, 'We marched or ran in extended order and met the Rothwell chaps at the brick kilns.'

Here the battle took place, and the wonder is that no one was killed. The Woodlesford miners were filled with a terrible anger at being interfered with, and they set upon the Rothwell men with their implements. The Rothwell men met the attack and the air resounded with shouts, and the sound of sticks meeting metal shovels. Considerably outnumbered and suffering from minor injuries, the Rothwell men, after putting up a game flight, eventually turned and raced across the fields with the opponents hot on their heels.

But, as in 1984, the dispute also empowered working class women. Wives and daughters who witnessed the extreme financial hardship of a lengthy strike set out to raise funds to support their men: which is where football comes in.

Women's football teams, which had been so successful in fund-raising during the Great War, turned to fund-raising on behalf of their own communities across the mining regions of South Yorkshire, Durham and Northumberland. All were strictly local affairs – money was not to be wasted on travelling expenses – but all were unequivocally acts of political defiance. This notice for a County Durham match makes the situation clear.

> On the Townley Park ground on Tuesday evening, a football match was played between teams representing Scotswood and Newburn ladies. Prior to the game a costume procession left Ridley Terrace and marched through the principal streets to the football ground. A collection was taken in aid of the relief fund.

There was, unequivocally, in these matches an attempt to re-kindle the spirit and the purpose of the munitionettes teams of the war years. But it was a sign of the times that although these women's games attracted sizeable crowds, they also drew trenchant criticism. The *Blaydon Courier* published a particularly vicious attack, in the form of what purported to be an open letter to a lady footballer from her elder sister – though since an identical letter was published a week later in the *Consett Guardian* (some miles away) the authenticity of these apparently warring sisters is at least open to question.

> Dear Sister,
> You ask what I think about you having joined the Ladies Football Club. Not much, and yet a lot. That may sound paradoxical, but allow me to explain. I blush with shame when I picture you, gentle Jennie, my youngest sister, in the habiliments of a football player.
> You cannot be the shy, blushing sister I remember of ten years ago, when you would have coloured at finding a hole in your stocking. You must have put on the brass since then, and if it really be true that you have developed

into a 'lady' footballer, then there must be sufficient brass in your face by this time to make a fender. You were never a smart figure – I always got lost in your corsets – and you must certainly be a true example of the ludicrous when clad in your football togs.

Think, gentle Jennie, what it would mean if a stitch or two gave way when you bumped the ground? Another reputation would be gone. What fit of mental aberration has prompted you to become a 'lady' footballer? Is there something in the game that appeals to the feminine instinct, or are you out for exercise? Surely, you cannot be seeking exercise – although I admit you would be better without some of your surplus fat – because whenever Mother asked you to dry the dishes you always had some excuse. Then whatever is there in this leather chasing that induces you to don men's garments and parade yourself before hundreds of watery eyes and gaping mouths?

You mention something about the sacred cause of charity. Is charity the only thing that is sacred? Is there not a beautiful flower called modesty? Have you no respect for your sex?

Dear, gentle Jennie, are you not aware that every time you enter the dressing room and discard your feminine attire for a pair of men's football knickers and a sweater you not only disgrace yourself, but lower your sex in the eyes of everyone with a sense of decency. Oh, my poor misguided sister, you have degenerated. And what an ass you must make of yourself when kicking and chasing a football, you panting and perspiring little fool.

What is this you say in your letter, '... and we all chew spearmint.' Try baccy the next time, it is more appropriate. Oh you horrid wretch. It's enough to make our dear dead grandmother of sacred memory turn in her grave. But you are still my sister Jennie, and I forgive you your little fling 'in the sacred name of charity.' Try knitting jumpers.

Your affectionate sister, NORA

Genuine or not, this was by no means an isolated attack. On Monday, 4 April 1921, one of Britain's most celebrated athletes gave an interview to the *Nottingham Evening Post* denouncing women's football. Walter Goodall George had been the unequalled star of amateur running when, in 1886, he turned professional to challenge the then-holder of the record for the measured mile. In August that year he won his race, and in the process set a record time which would last until 1931. All of which ensured that what he had to say was heard by a national audience. The following day his interview carried in newspapers throughout the country.

FOOTBALL FOR WOMEN
FAMOUS ATHLETE DISAPROVES [sic]

'With women who take up athletics the tendency is to overdo it,' said W. G. George, the famous athlete and world's record holder to a Press representative yesterday.

'Hockey and lawn tennis are all very well in their way, but the competitive element, from my observation, has a damaging effect on account of overstrain, mental and physical. As for women's 'Soccer' football, I scarcely think it conforms to the average woman's ideal of modesty, especially when staged as a public exhibition.

'We have to keep in mind the motherhood of the future, and, as a nation, to make up our minds as to whether this forcing process in women's sport, which is associated with a new mentality, is beneficial or detrimental. This point, I am inclined to believe, calls for an official investigation, under Government auspices, by medical authorities of the highest repute.

'In the long run, women might develop physically to such an extent as to compete in sport on equal terms with men. But will it be for good or ill?'

Within a week, George's interview started a debate, conducted in the letters columns of newspapers throughout Britain. In the West Country, by now a stronghold of women's football, the vice-president of Plymstock Ladies, one Mrs Lois Jackson, denounced her opponents as reactionaries from 'that class which breeds Bolshevism and revolution, and is sending our country more quickly to the dogs than anything else'. For good measure she rounded off her letter, published in the *Western Morning News* on Thursday, 14 April, by suggesting that the perceived threat to the sanctity of English womanhood cited by the game's critics was a mote which they should remove from their own eyes: '... there is a quotation: "To the pure all things are pure".'

The evidently formidable Mrs Jackson was not alone. The same edition of the newspaper carried a letter from someone signing himself (or herself) 'Spectator No. 1'.

The girls who play football are every bit as much ladies as those who swim, row, play hockey or tennis, and in spite of the annoyance it may cause to a few narrow-minded people, ladies' football is an established fact; it has come to stay, there being over 50 ladies clubs in Britain already, and they are increasing daily.

Six days later the *Western Morning News* had received sufficient response to justify devoting an entire column to the debate. Under the headline 'Ladies at Football', its correspondents were given space to give vent to their hostility.

> Sir, I have been expecting to see some word of protest against the latest development of so-called recreation football for ladies. I would be the last to say a word against recreation. I would rather encourage it, but surely there are plenty of other games; in fact, almost any other rather than football.
>
> I am surprised that mothers have not spoken out on this question. Is there not a great physical danger for ladies playing at a game of this kind? From a moral standpoint it is time to cry halt, too.

This fear – that women playing football was somehow a threat to morality as well as health – was re-enforced by other correspondents.

> Sir, Being in the service [The Royal Navy] I come into contact with hundreds of men every day and I can honestly say that up to the present I have not heard one of them say a nice word about lady footballers.
>
> One fairly broad-minded man, who has travelled the world and seen ladies under their best and worst conditions, stated to me in conversation about lady footballers that he would not care to marry among this class of women. Several other men have made similar statements in my presence. Ladies' football teams are decidedly destroying beautiful womanhood.

Nor was it only the regional press which voiced the concerns of

Middle England. Football Girl weighed in with her views in the national and widely read *Football Special and Sporting Pictorial*:

> It is an interesting question as to whether girls' schools should take up football. Personally I should hesitate to introduce football among very young girls. It has been done, however, in one or two schools and with success. Football is more strenuous than the usual games played at schools, and for very young girls to play might involve the risk of doing them harm internally.
>
> Most ladies' football clubs, I know, have young players and often they are very good. The Dick, Kerr's star player, Lily Parr, is only 16; and Miss Chorley, the clever little centre forward of the St Helens team, is 16. Indeed there are few clubs which haven't 16 and 17-year-old players.
>
> On the other hand, the Atalanta club have a rule that no girl under 18 may play football, and I think such a rule is wise. The girl may seem to stand the strain all right, but it is probable that she will suffer later in life.

Towards the close of the traditional football season at the beginning of May, that alleged strain was hardly evident. In addition to sides in the West Country, Wales, Scotland, the Midlands and North-East – all playing matches, all of them raising funds for charitable welfare – Dick, Kerr's Ladies was going from strength to strength. It had played 25 fixtures since the start of the year, in front of almost 400,000 spectators.

On 5 May 1921, Frankland's team turned out at Hull City FC's ground to play a match against the local women's team. As ever, the receipts were to go to charity, in this case the city's Children's Hospital. Ten thousand people paid the entrance fee. That same afternoon, just over a hundred miles away at

Manchester United's Old Trafford ground, two men's teams – Leicester City FC and Stockport City FC – played one of the last matches of the Football League season. Just 13 spectators turned out to watch.

That the women's game was so significantly more popular than professional men's football set it on an inevitable collision course with the guardians of the sport. Even were they immune to the voices raised against ladies football in newspapers up and down the country, in the stark differences between attendance figures lay a threat to the very survival of the game they had first tamed, then owned. Nor was it simply professional football which was suffering. Youth games, which were traditionally scoured for future talent by scouts employed by the major clubs, were facing dwindling support. Women's football threatened this source of new blood.

Did Alfred Frankland realise the forces slowly gathering strength and coalescing against Dick, Kerr's? He was, unquestionably, an astute political operator and cannot fail to have seen the voices raised against women's football. Yet there is no sign that he tempered his deliberately professional approach. On 17 May, in its penultimate game of the season, Dick, Kerr's played a one-off fixture against the Paris club *Fémina Sport* in front of a crowd of 15,000 at Stoke City FC's Longton Park ground. After a comfortable victory for his team, Frankland approached one of the French players, Carmen Pomiès, and successfully offered her a job, lodgings and match fees to transfer to Preston. Either English Electric (*née* Dick, Kerr & Co Ltd) was continuing to fund Frankland's ambitious plans or he was finding the money elsewhere.

Whatever the situation, Dick, Kerr's was now cemented in public consciousness as the country's top footballing attraction, with its stars regularly celebrated in the national and sporting press. Just how famous many of the players had become, by the end of the season, can be discerned from the football columns of the *Dundee Evening Telegraph*. Its round-up review of the 1920-21 season, on 24 May, led with a headline and story about Florrie Redford.

SCORING FEAT BY LADY FOOTBALLER

A remarkable scoring feat had been accomplished by Miss Redford, the centre forward of Dick, Kerr's Ladies team. Since New Year's Day she has registered no fewer than ninety-four goals, and is hopeful of reaching the century during the three or four remaining fixtures the team have to fulfil.

In fact, far from having 'three or four fixtures', Alfred Frankland's team calendar for the rest of the year was completely full, with games scheduled against the old rivals in St Helens, a representative Welsh XI, short tours of Scotland and the Isle of Man, as well as a fixture with the most glamorous and well-financed women's team in the country, Lyons' Ladies of London.

And yet the critical voices were becoming louder and more powerful. On Wednesday, 29 June, the *Dundee Evening Telegraph*, a paper which had devoted extensive and generally even-handed coverage to women's football, reported a speech given the previous day in Shropshire.

WOMEN FOOTBALLERS CRITICISED

'Degrading and Making Fools of Themselves'
A vigorous attack on the playing of football by women was delivered at Shrewsbury at the annual meeting of the Royal Salop Infirmary by Brigadier-General Arthur Lloyd.

Lord Berwick, treasurer, had alluded to a sum of £500 raised for the infirmary by a match between two teams of women, St Helens and Chorley, and Brigadier Lloyd said he was not a kill-joy, but he did say for heaven's sake do not let women degrade themselves by playing football, which was not a game for women and which made fools of them.

This was no mere burst of indignation from the outraged middle class of middle England. This was England herself speaking – the voice of the establishment, the country's *soi-disant* natural rulers raised to quell the unseemly behaviour of its subjects. And England, or that part of it which was represented in the comfortable armchairs of the Football Association, took note.

The FA, already alarmed by the threat women's football posed to the gate receipts of its professional men's clubs (and, not coincidentally, the risk of appearing impotent to its members) appears also have become concerned by the financial probity of ladies sides. At some point during the summer months of the closed season it began to consider tightening up the arrangements for matches to be played at the grounds of its professional clubs. On 3 October, the minutes of an FA committee meeting in London contained the following record of proceedings:

Item 36. Ladies' Football Match. Dick, Kerr's v. South of England. Permission for the match to be played on the ground of Bristol City FC upon the condition that the Club [Bristol City] be responsible for the receipts and payments, a Statement of Account to be sent to the Association showing how the whole of the receipts were divided.

A week later the full FA council, meeting in London, issued a new instruction to professional clubs:

> Ladies Football Matches. The Council decided that Clubs must not permit matches between ladies' teams to be played on their grounds unless sanction for such matters is first obtained from the Football Association. It will be a condition of any application granted that the Club on whose grounds the match is played shall be responsible for the receipts and payments and a Statement of Account must be sent to the Association showing how the receipts were applied.[32]

That the FA's concerns about money were grounded in some sort of fact became clear less than a week later. On Saturday, 15 October the *Western Morning News* reported a tawdry argument over gate receipts.

> Mr F. J. Lee last night presided at a meeting of the Camborne, Redruth and District Unemployment Relief Committee, when a much-improved financial position was reported. The reluctance of the Plymouth Ladies' Football Association [sic: no such 'Association' existed – it was, in reality, the Plymouth Ladies Team] to pay over the proceeds of the football match played at Redruth with the Marazion ladies was brought before the committee by the secretary Mr. W. A. Bryant.
>
> Mr. Stanley Wickett stated that the match was arranged 'in aid of local unemployment' and said they expected £25 or £30 [£5,000 to £6,000 today] as a result. The Plymouth Association [sic] had, however, written that they proposed to make a donation to the committee's

funds as an act of grace, and that the amount should be determined by that club alone. The local people at Redruth had a mistaken idea that the whole of the funds should be handed over.

It was only after reading the harrowing distress in the area that they decided at the last minute to allocate a portion of the proceeds to the Relief Committee's fund. The Plymouth ladies team could not allow any dictation from any persons as to what the amount of their donation must be.

It was an untimely and, as far as women's football was concerned, unhelpful incident. It fed into the potent cocktail of dislike and distrust felt by the FA – a hostility which increased when, later that autumn, Plymouth Ladies once again came to the Association's attention. Council minutes duly recorded another infringement of its rulings.

Item 60. Women's Football Match, Plymouth v. Seaton – Winchester City FC censured for having permitted the match to be played on their ground without having first obtained permission. The Club also ordered to pay to a local charity the amount received as their share of the gate receipts.

By the middle of October it was an open secret that the Football Association was gathering itself to take action. The women's cause wasn't helped by a newspaper account of another apparent instance of questionable finances, this time involving a Dick, Kerr game in Scotland. On 13 October, the *Dundee Courier* reported:

GIRLS WITH BALLS

DUNDEE EFFORT FOR THE UNEMPLOYED

In the efforts to raise money on behalf of the Lord Provost's Unemployment Fund it will generally be agreed that economy in administration expenses is a first essential. The 'Courier' learns that a curious result has emerged from a ladies' football match which was recently played at Dens Park [Dundee FC's ground].

The match was advertised on behalf of the Lord Provost's Unemployment Fund, and the teams which took part were Dick, Kerr's Ladies' Football Club, from Preston, and Dundee Ladies Football Club.

Naturally the expenses were fairly heavy so far as the visitors from England were concerned. The payments involved travelling expenses, loss of working time, and maintenance, and there were also certain expenses in connection with the appearance of the Dundee team, but allowing for all that and keeping in view the fact also that the Directors of Dundee FC gave free use of Dens Park, the cost of running the match has been somewhat heavy.

Out of a 'gate' which reached £200, including the sale of tickets, the fund will benefit to the extent of £50. In striking contrast to this effort in raising money is the result obtained by the Freemasons in the city on behalf of the funds of the Royal Infirmary. The Masonic brethren raised a sum of close on £2,000, and the expenditure amounted to only £107 4s 10½d

The usually astute Frankland was playing into the FA's hands. Dick, Kerr's was the most famous women's team in Europe. If it couldn't be trusted financially – and 'expenses' of three time the sum donated to charity unquestionably pointed in that direction – then who could? Five days later, on

222

Tuesday, 18 October, the *Dundee Evening Telegraph* carried the following report:

ARE FEMALE FOOTBALL EXHIBITIONS DOOMED?

English Association Look Upon Them With Disfavour

The women's football match on Bradford City ground tomorrow may be the last of the female football exhibitions, because the pundits of the English Football Association do not approve of it.

'Gates' of 30,000 and 40,000 have been so frequent at the matches in which the Dick, Kerr girls have played that charities of one sort and another must have benefited substantially from their exhibitions.

From that point of view, therefore, there will be some regret if women's football is banned by the English Association, who look upon it with disfavour.

Throughout October and November the FA evidently continued to leak hints that it was planning to take action. Dick, Kerr's meanwhile continued to claim the spotlight. On Wednesday, 23 November, Frankland's team staged what was billed as The Ladies Championship of England, taking on Lyons Ladies of London at Manchester City's Hyde Road ground. Newspapers carried prominent reports of a 13-0 drubbing handed out to Lyons, and the fact that Dick, Kerr's captain, Alice Kell, broke her wrist half way through the game. They also pointedly noted the size of the crowd – 10,000 – and the donation of £340 to the Lord Mayor's Fund for Mézières, a town near Rheims in France whose hospital had been completely destroyed during the war and with which Manchester was twinned.

At the start of December the Football Association announced

it was to hold a special committee meeting. Notices in the regional and national press left little room for doubting its intentions. The *Dover Express* was typical, reporting on Friday, 2 December:

> TO STOP WOMEN'S FOOTBALL MATCHES
>
> The Football Association propose to pass a regulation on Monday prohibiting playing of football by women on football enclosures controlled by the Association, which includes all grounds where affiliated clubs play.

The following day the football correspondent of the *Derby Evening Telegraph* assessed the public mood on the question and concluded:

> Those who disapprove of women football players will be dubbed old-fashioned, or regarded as jealous of the rivalry of the manly figures of the female sex. The women footballers took this sport up during the war to help the military charities and were accepted as something of a novelty.
>
> Fortunately, hitherto they have not entered into a challenge with male players, but no doubt even this will come in time. Although this country has accepted the equality of the sex, I do not think that there will be any unwillingness on the part of the Football Association to prohibit the playing of football on enclosures under the authority of the Association.

The FA council meeting was to take place in London on the evening of Monday, 5 December. With the Association's position so clearly signalled, supporters of women's football tried, largely in vain, to influence the newspaper editorials that morning. Only in Scotland did two papers carry their pleas. The *Dundee Courier* reported:

> There is very keen interest in the proposal which aims at banning the girl footballer from all Football Association grounds. It is said that the supporters of football for women are raising a plea for continuation of indulgence, on the grounds that the movement is just gathering strength, and with a little encouragement will eventually be able to provide separate grounds of its own. But a strong section of the FA utterly disapproves of football for women, and the ban is likely to be put up forthwith.

The *Aberdeen Journal* managed to be simultaneously more sympathetic and apocalyptic.

> Is there likely to be a sex war in the realms of sport? The answer to that question may depend on the result of a meeting of the Football Association. This body is discussing a subject which has a wider interest than merely that of professional football.
>
> The Council is to consider whether it should prohibit women footballers from playing on the grounds of clubs affiliated to the association. It may seem a small point. Far from it. Women footballers – amateur in name, at any rate – are more numerous than is generally realised. They swarm in the north and west of England, and not a few women's clubs are to be found in London, particularly connected with business firms.
>
> Now, these women have concentrated mostly on charity matches and it is estimated that something like £90,000 has been raised through that means.

If the Football Association places the ban upon the women the opportunities for raising as much money again will be lessened. Apart from this, the women players resent the 'stigma' underlying the proposal. Sex equality is claimed in sport as well as in economic and industrial life. A suggestion has been made that if the ban is made a movement will start to form an association for all sportswomen, including those who indulge in tennis, golf, cricket and hockey. Whether that would come about I would not care to say.

Would the Football Association really ban women's matches? Would it set its face against the progress of women's rights and emancipation? Would it, above all, risk killing such a golden goose – exhibitions which had apparently raised the modern equivalent of £18m at a time when a depressed and starving workforce needed this charity more than ever before?

CHAPTER TWELVE

'I consider football quite an inappropriate game for
women, especially if they have not been medically tested first.'
— EUSTACE MILES, PHYSICIAN

On the morning of Tuesday, 6 December 1921, newspapers across the country carried a syndicated report of
the FA Council meeting at its High Holborn headquarters the
previous evening.

The Football Association, at a meeting on Monday,
unanimously passed the following resolution:

'Complaints having been made as to football being
played by women, the Council feel impelled to express
their strong opinion that the game of football is quite
unsuitable for females and ought not to be encouraged.

'Complaints have also been made as to the conditions
under which some of these matches have been arranged
and played, and the appropriation of the receipts to other
than Charitable objects.

'The Council are further of the opinion that an
excessive proportion of the receipts are absorbed in

expenses and an inadequate percentage devoted to Charitable objects. For these reasons the Council requests the clubs belonging to the Association refuse the use of their grounds for such matches.'

In its terse communiqué the FA had delivered a triple-blow. Not merely had it banned its member clubs from allowing their stadia to be used – the delicate word 'request' being no more than a conventional politeness – but it had also given an official stamp of credence to the suggestions that all was not as it should be in the accounting of women's football. It had additionally, and shrewdly, fed the fires of concern about women's 'proper' role in society.

By accident or clever media management – and given the speed with which this happened it is more likely to be the latter – the same day's newspapers, such as this from the *Western Morning News*, were able to report support for the ban from influential medical doctors:

Dr. Mary Scharlieb, the Harley Street physician, briefly replied to a request for her views on the subject: 'I consider it a most unsuitable game, too much for a woman's physical frame.'

Mr Eustace Miles, discussing the subject, said: 'I consider football to be quite an inappropriate game for women, especially if they have not been medically tested first. In America in all the Ladies colleges, girls are not allowed to play games unless they have been medically tested, and the gymnastic instructor is always a qualified medical man. The trouble is that the type of woman who wants to play football will not be medically examined first. The kicking is too jerky a movement for women (just as throwing is in contrast to bowling at cricket), and the strain is likely to be rather severe. Just as the frame of a woman is more rounded than a man's, her movements should be more rounded and less angular.'

The FA was further supported by statements from officials of three of the leading professional men's clubs, reported in the *Hull Daily Mail*:

Mr. Peter William (manager to Tottenham Hotspur FC) – 'I have seen one or two women's matches, and these have left me convinced that the game can only have injurious results on the women.'

Mr. A. W. Turner (17 years secretary of Tottenham Hotspur FC) – 'Violent exercise such as football entails cannot be good for women'

Mr. A. L. Knighton (manager of The Arsenal FC) – 'Anyone acquainted with the nature of the injuries received by men footballers could not help but think – looking at girls playing – that should they get similar knocks and buffetings their future duties as mothers would be seriously impaired.'

And a statement issued by Frank Walt, secretary of Newcastle United FC, hammered home the FA's warnings about financial impropriety:

The game of football is not a woman's game though it was permitted on professional grounds as a novelty arising out of women's participation in war work and as a novelty with charitable motives. The time has come when the novelty has worn off and the charitable motives are being lost sight of, so that the use of the professionals' ground is rightly withdrawn. The women's games have developed into commercial concerns and the expenses they reckon it would cost to play would not have left much for charity.

The papers did carry the response of women players and their supporters, though generally as a final (or close to final) paragraph. The *Hull Daily Mail* was typical:

> In an interview on Tuesday, Miss T. Barkine, who has played for nearly five years for Fleetwood Ladies, Chorley Ladies, and Rochdale Ladies, said she considered the action of the Football Association scandalous, and thought they should study the money raised. She had never been ill since she commenced playing football and always had a good appetite after a match. The ex-servicemen of Leyland, and also of Preston, have sent a telegram of protest to the Football Association.

The *Western Morning News* sought out the views of the region's most celebrated female player.

> When the decision of the council requesting clubs to refuse the use of their grounds was communicated by one of our representatives to Mrs Boultwood, the captain of the Plymouth Ladies Club, she was unmistakeably aggrieved.
> 'The controlling body of the FA,' she declared, with emphasis, 'are a hundred years behind the times, and their action is purely sex prejudice. Not one of our girls have felt any ill-effects from participating in the game: in fact, they have enjoyed better health. Those who are swimmers and play hockey declare without hesitation

that nothing like the fatigue or nearly so dangerous as hockey. Despite the decision of the FA, we in Plymouth are determined to continue to play football, and we shall get our own grounds. If at all possible, we shall engage in weekly matches.'

And what of Dick, Kerr's – the most famous and well-supported women's team in the country, and whose bulging fixture list would be most affected by the FA's ban? Alfred Frankland issued a brief statement of defiance: 'The team will continue to play, if the organisers of charity matches will provide grounds, even if we have to play on ploughed fields.'

Team captain Alice Kell echoed her manager's resolution, and added a firm justification for the way in which its players were rewarded: 'We play for the love of the game and we are determined to carry on. It is impossible for working girls to afford to leave work to play matches all over the country and be the losers. I see no reason why we should not be recompensed for loss of time at work. No one ever receives more than 10 shillings per day.'

But public opinion, at least in so far as that was reflected by newspaper leader writers, was now apparently turning against women's football. Trenchant editorials supporting the FA appeared in several influential dailies, such as this in the *Hull Daily Mail*:

No one wishes to be a mere spoil-sport, but it is an excellent thing that the Football Association has considered the question of women playing football. The FA is really a sort of Venetian oligarchy in the best sense of the word. It is 'a pyramid of Soviets' – again in the best sense of the word; and we make bold to say that its rule and governance of its great game is a pattern and an example to all legislative bodies, Parliament not excepted.

This Council is so wise that its decisions are respected universally, and its prestige so high that disobedience never enters into the minds of its associates and followers. It can bind and loose, make or mar, suppress or exalt, and it controls not only the game, the clubs, the officials, and the players, but the crowd, too – and even the crowd fears it.

This august body has decreed that women's football is undesirable. It is a game 'not fitted for females'. It discourages its clubs offering or selling the use of their grounds. It deplores the fact that in some cases so large a share of the 'gate' receipts have gone in 'expenses'. All this is a pretty big mouthful for women's clubs and the public to be going on with!

We are not in the least enamoured of women's football. There have been one or two exhibitions which have not lacked a passing interest as a novelty, but it is to be feared that some, at least among the crowd, went in order to see the women 'make exhibitions of themselves'. It does not follow that the women did so, but it is far more certain that medical opinion, on the whole, is against the practice. Hockey is as vigorous a game as our girls and women should go in for.

The women's teams certainly have raised large sums for charity, but that is an agreeable fact, and not an argument. A bull fight for the same objects would do just as well – but it would be reprehensible. When news came from Australia the other day that women were starting to play the Rugby game, it was high time the governing bodies of the game gave the matter their attention.

The pronouncement by the Football Association will deal a very serious blow at women's football, although, at first, we may be sure that the better-founded women's clubs will make spirited protest against it.

The *Derby Daily Telegraph* focused its thoughts on the medical backing for the FA's decision:

However arbitrary the ruling of the Football Association may appear to be, we think they are right in their attitude towards the playing of the game by women. Football, they say, is quite unsuitable for females, and ought not to be encouraged, and they request Clubs belonging to the Association to refuse the use of their grounds for such matches. This, of course, does not make it impossible for women to play football, and the probability is that they will form an organisation of their own, but there are several reasons why the game is never likely to be very popular with the fair sex.

On physical grounds alone, football is harmful to women, a point upon which most doctors are in agreement, and the strongest argument in its favour appears to be the large amount of money that has been raised for charity. The great crowds that have paid to see women's matches have been largely influenced by the spirit of novelty, and with a few exceptions the exhibition has not been good enough to justify a second visit. Nor is a woman seen at her best on a football field, where she loses much of her natural charm in actions that are often devoid of grace. The Football Association must expect to be criticised over their latest decision, but on the whole we think the majority of the public will be on their side.

The FA's ban had two immediate outcomes. The first was the cancellation of forthcoming matches which had been scheduled at its member clubs' grounds – and a concomitant loss of funds to charities. In Devon, a game between Plymouth Ladies and Southampton Ladies had been agreed for 28 December, to raise funds for the local Royal Albert Hospital. But, under threat from the FA, the manager of Plymouth Argyle withdrew the club's facilities. 'In all probability,' he told the *Western Morning News*, 'the date allotted to the ladies for their game with Southampton would be given to the Plymouth schoolboys for their next cup match with Midsomer Norton.'

That the replacement fixture would be highly unlikely to raise much, if anything at all, for the hospital was bemoaned by the secretary of Plymouth Ladies, J E Boultwood (husband of the team's captain). Describing the cancellation as 'a crying shame', he pointed out that his club had raised at least £1,000 for charity in the year it had been in existence. Boultwood also drew a pointed comparison with women's football in France, and fired the opening salvo in what would become the second effect of the ban.

'The action of the English Association [Boultwood said] was in striking contrast to the French football authorities, who not only gave every encouragement to women footballers, but rendered them substantial financial aid. In France it was fully realised that football was a healthy recreation for women, and it was amazing to find that English sportsmen hold a different view.

'It is now up to clubs,' he continued, 'to organise their own affairs, to administer themselves, and to search for suitable grounds. This action of the FA may be a blessing

in disguise, as it is calculated to put the ladies' football
clubs on a sounder basis.'

There would be more to come from that link with France – a
nation for whose football officials the FA harboured a deep
distrust[33]. But Boultwood's prediction that at least some of the
150 women's clubs at home would take the laws of football into
their own hands was no mere casting of straws to wind.

At first glance the prospects did not seem promising, as
solidarity from other sportswomen had been noticeable only by
its absence. In the wake of the ban, the women footballers
received little support from other sportswomen. An official of
the Women's Golf Association declined to comment when
asked for her opinion of the FA ban, and when the left-leaning
national *Daily Herald* asked seven-times Wimbledon champion
Dorothea Lambert Chambers to condemn it, she too failed to
defend women's football. Undeterred, the ladies teams decided
to go it alone. On Wednesday, 14 December, less than 10 days
after the FA proclamation, the *Hull Daily Mail* carried the
following report:

An organisation has been set on foot styled the 'English
Ladies Football Association', and the acting secretary, Mr
W. Henley jun. of Grimsby last weekend obtained
national notoriety by his statement concerning a meeting
to be held last Saturday at Liverpool.

Such a meeting, it is understood, was held, but two at
least of the leading girls' clubs of the country – Dick,
Kerr's and Messrs Lyons – were not represented. Mr.
Henley, in an interview, reveals how the girl players
propose dealing with the situation.

Mr. Henley states: 'Since the official ban was declared

we have had letters from ladies' clubs in all parts of the country asking for affiliation with our association, which was formally inaugurated at the meeting in Liverpool last weekend. A league of ladies' clubs is being formed in the Doncaster district, and another in the Coventry area. An East Riding and North Lincolnshire League is in contemplation.

'Representatives of some sixty clubs will meet this weekend to draft rules and to decide upon modifications of the game which are considered desirable. These probably will include the elimination of charging, latitude with regard to hands for protective purposes, a smaller playing area, and a lighter ball. The Football Association condemned certain financial aspects of women's football. We hope to conduct our charity matches as to leave no ground for criticism.'

Mr. Henley, however, does not state how his association are going to overcome the all-important matter of finding suitable grounds for their matches.

The following Saturday, representatives of 57 women's teams – players as well as managers – met in Grimsby to put flesh on the bones of the plan. With a declared aim 'to popularise the game among girls and to assist charity', the meeting resulted in an announcement designed to allay fears about its probity.

The Association is most concerned with the management of the game, and intends to insist that all clubs in the Association are run on a perfectly straightforward manner, so that there will be no exploiting of the teams in the interests of the man or firm who manages them.

This had all the appearance of a sharp dig at Alfred Frankland and his team of semi-professional all-stars. The new guardians of the women's game also proposed to keep a register of players and to ban any woman from playing for a team more than 20 miles from her home without its express and written permission. This, too, struck at the heart of Dick, Kerr's 'poaching' of players from other clubs and could potentially have prevented a player like Alice Woods, still living at home in St Helens, from appearing in the Preston-based side. Frankland, like the teams from Lyons Corner Houses, kept his distance, and in doing so, he – and they – created fundamental cracks within the previously united front of women's football.

In any event, Frankland had his own plans. Although Dick, Kerr's were now barred from their traditional home at Preston North End's Deepdale ground, he had secured the agreement of Rugby League clubs to host the team's matches. And, ever the political operator, he arranged a publicity stunt for the first game following the FA ban.

On Wednesday, 28 December, around 3,000 spectators travelled to Dick, Kerr's company-provided training ground at Ashton Park to watch them play Fleetwood Ladies in aid of the Preston Poor Children's Clog Fund. Among them were 20 doctors and a Methodist minister, specifically invited by Frankland to observe the action and pronounce on the suitability of football for women. After watching Dick, Kerr's win by three goals to one (two for Lily Parr, one for Florrie Redford) the medics' spokeswoman, Dr Mary Lowry, duly gave the sport a clean bill of health: 'From what I saw, football is no more likely to cause injuries to women than a heavy day's washing.' And the minister (sadly unnamed in contemporary reports) pronounced that 'there was nothing to disapprove of in women's football'.

It was a clever and cheeky act, designed to poke the sharp stick of press publicity into the comfortable midriff of the Football Association. In fairness, though, Frankland wasn't the first to try this sort of ploy. Two weeks earlier, on 13 December, Lyons Ladies' FC staged an exhibition match at Sudbury Hill between two teams from the Strand Corner House and the Regent Palace Hotel. Invitations were issued to 30 representatives of the press to attend and 'form an opinion of the desirability of ladies playing this game'. The subsequent reports were not particularly complimentary about the standard of play, but most reported that football was no more strenuous for women than tennis or hockey.

The FA, however, remained unmoved and, as the new year approached, took action to tighten its grip. Frederick J Wall, the Association's secretary, wrote to clubs and the referees' organisation with a firm new edict, designed to further suppress the women's game: 'No official referee should take charge of a game not recognised by us.'

Modern historians have not been kind to either Frederick Wall or to the Football Association. Their campaign to shut down women's football has been perceived as an anachronistic vendetta – a product of a less emancipated era by a resolutely misogynistic organisation. And, in truth, it is hard to deny the charges. But to condemn the FA on these grounds alone is to miss both a genuine problem in football – both male and female – and the first stirrings of a contemporary moral panic.

Although the FA had abandoned its opposition to professionalism a generation before, it had retained a sharp determination that money should not illicitly control football

– and with good reason. The routine system of unlawful payments, which it had uncovered at Manchester City in 1906, had been followed four years later by a succession of match-fixing scandals.

The first, in Middlesbrough in January 1911, had led to an FA commission of enquiry, led by Frederick Wall, which duly banned a club official for offering a £30 bribe to the captain of a rival team to 'throw' an important derby match. The second, which dragged on for two years between 1918 and 1920, led to a former Manchester United star being charged in police courts with conspiracy to defraud. It emerged that he player had been part of a systematic, and then criminal, gambling syndicate which used underhand payments to ensure successful bets for its members. Nor was this a scandal confined to the sports pages. As a direct result of the case, Parliament introduced a new law – The Ready Money Football Betting Act, 1920 – to crack down on the problem. As an editorial in the *Derby Daily Telegraph* (in its issue of Friday, 13 August) made clear, the fact that the Commons and The Lords had to intervene was a sure sign that the FA could not keep its own house in order: 'The Football Association have endeavoured to cope with the evil for years past, but as scandal after scandal was brought to light they realised how helpless they were.'

Financial mismanagement, and frequently fraud, was therefore an open and sensitive sore for the FA. Allegations that money meant for charity was being misappropriated by women's clubs (who were completely outside the Association's control) could not be ignored. The question is: was it? Contemporary newspaper accounts have made clear that there were certainly individual instances of disputes over the amount of money handed over to charities. But these were, even in the heightened sensitivity of the time, both isolated and small-scale. The big money was being generated by the most famous women's side in the country; and the vital question was, what exactly was happening to it?

The extraordinarily high level of expenses incurred in Dick, Kerr's game with Dundee Ladies the previous October – £250 from gross receipts of £300 (the equivalent today of £50,000 and £60,000 respectively) would certainly suggest that something untoward was going on. Barbara Jacobs, in her passionately supportive book, *The Dick, Kerr's Ladies*[34], argues that Frankland deducted between £28 and £38 from the gate receipts of each match to pay for transport, laundry and the 10 shillings per head match fees (as well, apparently, as the cost of 100 Woodbines for Lily Parr). A more disturbing picture emerged from an analysis of the club's 1918 and 1921 accounts. Gail Newsham – Dick, Kerr's Ladies original and highly supportive biographer[35], and therefore not one to cast unwarranted stones – found significant discrepancies in the team's accounts for those years.

In 1918, Alfred Frankland had declared that Dick, Kerr's Ladies had raised and donated to charity £800 10s 5d from its first four games. Yet records also show that the first and fourth games, attended by a total of 16,000 spectators, generated £800 alone; and the second and third fixtures, for which no financial accounting is available, were played in front of a combined crowd of 7,000 people. Could that substantial attendance yield the remaining declared gate receipts of just £4 10s 5d? It seems scarcely credible.

The accounts for 1921 seem even more damning, given the sheer scale of money unaccounted for. Dick, Kerr's played 67 matches in that year, handing over approximately £50,000 to various charities. For 25 of those games, Alice Woods assiduously noted the gate receipts in her diaries: a total of £22,525, accounting for almost half the entire sum raised. This suggests that the remaining 42 matches, unfortunately financially undocumented, yielded only slightly more than the preceding 25. Given the vast numbers of paying spectators in a year that the team drew crowds totalling almost 1m, it is a highly improbable result.

The wording of the FA's communiqué also suggests that there was contemporary concern about the accounting of major sides like Dick, Kerr's: 'Complaints have also been made as to the conditions under which some of these matches have been arranged and played, and the appropriation of the receipts to other than Charitable objects.' And given Alfred Frankland's determination to create a serious women's team, a team which was professional, or at least semi-professional, in all but name, it would hardly be a surprise if he had diverted the profits from some games to fund his protégés.

There is no evidence that Frankland lined his own pocket – indeed, every written account paints him as a largely avuncular figure. But Gail Newsham spoke with several of his players, one of whom, Lydia Ackers, poached from St Helens, recalled an incident (quoted in *In a League of Their Own*) involving another team.

'Well, there won't be many people remember this, but I witnessed it and this is the truth. We were playing a match near Manchester against the West Cheshire's. As we were getting dressed, the man who had brought the West Cheshire team came in and asked how much we got when we played. We told him 10 shillings each match. But he was asking for much more... He must have thought that because there had been a big crowd at the game, he would put in for a big lump sum and get more than he was entitled to, but he didn't get it.'

If this was the stuff of changing room gossip, the FA and its secretary Frederick Wall, already smarting from the match-fixing and betting scandals which dogged the professional men's game, are highly unlikely not to have known about it. Wall was an adept and professional administrator. He served as FA secretary from 1895 to 1934, and Pathé News showed him being presented with a silver trophy, paid for by subscriptions from other football associations and the British press for 'long and valued service to the game'. The Pathé introductory caption pronounced him the 'Prince of Secretaries', and Wall wrote detailed histories of both the Football Association and the demands of safeguarding its role in the sport, including the following:

> We are the guardians of the game, but our zeal as trustees must not over-ride our sense of justice and our responsibility to the public. We must always do our duty without fear or favour and retain the confidence of the public. That is the spirit in which all enquiries and commissions have been conducted and the basis of all findings.[36]

The FA's actions in banning women's football seem to sit uncomfortably with this self-proclaimed mission of duty and justice. If financial irregularities were the problem, logic and the Association's own history would surely have dictated that it carry out a formal investigation before issuing its diktat. But Wall's phrase 'our responsibility to the public' suggests a patrician desire to protect the country. And to the mind of the 1920s male, women's football represented something very real threatening the fabric of the nation – a 'disease' that was, as yet, unnamed.

In the months before the FA passed its ban on women's football, Parliament had debated an amendment to Section 11 of the 1885 Criminal Law Amendment Act. This law, more commonly known as the Labouchère Amendment,[37] made gross indecency between two (or indeed more) men an offence punishable by two years hard labour. The debate in 1921 centred on whether to also proscribe lesbianism an act of gross indecency, with the same punishments as were imposed on homosexual men. The proposal was defeated, with MPs reasoning that the public could not comprehend that such acts existed, and codifying them in law would only serve to increase the incidence of such a moral hazard.

In fact, the public was all too aware of lesbianism, though the word itself would not enter the language until several years later. In the first two decades of the 20th century the writings of two influential sexologists – Richard von Kraft-Ebbing and Havelock Ellis – had drawn widespread attention to what they termed 'Sapphism', and suggested that sexual relationships between women were far from uncommon. For good measure, they pronounced that the behaviour of these 'inverts' was both a form of insanity and frequently 'incurable'. The result was that in the years immediately following the First Wold War, years in which sexuality itself was escaping from the stifling cloak of Victorian hypocrisy and into the public arena, a moral panic emerged.

In the prevailing climate of opinion, women were under a duty to both their husbands and the nation to bear children. Lesbianism, therefore, posed a significant threat to the very fabric of society. This coincided with the advance in women's emancipation as unemployment benefits were extended to include allowances for wives, and a new Law of Property Act, which for the first time allowed women to inherit property on an equal basis with their husbands, was about to enter the statute books. Combined with the arrival of the 'Flapper' era, these developments ensured a fertile soil in which the moral panic could grow.

Flappers, a new breed of young women who wore short skirts, cut short and bobbed their hair (previously an unthinkably barbaric act) and flaunted their disdain for what society considered acceptable behaviour , were perceived as the harbingers of the end of traditional British values. They wore 'excessive' makeup, drank and smoked publicly and enthusiastically, drove motor cars and treated sex as both a right and a pleasure.

In short, they were the visible antithesis of social and sexual norms. And, it was an article of faith for society (or at least that part of it still clinging to the moral certainties of the Victorian and Edwardian eras) that where there were flappers so there would be 'inverts' with 'Sapphic' desires and practices. After all, both shared (or were perceived to share) the same styles of mannish dress and coiffeur.

Women's football teams would have slotted neatly into this perception of moral confusion. Here were girls, the future mothers of the nation, cutting their hair short and parading themselves in manly attire on football pitches, the very temples of masculinity. But there was an additional reason for them to be feared. It being common knowledge that some players were 'inverts', the thinking went that women's football must be a breeding ground for these perceived dangerous and immoral tendencies. This absurd stereotype of the 'dyke' footballer would plague the women's game for decades to come.

It could not have helped that the most celebrated woman footballer, Lily Parr, was openly lesbian. Parr, never one to shrink from a fight or pay any great heed to prevailing norms, was the darling of the press and a regular feature in the Pathé newsreels playing at Kinemas up and down the land. By the end of 1921 she had lost her job at English Electric (Dick, Kerr's) and begun work at the local Whittingham Hospital and Lunatic Asylum, a charitable institution for which Dick, Kerr's Ladies had raised considerable funds, and which, as a mark of gratitude, provided jobs and accommodation to women from the team who had been made redundant. In her first few days at the hospital Lily met a woman employee called Mary and the two fell in love and became life-long partners.

Parr and Mary refused to hide their relationship and their sexuality was common knowledge among friends and teammates. In fact, they were so forthright they bought a house together (Parr was the only woman on the team to own her own house) and set up home as what would now be termed an 'out' lesbian couple[38]. Did the Football Association know? Had word of this 'unnatural behaviour' reached the be-whiskered ears of Frederick Wall, the embodiment of probity and the zealous guardian of the game's morals? No documents survive concerning this, but it was certainly no secret within the women's game, and would equally certainly have been cause for significant concern to the FA's secretary and council members. Whether this moral panic played a part in the decision to stamp out women's football is sadly lost from history, but in 1922, the FA's determination to suppress it was now out in the open.

CHAPTER THIRTEEN

*'And why shouldn't girls play football anyway?
We're going to show everyone that the girls at
Blake Mills can run a football team.'*
– MEG FOSTER: FOOTBALLER, FOOTBALL AND
SPORT LIBRARY, 1921

In January 1922, with the fixture list for Dick, Kerr's now in jeopardy, Alfred Frankland gave an interview to *Sports Picture* magazine in which he emphatically refuted the FA's allegations of financial impropriety – at least as far as his team was concerned.

> We have always made a special point – in fact it is a resolution of our club committee – that we must never apply for a ground for a charity match. Those responsible for the charity must make all the arrangements themselves and accept all responsibility for payments made in connection with the match. All we have received wherever we played has been just our expenses, and in no way include any pecuniary recompense for playing.
>
> Never has any of our players received any payment which could be regarded as a match fee. The biggest sum any girl has ever received is 10 shillings a day to

compensate her for loss of work. No official of the club has ever received a penny-piece in the shape of honorarium, so that there can be no suggestion on any grounds whatsoever, that anyone associated with club has ever made anything out of it.

Our sole ambition has been to help as much as we possibly could the numerous charities on whose behalf we have been asked to play. We have all given our services gladly and the girls have revelled in the football.

But who were they to play – and where? The FA's draconian action had already ensured that the pitches usually available to women's teams had closed their turnstiles. For clubs like Dick, Kerr's – embedded within strong Rugby League communities – it would be possible to hire alternatives. But apart from Lyons Ladies, for teams in the south there was little such scope. Inexorably, the official noose began choking the women's game to death, as the FA must have hoped.

The journalist writing as Football Girl summed up the problem in her latest column: 'As far as I can see there are two alternatives. The first is that inter-club matches be abandoned altogether, each club having two teams of its own and playing privately: the other is that matches be arranged to take place between neighbouring clubs on the practice ground of one of the clubs.'

Of the two options, the latter was more likely to ensure competitive matches; it was also close to the game-plan of the English Ladies Football Association (ELFA). On Saturday, 7 January, its committee met in Manchester to finalise the rules and structure of its version of women's football. These included uncontroversial decisions about the use of a lighter ball and discretion being given to referees on handling and charging.

The committee also expressed the opinion that the management committee of each club should consist of at least three married ladies.

But other pronouncements from that meeting were to prove much more divisive. Firstly, ELFA carved up the country into five geographical regions, each with the power to arrange fixtures under the supervision of a district committee, and the champions of each section would play off in a cup competition. Next, there was to be far stricter regulation of who could play. Clubs would have to sign on and register their players, all of whom had to be strictly amateurs, with the Association.

Worse still, at least from Alfred Frankland's point of view, member clubs would be forbidden to play against non-affiliated teams, and it was confirmed that no player would be allowed to play for a side further than 15 miles from her home town (at least without the permission of the Association). The following Monday, the *Midland Daily Telegraph* shrewdly identified this as a threat to the women's game's biggest stars: 'This will mean the general breaking-up of the famous Dick, Kerr's team, as the players are drawn from all parts of the country.'

The newly-elected president of ELFA, Len Bridgett, a former Northern Counties athletics champion turned Stoke-on-Trent fishmonger, also wrote to the Football Association and requested that it lift the ban on the use of professional clubs' grounds. But by the time of ELFA's next committee meeting on 4 February – at which the fixtures for its inaugural English Ladies' Challenge Cup would be discussed – the FA had replied only that 'the matter was under consideration'. If indeed Frederick Wall and his fellow worthies were having second thoughts, there remain no minutes of any FA committee or council meeting which reflect this. At its High Holborn offices, 'under consideration' evidently meant being ignored.

GIRLS WITH BALLS

Two weeks later, Bridgett was able to report back to his committee that ELFA had secured the agreement of rugby's Northern Union (as rugby league was then known) to stage matches at the grounds of its affiliated clubs. And in the august surroundings of the Queen's Hotel in Birmingham, the first round draw for the women's cup competition was announced. Disappointingly, just 23 of the 58 teams who had signed up to ELFA had put their names into the competition hat, leaving one club with a bye to the next round. It was hardly an auspicious start.

There were two other notable features of this first round draw. All 11 matches, to be completed by mid-March, were between sides geographically close to one another. This may have been done to minimise the cost and difficulties of travel, but it also may have led to the stark absence of Dick, Kerr's Ladies. Alfred Frankland had evidently looked at ELFA and however much he might have been impressed by its ambition, he plainly wanted no part of its bureaucracy. His team of mill and factory girls were, to all intents and purposes, at least semi-professional, and their burgeoning fixture list was an established money earner. That this money went to charity rather than into Frankland's pockets is to miss the point. The currency he sought was local influence and power – and Dick, Kerr's fundraising efforts guaranteed both.

By the time the clubs associated with ELFA were playing their local first round cup matches, Dick, Kerr's Ladies were once again on international duty. On Wednesday, 22 March they were in Cardiff to play the first of four matches against *Olympique de Paris*. Fifteen thousand spectators paid to watch, raising £655 (equivalent to £131,000 today) for charity. Over the next eight days the sides would face each other again at

Ashton Park, Preston, Stanley Athletic Grounds, Liverpool and Hyde in Manchester.

But the matches showed ominous signs of public fatigue. No record exists of the final crowd, but the second and third fixtures drew a total of just 4,000 paying spectators. Nor was there any sign of the previously ever-present Pathé Newsreel cameras. Did Frankland realise that a new PR gimmick would be needed? Certainly, what would ensue in the autumn of 1922 had all the elements to ensure worldwide publicity, and it is highly improbable that a manager as astute as he would not have predicted at least some of the drama which was about to unfold.

Meanwhile, away from Preston, the ELFA Cup staggered on. Second round matches were scheduled to take place before 22 April, but at least one – the game between Mersey Amazons and Rochdale – was cancelled at the last minute, with the organisers facing a £20 (the equivalent of £4,000 today) loss. No explanation was offered for the cancellation, though it appears that the owners of the ground on which the fixture was due to take place – an amateur football club – may have been warned against allowing it by the FA.

By the time of the third round draw on 22 April, newspapers reported that only three teams remained in the competition. Bizarrely, this number was increased to four by the time the semi-final fixtures were announced. The final, in theory the pinnacle of women's football, was supposed to take place in Bradford, but opposition from the Rugby Union (in sharp contrast to the support from rugby league) made it impossible to secure the use of a suitably large ground. The Yorkshire branch of the Rugby Football Union (RFU) had previously rejected an application to stage a women's football match the local Lidget Green stadium, on the grounds that football was

251

'not suitable for women' and that when they tried to play it 'they made a ridiculous exhibition of themselves'.

One rugby worthy, the Rev Huggard of Barnsley pronounced that 'they respected, and loved their women, and therefore ought not to encourage them to do anything derogatory to their position, or anything that would be unseemly'. As a result, the ELFA Ladies Cup Final had to relocate to Cobridge, in the Midlands. It eventually took place on 24 June, in front of a meagre crowd of 2,000. Len Bridgett's Stoke Ladies beat Doncaster, thus ensuring that Bridget, as president of ELFA, effectively presented the Cup to himself.

If this was hardly the stuff of footballing dreams, by 1922 a succession of female sporting role models had emerged. All were young working class women, determined, often against impossible odds, to play football and to play as well, if not better than men. Meg Foster was the first. Girls across the country were treated to accounts of her pluck and skill, delivered in regular instalments by the newly emerged illustrated sports weeklies.

Meg Foster stood on the platform in the recreation room of Blake's Mills. She was a very pretty girl of eighteen – fairly tall and well-made. And just at present her cheeks were flushed, and her eyes sparkling – she was heart and soul in her subject.

Since the visit of the French team of lady footballers to Preston, the idea of playing football herself had taken a very firm hold in Meg's mind. And now, it seemed, was her great chance. For the first Girl's Football League had been formed. Some twenty clubs all over Lancashire had been got together. For the first time in Great Britain, football for girls was about to come into its own, and it was Meg's great idea that Blake's should form one of the League.

'Oh, I know we've got plenty o' difficulties to overcome, but we'll manage 'em all reet. So long as I can keep the team together, I don't care a snap o' t' finger. We're going to show everyone that the girls at Blake Mills can run a football team – ay, and run it successfully. Time season is over we'll be top o' t' League!^{39}

There was, of course, something about Meg. She was a work of fiction. The exploits of Meg Foster were chronicled in what we would now recognise as the forerunners of boy's football comics. And she wasn't the only female footballer to have her own pulp fiction: other comics featured Bess O' Blacktown, Nell o' Newcastle and even Ray (short for Rachel) of the Rovers – thus pre-dating the rather more celebrated Roy of The Rovers by three decades.^{40} Each of these follows essentially the same stock plot lines: honest, hard-working mill girl leads plucky team of fellow women footballers, but is forced to overcome male prejudice as well as thwart the wicked (and often criminal) scheming of their dastardly mill-owning employer.

But the importance of these larger than life characters goes well beyond the pages of the 'penny dreadfuls' in which they featured. Their existence, and their clear commercial popularity, speaks to some innate acceptance or desire amongst the target audience. At a time when football's guardians were successfully clamping down on the staging of women's games – and the first attempt at a serious competitive competition was evidently floundering – here was evidence that girls still dreamed of playing soccer, and that in those dreams lay profit.

In Preston, Alfred Frankland was finalising plans for what would be the most ambitious and innovative event in international football – male or female. He was going to take his squad of women away for a two-month tour on the other side of the Atlantic. Dick, Kerr's Ladies was to play a succession of matches in Canada and the United States.

Quite how Frankland came up with the idea, or how he met the two men he entrusted to organise it, has never been explained. Whilst several of his players appear to have had relatives (of varying degrees of distance) in North America, none has left any record which indicates that families played a part in the decision. Nor was football a dominant sport in either Canada or America. The former did have a functioning hierarchy, headed by the Dominion Football Association, but in the United States, soccer had not been successfully imprinted on the national psyche, unlike rugby which had been transformed into American football, and cricket, which had become (via rounders) baseball. Association football remained the preserve of rich college elites on the one hand, and impoverished immigrant communities at the lower end of the social scale.

It is, though, possible that Frankland knew of the two men who promised to make the tour a sporting and financial success. The first was an expatriate clothing salesman from the New York borough of Brooklyn. Abe Zelickman's family were hard-working Jewish tailors who, in the late 19th century, had fled anti-Semitic pogroms in their native Russia and settled in England. Abe was brought up in Sheffield, where he had developed a keen interest in football. When he packed up his bags and headed for the new promised land of New York, he brought with him the game he loved and began organising teams among Brooklyn's Russian émigré population. His day job also took him to Europe and Britain, where he sold

American finery into the drab and depressed post-war clothing markets. Whether this brought him in contact with Alfred Frankland remains unknown, but by September 1922 he was arranging fixtures for Dick, Kerr's Ladies across Canada and the north-east seaboard of the United States.

The second member of the organising committee had at least some experience of women's football matches overseas, albeit the relatively short distance between Newcastle and Belfast. David Brooks (who we met earlier in Chapter Eight) had been team manager of the squad of English munitionettes who played exhibition matches against Ireland in 1917. His chief contribution, history records, was getting startlingly drunk on a ferry and regaling fellow passengers with the popular ditty 'Waiter, waiter, bring me some paper to wipe me bumbelator', from behind the locked door of a toilet. This was the man Frankland put in joint charge of the North American adventure.

It was perhaps not surprising that the fixture list the pair drew up was eccentric in the extreme. Having secured from each of their proposed opponents agreement to pay a minimum of $1,000 to host a match, the schedule was both physically and geographically demanding. The tour was to start in Quebec, then move on to New Jersey, New York, Washington, Philadelphia, Detroit, before travelling to Akron (in the mid-western state of Ohio), St Louis, Missouri, Chicago and Pittsburgh. From here it would cross back over the border into Canada for a whistle-stop succession of games in Edmonton, Toronto, Ottawa and Montreal. It was, quite simply, madness.

Nonetheless, in mid-September, Dick, Kerr's Ladies, accompanied by Messrs Zelickman and Brooks, along with Alfred Frankland and his newly appointed aide-de-camp,

Herbert Stanley (soon to be husband of star player Alice Woods) travelled to Liverpool and boarded *RMS Montclare* – the pride of the Canadian Pacific Steamship Company – for her maiden commercial voyage. The crossing would take 10 days, with a scheduled landing in Quebec on Friday, 22 September. If nothing else, Frankland's unique tour had caught the attention of the press. Contemporary newspapers contained photos of the team on the deck of the *Montclare* along with suitably excited headlines and captions.

SOCCER GIRLS OFF TO CANADA

Fresh fields to conquer! Dick, Kerr's famous team of lady footballers have been looking out for new places to show their skill, and decided on Canada. Here they are, just about to leave Old England.

Pathé News, too, had returned and cinemagoers across Britain were treated to a one-minute film, shot on board the ship. After an opening caption proclaiming 'Good Luck – Girls!' the newsreel captured the women group-skipping and kicking a ball about on the main passenger deck, before waving their goodbyes with fluttering white handkerchiefs.

The crossing was to prove suitably eventful. On the first day, the women, flanked by Frankland and Herbert Stanley, stood in silent tribute as the ship passed the point where the passenger liner *Lusitania* had been sunk by a German boat seven years earlier. Twenty-four hours later, storms battered the *Montclare* confining all but Lily Parr to their cabins for two days. And then David Brooks was to ensure that financial scandal was once again linked with women's football.

Both of Dick, Kerr's biographers, Barbara Jacobs and Gail Newsham, recount the same story, but Newsham sources it

directly from the transcript of a tape recording made by
Herbert Stanley several decades later. He had a particularly
clear memory of Brooks and his antics:

> He was a very fit, fine upstanding figure of a man; good
> looking, curly hair and I was apportioned the same cabin
> as him when we got on board ship. There were only two
> classes, Cabin and what was known as Second Class. We
> travelled Cabin... [Brooks] was, I afterwards learned, a
> man who had left his wife and family and cleared the
> country without saying a word. He had been doing all the
> negotiating for the tour in secret, and this was his
> getaway... His one ambition in life, I soon learned, was to
> make love to women: any woman, provided he could gain
> his own ends.
>
> David, I learned, was broke. Now, in those days, before
> you could land in Canada you had to have in your
> possession at least £25 in English money. I knew David
> had nothing but he said 'Don't worry'. He was happy and
> carefree; he didn't mind. He would make out.
>
> He asked me how much money I had... and, by his
> charming manner, he borrowed £2 from me. I didn't see
> much of him for the next two or three days except at meal
> times, but I knew he was making love to an elderly
> woman: a very rich woman, and the way he was carrying
> on anyone would have thought they were teenagers.
>
> One day, soon after breakfast, David came to me and
> said, 'When I beckon you on deck, come to me and stand
> between the cabin and where I am stood. I'll tell you my
> reasons for it afterwards.' Sure enough, he had his lady-
> love engaged in the usual loveable dialogue leaning over
> the ship's rail. Presently he pulled out his wallet,

extracting one of the photographs of the team and said he would get all the players to autograph the picture for her.

He called me over and I stood where he had told me to stand, and he said 'Will you get this photograph signed by the rest of the party?' I said I would. He half turned, and with a deft flick of his right wrist, he flicked the wallet into the sea with a cry, 'My wallet !' I was the only one who had seen this action. He attracted the attention of some of the crew and a number of passengers and we all watched the wallet as it was swallowed up in the waves.

Then came the most pathetic story you have ever heard: about him being destitute, his world of wealth was in that wallet, how would he pass the authorities on the other side? The Purser organised a collection amongst the passengers and when David was asked how much he had in the wallet [he] said it was just over £50. The collection raised about £45, and during the dance on deck that night the money that had been collected was presented to David. With grateful thanks and with something of an apologetic manner, he said the remainder of the money did not matter. In the cabin that night he returned me my £2. The whole of his scheme had been really well organised.

To a modern ear, the sums involved don't sound particularly significant. But given the steep inflation in the intervening 90 years, Brooks had apparently conned his fellow passengers of £9,000. It was precisely this sort of financial chicanery – fraud – which clung to the cash-dispenser of women's football, and which the FA claimed as justification for its actions.

In view of the speed (or rather, slowness) of communications in 1922, it is highly unlikely that Brooks' shipboard antics would have reached the London offices of the game's doggedly upright guardians. But by the time the *Montclare* docked in Canada the Football Association would have already taken action to torpedo Dick, Kerr's North American tour. On the morning of Saturday, 23 September, the *Washington Post* carried the following report:

> Quebec, September 22nd: The Dick, Kerr's team of English women soccer football players arrived today on the steamship Montclare en route to the United States where they will play a series of games. The girls will not be allowed to play Canadian soccer teams under order from the Dominion Football Association which objects to women football players. The team's first game will be at Patterson, N.J., on September 24th.

With this dry announcement, half of Dick, Kerr's tour had been cancelled. What had changed in the 10 days between leaving Liverpool and arriving at Quebec? The answer was the annual general meeting of the Dominion of Canada Football Association. Its all-male committee had assembled in Winnipeg to debate the forthcoming coming arrival of the Dick, Kerr's Ladies. The result was a motion, put to the vote and carried: 'We do not approve of the proposal of Ladies Football'.

It would be tempting to read into this abrupt volte-face the hidden hand of the FA: certainly the minutes of the meeting reflect the same bias against the women's game as shown in England. But they do not record any communication from London and it could simply be that Canada suffered from the same misogyny as the mother nation. And there was worse to come.

Within hours of the Dominion Football Association blow,

Abe Zelickman confessed to Alfred Frankland that the American leg of the tour had one small glitch: all the teams that Dick, Kerr's would face were men's sides. There were not, he insisted, enough women's teams either to provide fixtures or (perhaps as importantly) able to stump up the required $1,000. With the schedule already in tatters, Frankland and his charges reluctantly agreed.

They arrived in Clifton, New Jersey, on the morning of Sunday, 23 September. The 550-mile journey had taken more than 24 hours, night and day on rattling steam trains. Within three hours of checking into their hotel – a cheap boarding house in the rough textile district – they ran out on to the field at Olympic Park. Five thousand spectators had turned up to watch their local (male) side, Patterson Silk Sox take on what press notices and billboards proclaimed to be 'Newcastle United Ladies Team from Preston, Lincolnshire'. It seemed that the combined PR efforts of Zelickman and Brooks were as reliable as their tour scheduling had been.

Perhaps, given the effects of overnight travel so soon after a lengthy sea crossing, Dick, Kerr's lost by 3 goals to 6. But not, according to a report in the local press the day after, before Dick, Kerr's had proved they were up for, and to, the physical challenge of playing against men.

> There were few falls, McGuire, the noted one-armed forward from Brooklyn, being the first to measure his length on the green-sward. For this Annie [sic – it would have been Alice] Woods, the sturdy centre halfback, was responsible, and seemed just a little proud of it.

From New Jersey the tour travelled on to Rhode Island for three games in five days. Press reporting reflected the less stuffy approach of American newspapers to sportswomen (pictures of whom in their various disciplines were routinely splashed on the back pages). The *Pawtuckett Times* reported:

> Jauntily togged out in light athletic suits familiar to the followers of soccer football, the women, bobbed hair held in restraint by caps, trotting out on to the field before 4 o' clock to the tooting of horns and wild acclaim of the crowd... The outstanding figure among the English girls was Lillie [sic] Parr at outside left. Her driving from the wing and the accuracy of her shots left little to be desired.

It was a similar story three days later when the *Pawtuckett Times* told its readers:

> The contest [against J P Coats] was one of the biggest attractions ever staged on Coats Field. When the girls team ran out... a battery of cameras were trained on the black and white figures. Every fan stretched his neck to get his first glimpse of the team that has conquered the best in Europe and is over here to garner further laurels. The girls were real business-like and did no more posing than was required by the persistent photographers.

Despite the attentions of America's proto-paparazzi, it was the quality of Dick, Kerr's football which was most widely, and favourably, reported. After their match with the Washington Stars on 4 October, the august and respected *Washington Post* noted:

> The fair kickers of the Dick, Kerr's women's soccer club of Preston, England, lived up to their reputation yesterday at American League Park when they battled the Washington

soccer eleven to a 4 to 4 draw. The women showed a fairly good dribbling game, but their kicking lacked both speed and force. The Washington kickers were extended most of the way.

Although the men players, through good team work were given many opportunities they were not successful in registering goals, due to the brilliant defence of Miss Carmen Pomiès, the Preston goalkeeper. She checked eleven of the fifteen attempts made by the local booters. Miss Lilly Parr, at outside left, put up an aggressive game registering two goals in seven tries she had at the net. The girls were able to penetrate the Washington right wing with success, but were checked several times on attempts at the left wing and midfield. The District kickers counted first, Green placing one past Miss Pomiès after 26 minutes of play. Miss Parr evened it up shortly before half time. The second half was rather loosely played by both clubs, but the women showed to better advantage with teamwork.

By the time they left New York on 9 November for the journey home on board the *SS Adriatic*, Dick, Kerr's Ladies had travelled 15,000 miles, played nine matches against men's teams (won 4, drawn 2, lost 3) in front of an estimated 75,000 spectators. They arrived back in Liverpool on Friday, 17 November, carrying with them a football signed by US President Warren Harding.

Exactly two weeks later the management of English Electric Ltd welcomed its international stars home with a social evening and dance in the works canteen. Amid toasts to the health and continuing success of the most successful women's football side in the world, a local dignitary and former mayor of the neighbouring mill town of Burnley, roundly criticised the Football Association and hoped it would soon 'see the error of its ways' by rescinding its ban.

But the music and the dancing that night were to be the swansong for women's football – the last rites for an epoch which had enabled women to claim their right to be treated as equals on the pitch. Women's football was dying on its feet – killed by a lethal combination of its own mismanagement and the FA's diktat. It would be more than half a century before the sport could once again be celebrated.

CHAPTER FOURTEEN

'The law would be an ass and an idiot if it tried to make
girls into boys so that they could join in all-boys' games.'
— LORD DENNING, COURT OF APPEAL, 1978

The years from 1923 onwards were not kind to women's football. Teams which had once been strong and well-supported gradually shut down. Lyons Ladies would disappear long before their eponymous company with its iconic Nippy. Huddersfield Atalanta is slowly erased from the pages of history. There would be no second season for the English Football Ladies Association Cup. The Pandora's Box of female soccer had been closed and the FA had securely fastened the locks.

Women did still play football, but the best years were over. ELFA had been turned into a limited company in October 1922; but if it traded at all – which is to say, if it ever arranged women's matches – no accounts were ever filed and on 22 December 1931 the company was dissolved by order of the Registrar of Companies and struck off the lists of active businesses.

In part, of course, the demise of ladies football teams was the gradual decline in requests for their services. As 1923 dawned, the Great War had been over for four years and if the plight of injured ex-servicemen, military widows and orphans (in addition to the needs of the unemployed) lingered on, they had to an extent drifted from the front of the public mind. The 1926 General Strike did cause a brief re-kindling of the flame, with soup-kitchen soccer, as women's games played for the benefit of strikers and their families were termed, but it was little more than the last kicks of a dying horse.

In Preston, Dick, Kerr's was one of the last stubborn outposts of the women's game. But here, too, the FA's choke-hold was having an effect. In 1923, Frankland's team managed to play just three matches – a far cry from the heydays of two games a week. This extract from a surviving souvenir programme for one of those, a fixture against Len Bridgett's Stoke Ladies, on Saturday, 22 September, captures some of the team's lingering defiance:

> No sane person dreams that football matches are played between women and men. Woman meets woman, and if the fair sex desire to play this game, and continue to play it, they will do so, and nobody can stop them.
>
> Our complexions disprove that football is bad for us. Our complexions are our own. We have no need for powder puffs or toilet cream, and we don't keep late hours.

The following year, Dick, Kerr's do not appear to have played at all, and the only fixtures in 1925 were six matches against *Fémina*, the Paris-based team they had first met (in its guise as a French XI) five years earlier. But in France, too, the women's game was beset with problems: prejudice to be sure, but also repeated violence both on and off the field, and here the best years for the game were drawing to a close.

At some point during 1926, Alfred Frankland parted

company with English Electric Ltd (Dick, Kerr). No completely convincing reason has been offered, but Gail Newsham, the team's most sympathetic and earliest biographer, suggests that once again the old problem of financial misbehaviour may have been responsible. She quotes several of the team's players – Alice Norris, Lydia Ackers and Elsie Yates – reporting that it could be uncomfortably difficult to prise from Frankland the expenses he owed them. And, shortly after leaving his former employers, Frankland found the money to purchase a greengrocery business in Preston. According to Alice Norris, quoted in Newsham's book, *In a League of Their Own*: 'No one could ever prove anything but I think there was something in the rumours. The older players used to say that when he first came down here he didn't have two halfpennies to rub together. There was all that talk going around.'

When Frankland left English Electric, Dick, Kerr's Ladies lost the use of the company's recreation ground. They also lost their name, being re-christened Preston Ladies. Many of the players (though not Alice Kell, who valued her job at the company too much to cross its management by being seen to side with Frankland) played on. Lily Parr, in particular, would be a fixture in the team until 1951. But competitive matches were few and far between, and press reports all but non-existent. From their status as international celebrities – the David Beckhams of their day – Parr and her team-mates had fallen off football's radar. Preston Ladies, then a depleted and forlorn shadow of its once imperious side, finally folded in 1965.

And what of the Football Association? It would take 48 years for the first hints of remorse over its actions to emerge. FA records show that on 1 December 1969, the Association's council considered repealing its ban:

GIRLS WITH BALLS

Ladies Football – recommendation to delete decision of council in 1921... and that ladies' football no longer be considered to be classed as unaffiliated football, and that any ladies' team which wished to affiliate to county Association might be permitted to make such an application.

But the records also show the FA's decision on this recommendation: 'Deferred'. The ban stayed in force. Six years later, the Sex Discrimination Act 1975 came into force, making it illegal to treat men and women differently (or at least to treat one less favourably than the other). But Section 44 of the Act contained a little-noticed clause:

Nothing... shall, in relation to any sport, game or other activity of a competitive nature where the physical strength, stamina or physique of the average woman puts her at a disadvantage to the average man, render unlawful any act related to the participation of a person as a competitor in events involving that activity which are confined to competitors of one sex.

Behind this tortured prose lay a rich seam of potential litigation. Who, or what, was 'the average woman'? Likewise, 'the average man'? And what might be the definition of 'competitive'? However arcane these questions might appear, British (and subsequently, European) courts would devote considerable time and no little legal expense to debating them.

But for women's football, the most important case to reach the courts centred on a highly talented 12-year-old girl called Theresa Bennett. In 1975, she was picked, on merit, to play for her local boys' football team. FA rules forbade girls to play football in boys' teams, and the unfortunate Ms Bennett was prevented from taking the field. Three years and several court challenges later (Bennett's parents sued the FA and won in the County Court – a decision the FA appealed) the case came before Lord Denning, then Master of The Rolls and the most celebrated judicial mind of the 20th century. In the gloomy gothic sub-fusc of the Royal Courts of Justice, Denning listened to days of legal argument before bestowing upon the world his great wisdom.

> Women have many other qualities superior to those of men, but they have not got the strength or stamina to run, to kick or tackle and so forth. The law would be an ass and an idiot if it tried to make girls into boys so that they could join in all-boys' games.

These judicial *bon-mots* delivered, he upheld the FA's appeal and Ms Bennett (along with any other female footballer) lost once again her right to play football with the boys. It would take another 13 years for the FA to allow mixed football (and then only for children of 11 or under) and until 1992 for it to abandon its hostility to the women's game and bring it, finally, under its formal control.

A year earlier, FIFA had launched the very first women's world cup: twelve teams qualified for the final stages, held in southern China, five of them from Europe. England was conspicuous by its absence – as were Scotland, Wales and Ireland. Each of the 26 matches attracted almost 20,000 spectators – a reminder of just how popular the women's game once was, and could be again.

Over the ensuing 20 years England – the pioneer of women's football – got through to three of the five World Cup Finals, but failed to come home with any silverware. In 2011, the

English team were beaten in the quarter finals, on penalties, by France. It was a far cry from the triumphant days of Dick, Kerr's victories in Paris.

What had the FA been doing in the years since it belatedly accepted that women could, should and did play football ? In truth, relatively little. Under its auspices, a Premier League of women's clubs had been formed in 1992, but the sport attracted little interest and almost no television coverage.

It was not until 2011 – when women's football had become established globally and international tournaments had been proven to attract sponsorship and broadcasters as well as large crowds - that the FA finally heeded Sepp Blatter's prophecy that the future will be feminine. In some style and with no little publicity it launched a Women's Super League – a championship, played in summer, contested by eight semi-professional sides.

Few of the original stars lived to see justice, so long denied, at last delivered. Lily Parr, perhaps the greatest woman footballer ever to set foot on a pitch and the player who would most have welcomed the FA's volte-face, died in 1978, a victim of lung cancer caused by her inexhaustible appetite for cigarettes. She, and the women she played with, were pioneers in a misogynistic, narrow-minded sport, and the forebears to whom today's increasingly famous female footballers owe an immense debt.

They were working class mill and factory workers who dared to take on the weight of a prejudiced male establishment in – and indeed beyond – an era when women of all classes were fighting for freedom. They were, in the most important sense, sporting giants, as brave in real life as the comic book soccer heroines were in print.

They were truly Girls With Balls. And this was their story.

POSTSCRIPT

In February1995, William David Charles Carling managed the relatively rare feat of putting English sport on the front page of every newspaper in the country (and several more internationally). The handsome Carling was the celebrated captain of England's Rugby Union team, and a friend of Princess Diana to boot. English rugby was then in its final season of official amateurism, with the professional era waiting to begin six months later.

What propelled Carling and the game of rugby into splash headlines, innumerable editorials and hours of broadcast hand-wringing, was a TV documentary broadcast on Channel 4. The film, fronted by Greg Dyke, who would later go on to be Director-General of the BBC, followed the English team in its preparations for the annual Five Nations (now Six Nations) Championship. It focused an unforgiving eye on the vast wealth being accumulated by the Rugby Football Union – a fortune built on the toil, sweat and (frequently) blood of players who were not paid a penny for their efforts. Will Carling was, from the outset, a key and a keen participant. I was the producer.

Carling's main interview in the film included his less than flattering view of the RFU as '57 old farts'. It was a phrase which would instantly become part of the sporting lexicon. It was also a phrase which, when the film (including this description of official flatulence) was broadcast, would cause an almighty row. Twenty-four hours later, Carling, who had led England to the Five Nations Grand Slam (all games won) in 1991 and 1992, was sacked both as the captain and as a player. RFU president Dennis Easby declared that it was 'inappropriate' for him to continue.

Dudley Wood, the Union's General Secretary, who had happily been filmed accepting an oversized cheque for the documentary, whilst maintaining that players simply couldn't be trusted with money, said: 'It is a very sad day for English rugby. It was strongly felt by the committee that his position as captain was untenable. His attack on the committee who had appointed him gave them no alternative but to dismiss him.'

It took 48 hours of frantic negotiation (during which several press photographers turned up to stake out my somewhat remote home on the edge of the Yorkshire Dales) before the RFU blinked, backed down and re-instated Carling to the team and to the captaincy. He led England to another Grand Slam a few weeks later, by which time the RFU was busy trying to sabotage the advent of professionalism.

There is an all-too-obvious parallel between the absurd behaviour of the Rugby Football Union in 1995 and the vengeful determination of the Football Association to eliminate women's football from 1921 onwards. Both decisions were taken by men out of touch with the sport they professed to love; both were self-appointing (and self-aggrandising) oligarchies who claimed for themselves the right to determine just who could play the game they governed. And both the RFU and the FA, in their turns, hindered the progress of their respective codes.

Just as English rugby took years to catch up with southern hemisphere nations, which had adopted professionalism in all but name some years before, so the Football Association squeezed the life out of a game England invented. Women's football, yes, for the FA certainly smothered that shortly after its birth, but men's football, too. The history of English soccer (the 1966 World Cup notwithstanding) is a sad, slow decline while other, less hidebound countries take it on apace.

The same reactionary attitudes which killed women's football for more than 70 years have also been at play in the history of the FA's governance of Britain's national sport. That story is one for another author, another book, but it is not unreasonable to ask: what if?

What if football had moved with the times and embraced the coming of a new era – at least when that era was still breathing? What if the petty bourgeoisie of the sporting establishment paid less attention to committees, and meetings and the delights of corporate management, and more to fostering excellence on the field in whatever form it comes? And what if they recognised that men are not naturally more gifted, more agile, more able than women, and – nearly 100 years after the golden era of Dick, Kerr's Ladies – allowed women to govern football?

Now, there's a thought.

Tim Tate
July 2013

END NOTES

CHAPTER 1

1. In the earliest days of the fight for women's rights, 'suffragist' was the word used. The term 'suffragette' would emerge a decade later.
2. shilling = 5 pence in modern decimal coinage.

CHAPTER 2

3. The Riot Act was first introduced by Parliament in 1714. The Act created a mechanism which empowered local officials to make a public proclamation ordering the dispersal of any group of more than 12 people who were 'unlawfully, riotously, and tumultuously assembled together'. If the group failed to disperse within one hour, anyone remaining gathered was guilty of a felony and punishable by death.

CHAPTER 3

4. *Football Facts & Fancies*, Percy M Young, 1950.
5. *Seven Years at Eton, 1857-1864,* Brinsley Richards (Pub: 1883).
6. FA rules still required the presence of two umpires, provided by

each of the competing teams and a neutral referee to mediate
between them.

CHAPTER 4

7.   The fainting and attacks of 'the vapours' associated with
     Victorian women were often symptoms of chlorosis, a
     syndrome connected with disruption in blood flow. In some
     cases this led to uterine prolapse, in which the womb itself
     was pushed outwards and downwards by the force of
     tight lacing.
8.   For an admirably exhaustive account of who scored what goals,
     where, when and how, football obsessives can find details at
     Patrick Brennan's excellent website: www.donmouth.co.uk
9.   As telegrams have not existed in Britain for more than 30
     years, it's worth noting that in Nettie's age of very slow
     communication (telephones were then in their infancy)
     telegrams were the quickest means of contact.
10. Patrick Brennan, Op. Cit.

CHAPTER 5

11. *London During The Great War, Michael MacDonagh,*1935.
12. The only political or military leader who said anything close to
     this was Kaiser Wilhelm. He announced that German troops
     would be *'Home before the leaves fall'* – a confidence based on
     the belief that his key military Schlieffen Plan dictated the
     defeat of France within six weeks, i.e. by mid-September 1914.

CHAPTER 7

13. Few people have done more to highlight the role of Dick,
     Kerr's Ladies team in the development of women's football
     than Ms Newsham. Her 1994 book, *In a League of Their Own*,
     is heartily recommended.
14. Football in England was divided along regional lines. There
     were two major league organisations at this point: the Football
     League itself and the Southern League.

15. The Victoria Cross is Britain's highest military honour awarded for valour 'in the face of the enemy'.
16. Lest this be misunderstood, 'knickers' was the term used for all football shorts of the era – men or women's.
17. 'Unco Guid' means the rigidly righteous. It comes from a poem by Robert Burns, 'Address to the Unco Guid' in which Burns targets hypocrites, 'sae pious and sae holy' who seek to repress and condemn natural instinctive feeling and behaviour.
18. Wills' Woodbines was the most widely smoked brand of cigarettes by working men and women, and also became indelibly associated with British soldiers in the trenches of the First World War.
19. Fry's 'Five Boys' chocolate, launched in 1902, became one of the most popular chocolate bars over more than six decades. Its wrapper featured the face of the photographer's son, captured in five different expressions.

CHAPTER 8

20. Calculating today's relative equivalents of First World War money is peculiarly complicated. The Bank of England official inflation calculator suggests that £1 in 1917 would be equal to almost £59 in 2013. But this only takes into account average annual inflation of 4.3 per cent. A rather more relevant guide is that in 1913, a Fabian Society study showed that the average working class weekly wage was £1. Today it is at least £200.
21. Although some of the British Ladies' Football Club games, particularly those involving Mrs Graham's XI, were billed as England v Scotland, the reality is that this was nothing more than an advertising gimmick with little or no factual basis.
22. *In a League of Their Own*, Gail J Newsham, Pride of Place Publishing, 1994.

CHAPTER 9

23. Exploding fireworks, normally used by the military as a warning signal.

24. To maintain morale wartime censors minimised early reports of illness and mortality in Germany, Britain, France, and the United States, but newspapers were free to report the epidemic's effects in neutral Spain (where King Alfonso XIII had already been struck down) creating a false impression of Spain as being especially hard hit.

CHAPTER 10

25. Although the company's name had changed, the football team carried on playing under the name of Dick, Kerr's. For that reason, it will be referred to here by its original name.

26. *The Dick, Kerr's Ladies*, Barbara Jacobs (Robinson Publishers, 2004).

27. *Belles of the Ball*, David J Williamson (R & D Associates, 1991.) Unfortunately there is no detail listed for the origin of this contemporary report about Selman's technique.

28. Williamson: Op cit.

29. Despite its initial high hopes, the League of Nations was to prove a sorry failure, proving itself hopelessly incapable of stopping German re-armament and aggression in the 1930s. Its direct descendant, the United Nations, was founded at the close of the Second World War with the stated determination to avoid the mistakes of its predecessor. Whether it has done so, is a matter of international dispute.

CHAPTER 11

30. Notionally, at least, Wintringham was the second female MP. But the first, revolutionary Irish republican Constance Markievicz, never took up the seat in Parliament which she had won in 1918.

31. One previously overlooked result of the carnage of World War I – which killed millions of men irrespective of their sporting history – was to leave both professional and amateur football with a dearth of qualified referees.

32. FA Council minute, Monday, 10 October, 1921.

CHAPTER 12#

33. The FA had refused to join the new international organisation
FIFA (the Fédération Internationale de Football Association)
when it was founded in the headquarters of the FA's equivalent
body, *L'Union Française de Sports Athlétiques* in the Rue Saint
Honoré, Paris, on 21 May 1904.
34. Barbara Jacobs, Op. Cit.
35. Gail Newsham, Op. Cit.
36. *The Book of Football: A Complete History and Record of the
Association and Rugby Games* (Amalgamated Press, London,
1906).
37. Named after Henry Du Pré Labouchère, the Liberal MP,
writer, publisher and theatre owner who drafted the Act's
clauses. The Act claimed many high-profile victims, including
Oscar Wilde.
38. In 2007 an annual lesbian football cup – The Lily Parr
Exhibition Trophy – was established to honour the only
woman ever to be included in football's Hall of Fame. The
inaugural match, against a Paris-based lesbian team, re-enacted
the first match between Dick, Kerr's Ladies and Mme Milliat's
French XI.

CHAPTER 13

39. *Meg Foster – Footballer: Absorbing Tale of a Mill-Girls' Football
Club. And Their Plucky Fight for Fame and Fortune* (The
Football and Sports Library, London, No. 2, 1921).
40. *Roy of the Rovers* was the most iconic football comic hero, first
published in 1954.

FURTHER READING

Belles of the Ball, David J Williamson (R&D Associates, Devon, 1991)

In a League of Their Own!, Gail J Newsham (Pride of Place Publishing, 1994)

The Dick, Kerr's Ladies, Barbara Jacobs (Robinson Publishing, 2004)

The Munitionettes, Patrick Brennan (Donmouth Publishing, 2007)

A Game for Rough Girls?, Jean Williams (Routledge, 2003)